EXAM CRAM™ 2

Windows® Server™ 2003 Network Infrastructure

Diana Huggins

que®

CERTIFICATION

Windows® Server™ 2003 Network Infrastructure (Exam Cram 70-291)

International Standard Book Number: 0-7897-2947-4

Library of Congress Catalog Card Number: 2003100986

Printed in the United States of America

First Printing: October 2003

06   05   4   3

Que offers excellent discounts on this book when ordered in quantity for bulk purchases or special sales. For more information, please contact

U.S. Corporate and Government Sales

1-800-382-3419

corpsales@pearsontechgroup.com

For sales outside of the U.S., please contact

International Sales

international@pearsoned.com

Trademarks

Warning and Disclaimer

Publisher

Paul Boger

Executive Editor
Jeff Riley

Acquisitions Editor
Jeff Riley

Development Editor
Ginny Bess Munroe

Managing Editor
Charlotte Clapp

Project Editors
Bonney Hartley
Tricia Liebig

Copy Editor
Krista Hansing

Indexer
Erika Millen

Proofreader
Katie Robinson

Technical Editors
Marc Savage
Jeff Dunkelberger

Team Coordinator
Pamalee Nelson

Multimedia Developer
Dan Scherf

Interior Designer
Gary Adair

Cover Designer
Anne Jones

Page Layout
Kelly Maish

Graphics
Tammy Graham

The 70-291 Cram Sheet

This Cram Sheet provides you with the distilled facts about Exam 70-291: "Implementing, Managing, and Maintaining a Windows Server 2003 Network Infrastructure." Review these important points as the last thing you do before entering the test center. Pay close attention to those you feel that you need to review. A good exam strategy is to transfer all the facts you can recall from this Cram Sheet onto a piece of paper after you enter the testing room.

DHCP/DNS

- TCP/IP is automatically installed with Windows Server 2003 when a network adapter is detected.

- The default configuration for a computer running Windows Server 2003 is to automatically obtain an IP address from a DHCP server.

- IP addresses can be assigned either dynamically using a DHCP server or statically (manually).

- Clients use automatic private IP addressing if they are enabled for DHCP but no DHCP server is available. DHCP clients using APIPA assign themselves an IP address in the range of 169.254.0.1 to 169.254.255.254.

- Clients using APIPA are limited to communicating on the local subnet because only an IP address and subnet mask are configured.

- A computer can be configured with multiple gateways. The gateway with the lowest metric is preferred.

- Windows Server 2003 supports WINS to remain backward compatible with legacy clients.

- LMHOSTS is a static text file that maps NetBIOS names to IP addresses.

- TCP/IP filtering is used to filter network traffic based on TCP/UDP ports and IP protocols.

- The Dynamic Host Configuration Protocol (DHCP) is used to dynamically assign IP addresses and other parameters to DHCP clients.

- The DHCP lease process includes the following four phases: Discover, Offer, Request, Acknowledge (remember "DORA").

- A DHCP server must be configured with a static IP address.

- Every DHCP server requires a scope. For fault tolerance, use the 80/20 rule with multiple DHCP servers. Scopes must not overlap because DHCP servers do not share scope information.

- Superscopes enable a DHCP server to assign IP addresses from multiple scopes to DHCP clients on one physical network. Multicast scopes enable messages to be sent to a group of computers.

- DHCP can be integrated with DNS. DHCP can update the resource records on behalf of DHCP clients and clients that do not support dynamic updates.

- Dynamic update registration credentials specify the user account under which a DHCP server performs updates to the DNS database.

- A DHCP server must be authorized within Active Directory before it can lease IP addresses to DHCP clients. You must be a member of the Enterprise Admins group to authorize a DHCP server.

- Optional parameters can be configured at the server, scope, class, and client levels. Settings are applied in the following order: server, scope, class, and client. Settings configured at the client level override those configured at any of the other three levels.

- DNS is a distributed database that maps domain names to IP addresses.

- Recursive queries require the DNS server to respond with the IP address of the request or an error message that the requested name does not exist.

- With iterative queries, the DNS server uses zone information and its cache to return the best possible answer.

- Zone files contain configuration information for the zone as well as the resource records.

mation such as the computer name, where the instance is installed, and who is currently logged onto the computer.

- Capture filters can be created using the following criteria: protocol, address pairs, and pattern matches.

- System Monitor can be used to monitor the real-time performance of the local computer or another computer on the network.

- The capability to control which users can view data using the Performance Log Users and Performance Monitor Users groups is a new feature in Windows Server 2003.

- Windows Server 2003 supports four service recovery actions: take no action, restart the service, run a program, and restart the computer.

- Task Manager is used to view information about the local computer, such as the applications and processes currently running.

- System Information is a utility that provides configuration information about a local or remote computer.

- Event Viewer is used to view the contents of the event log files.

- Every computer running Windows Server 2003 has at least three log files by default: Application, Security, and System.

- Shutdown Event Tracker is used to monitor why users shutdown and restart their computers.

- The GPUPDATE command can be used to manually refresh security settings.
- Software Update Services (SUS) is used to distribute software updates to servers and workstations.
- The updated version of automatic updates can be installed on Windows 2000, Windows XP, and Windows Server 2003.
- As part of managing and maintaining network security, administrators can use the IP Security Monitor tool to ensure that communication between hosts is indeed secure.
- The version of IP Security Monitor included with Windows Server 2003 cannot be used to monitor computers running Windows 2000.
- Network Monitor is used to capture and analyze network traffic. The information can be used to troubleshoot and optimize network traffic.
- Network Monitor consists of two components: the network monitor driver and network monitor tools.
- Capture filters can be defined to specify the type of network traffic that should be captured.
- netsh is a command-line utility that can be used to view or modify the network configuration of the local computer or a remote computer.

REMOTE ACCESS

- Remote access enables users to dial into a server and access the network as though they were physically connected to it.
- Windows Server 2003 supports two remote access connectivity methods: dial-up and VPN.
- Remote access clients can be assigned IP addresses using a DHCP server. Alternatively the remote access server can be configured with a pool of IP addresses.
- The two main dial-up protocols are PPP and SLIP. Windows Server 2003 supports the use of SLIP for outbound connections only.
- The DHCP relay agent enables DHCP clients to obtain an IP address from a DHCP server on the network when they dial in.
- Remote Access Policies determine who has permissions to dial in and also define the characteristics of the connection. Remote Access Policies consist of conditions, permissions, and profiles.
- Remote access policy elements are evaluated in the following order: conditions, permissions, and profiles.
- Remote access permission can be granted through the properties of a user account and through a remote access policy.
- If no remote access policy exists, all remote access connection attempts will be denied.

- Multilink enables multiple phone lines to be combined into a single logical connection to increase available bandwidth.
- BAP enables multilink connections to be dynamically added and dropped based on bandwidth requirements.
- The following protocols can be used for authentication: PAP, SPAP, CHAP, MS-CHAP, and EAP.
- Windows Server 2003 supports two types of encryption: MPPE and IPSec.
- Windows Server 2003 Internet Authentication Services (IAS) is used to centralize user authentication, auditing, and accounting information.
- VPNs are created using a tunneling protocol. A tunnel can be established using either PPTP or L2TP.
- Routing can be configured within the Routing and Remote Access MMC snap-in.
- Static routing is good for small networks in which the topology does not change often.
- Use the route command to add static entries to the routing table. To add persistent routes, use the -p parameter with the command.
- RIP routers periodically send their entire routing table to other routers. RIP causes an increase in network traffic. Routing is based on hop counts.
- OSPF routers only transmit updates. Routing is based on metrics.
- The IP Security Policy (IPSec) is used to protect data that is sent between hosts on a network, which can be remote access, VPN, LAN, or WAN.
- The three default IPSec policies are Client (Respond Only), Server Secure (Require Security), and Server (Request Security).
- IPSec supports Kerberos, certificates, and pre-shared key authentication methods.

NETWORK MAINTENANCE

- Display filters can be created to locate specific types of traffic from a capture. Capture filters can be created to specify the type of information to capture.
- Triggers enable certain actions to be performed based on the content of a packet.
- When the criteria of a trigger is met, any of the following actions can be configured to occur: the computer can beep, Network Monitor will stop capturing frames, and a command-line program can be executed.
- The network monitor driver captures the frames coming to and going from a network adapter. The Network Monitor tool is used to view the captured information.
- To prevent unauthorized users from running it, when Network Monitor starts up, it can detect other instances on the network and display infor-

- The process of replicating a zone file to a secondary server is referred to as a zone transfer.
- Pre-Windows 2000 implementations of DNS supported a full zone transfer (AXFR) only, in which the entire zone file is replicated to the secondary server. This type of zone transfer is supported by most implementations of DNS.
- Windows 2000 and Windows Server 2003 support incremental zone transfers where only the changes are replicated instead of the entire zone file.
- DNS can be installed during the installation of Windows Server 2003, using the Add or Remove Programs applet, or when promoting a server to a domain controller.
- A DNS zone is a portion of the DNS database that is administered as a single unit.
- Caching-only servers do not maintain any zone information. They resolve names on behalf of clients and cache the results. Caching-only servers are useful when network traffic needs to be reduced.
- Primary DNS servers maintain the working copy of the zone database file, whereas the secondary DNS servers maintain a replica.
- BIND 4.9.6 supports SRV records. BIND 8.1.3 supports dynamic updates.
- A forward lookup zone maps hostnames to IP addresses. A reverse lookup zone maps IP addresses to hostnames.
- Three zone types are supported: standard primary, standard secondary, and stub. Primary and stub zones can be converted to Active Directory-integrated zones.
- Stub zones maintain a list of authoritative name server for a zone.
- A zone file is replicated from a master name server to a secondary DNS server. A master name server can be a primary DNS server or another secondary DNS server.
- Host Address (A) records map DNS names to IP addresses.
- The Serial Number lists the number used to determine whether the zone file has changed. Each time a change is made, this number is incremented by 1. You can force a zone transfer by manually increasing this number.
- The Refresh Interval determines how often the secondary server polls the primary server for updates.
- The Time-To-Live (TTL) specifies how long DNS servers are allowed to store a record from the zone in their cache before it expires.
- A forwarder is a DNS server that receives DNS queries that cannot be resolved locally and forwards them to external DNS servers.

- When configuring zones, use the Name Servers tab and the Zone Transfers tab to limit which servers can receive DNS updates and transfers.
- DNS servers that store information within Active Directory poll Active Directory at 15-minute intervals to check for updates.
- DNS supports dynamic updates so that clients can dynamically register and update their own resource records. Secure updates can also be configured so that only those clients with permission to use the zone file can perform updates.
- When configuring dynamic updates, the zone must be standard primary (information is stored locally in files) or Active Directory-integrated (information is stored on all DCs). Also, to use secure updates, the zone must be Active Directory-integrated. This feature is not supported by standard primary zones.
- Using delegation, administrators can divide a namespace among multiple zones.
- The DNS service can be monitored using various tools, including System Monitor, Event Viewer, and Replication Monitor.

NETWORK SECURITY

- A secure baseline or build involves installing the operating system, applying service packs and hot fixes, and configuring various operating system settings.
- Service packs and hot fixes eliminate security issues on an operating system.
- There are risks associated with installing service packs. They should be tested before being deployed in a production environment.
- System hardening refers to configuration changes made to make an operating system more secure.
- Windows Server 2003 does not allow you to create non-complex passwords.
- The principle of least privilege is based on the idea that a user who is logged on should have only the minimum privileges required to perform a task.
- The Security Configuration and Analysis tool can be used to compare the existing security settings configured on a server against those settings within a template.
- A security template holds a number of security settings considered to be appropriate for a server, domain controller, or workstation. Windows Server 2003 ships with predefined templates, or custom templates can be created.
- Security templates can be deployed locally or through group policy.
- Security settings are automatically refreshed on a domain controller every 5 minutes. Security settings are automatically refreshed on a server or workstation every 90 minutes.

CERTIFICATION

Que Certification • 800 East 96th Street • Indianapolis, Indiana 46240

A Note from Series Editor Ed Tittel

You know better than to trust your certification preparation to just anybody. That's why you, and more than two million others, have purchased an Exam Cram book. As Series Editor for the new and improved Exam Cram 2 series, I have worked with the staff at Que Certification to ensure you won't be disappointed. That's why we've taken the world's best-selling certification product—a finalist for "Best Study Guide" in a CertCities reader poll in 2002—and made it even better.

As a "Favorite Study Guide Author" finalist in a 2002 poll of CertCities readers, I know the value of good books. You'll be impressed with Que Certification's stringent review process, which ensures the books are high-quality, relevant, and technically accurate. Rest assured that at least a dozen industry experts reviewed this material, helping us deliver an excellent solution to your exam preparation needs.

Best Study Guides

We've also added a preview edition of PrepLogic's powerful, full-featured test engine, which is trusted by certification students throughout the world.

As a 20-year-plus veteran of the computing industry and the original creator and editor of the Exam Cram series, I've brought my IT experience to bear on these books. During my tenure at Novell from 1989 to 1994, I worked with and around its excellent education and certification department. This experience helped push my writing and teaching activities heavily in the certification direction. Since then, I've worked on more than 70 certification-related books, and I write about certification topics for numerous Web sites and for *Certification* magazine.

In 1996, while studying for various MCP exams, I became frustrated with the huge, unwieldy study guides that were the only preparation tools available. As an experienced IT professional and former instructor, I wanted "nothing but the facts" necessary to prepare for the exams. From this impetus, Exam Cram emerged in 1997. It quickly became the best-selling computer book series since "...*For Dummies*," and the best-selling certification book series ever. By maintaining an intense focus on subject matter, tracking errata and updates quickly, and following the certification market closely, Exam Cram was able to establish the dominant position in cert prep books.

You will not be disappointed in your decision to purchase this book. If you are, please contact me at etittel@jump.net. All suggestions, ideas, input, or constructive criticism are welcome!

Ed Tittel

This book is dedicated with all my love to my son, Brandon.

&

About the Author

Diana Huggins is currently an independent contractor providing both technical writing and consulting services. Before this, she worked as a senior systems consultant. Some of the projects she worked on include a security review of Microsoft's official curriculum, content development for private companies, and network infrastructure design and implementation projects.

Diana's main focus over the past few years has been on writing certification study guides, including *Windows 2000 Directory Services Design (Exam Cram 70-219)* as well as *Windows 2000 Network Infrastructure (Exam Cram 70-216)*. To complement her efforts, she also spends a portion of her time consulting for small to medium-size companies in a variety of areas and continues to work as an independent technical trainer.

Diana currently has her Microsoft Certified Systems Engineer (MCSE) and Microsoft Certified Trainer (MCT) certifications, along with several other certifications from different vendors, including A+, I-NET+, and Server+. Although her focus is on the information technology industry, she also holds a Bachelor's degree in education. Diana runs her own company, DKB Consulting Services. The main focus of the company is on developing certification training courseware and online practice exams, as well as content delivery.

About the Technical Editors

Marc Savage, MCT, MCSE, MCSA, CNE 4.11, A+, Network+, is the senior national technical advisor and technical trainer for Polar Bear Corporate Education Solutions in Ottawa, Canada. With more than seven years experience in microcomputer training and systems development in the private, public, and nonprofit organization sectors, Marc's professional expertise is focused particularly on providing companies with a clear vision in regard to

Microsoft products and directions. He has also recently been selected to deliver a series of TPREPs on Windows 2003 in Canada. Marc lives in Ottawa, Canada, with his wife, Lynne, and two daughters, Isabelle and Carolyne.

Jeff A. Dunkelberger, MCSE, MCT, is currently a Solution Architect in the Hewlett-Packard Enterprise Microsoft Services practice, where he works with HP's large Federal government and commercial customers, helping them solve their business problems with Windows and Exchange solutions. Most recently, Jeff completed a special assignment as the Lab Master on the design and delivery team for the HP Windows 2003 Academy series. HP's Windows 2003 Academy program is an intense, practical field-training exercise attended by hundreds of HP's Windows consultants around the world.

Jeff completed his master's degree in business management at the McGregor School of Antioch University and acts as a technical editor for several computer-book publishers. He lives in the Washington, D.C., suburb of Alexandria, Virginia, in a very small house with his attorney wife, two dogs, and three cats, and he can be reached at `jeffd@hp.com`.

Acknowledgments

First and foremost, I'd like to once again thank my son for being so patient and understanding when things get a little hectic. And, of course, my dad, who probably doesn't know how much he is appreciated.

Once again, thanks to Dawn Rader, managing editor at LANWrights, Inc., for her assistance and dedication in keeping the project up-to-date and on track, as well as for her flexibility and understanding with the tight deadlines. Working with Dawn is always a pleasure.

Finally, to all those people in my life who support me and encourage me when I'm struggling to get things done and that one person who always manages to drag me away from work when I do need to get things done. Thanks to you all!

Contents at a Glance

Table of Contents

We Want to Hear from You!

As the reader of this book, *you* are our most important critic and commentator. We value your opinion and want to know what we're doing right, what we could do better, what areas you'd like to see us publish in, and any other words of wisdom you're willing to pass our way.

As an executive editor for Que Publishing, I welcome your comments. You can email or write me directly to let me know what you did or didn't like about this book—as well as what we can do to make our books better.

Please note that I cannot help you with technical problems related to the *topic* of this book. We do have a User Services group, however, where I will forward specific technical questions related to the book.

When you write, please be sure to include this book's title and author, as well as your name, email address, and phone number. I will carefully review your comments and share them with the author and editors who worked on the book.

Email: feedback@quepublishing.com

Mail: Jeff Riley
         Executive Editor
         Que Publishing
         800 East 96th Street
         Indianapolis, IN 46240 USA

For more information about this book or another Que title, visit our Web site at www.quepublishing.com. Type the ISBN (excluding hyphens) or the title of a book in the Search field to find the page you're looking for. For information about the Exam Cram 2 series, visit www.examcram2.com.

Introduction

Welcome to the *70-291 Exam Cram 2*! Whether this is your 1st or your 15th *Exam Cram 2* series book, you'll find information here that will help ensure your success as you pursue knowledge, experience, and certification. This introduction explains Microsoft's certification programs in general and talks about how the *Exam Cram 2* series can help you prepare for Microsoft's Certified Systems Engineer (MCSE) and Microsoft's Certified Systems Administrator (MCSA) exams. Chapter 1, "Microsoft Certification Exams," discusses the basics of Microsoft certification exams, including a description of the testing environment and a discussion of test-taking strategies. Chapters 2–6 are designed to remind you of everything you'll need to know to take—and pass—the 70-291 Microsoft MCSE/MCSA certification exam. The two sample tests at the end of the book should give you a reasonably accurate assessment of your knowledge—and, yes, we've provided the answers (and their explanations) to the tests. Read the book and understand the material, and you'll stand a very good chance of passing the test.

Exam Cram 2 books help you understand and appreciate the subjects and materials you need to pass Microsoft certification exams. *Exam Cram 2* books are aimed strictly at test preparation and review. They do not teach you everything you need to know about a topic. Instead, I present and dissect the questions and problems I've found that you're likely to encounter on a test. I've worked to bring together as much information as possible about Microsoft certification exams.

Nevertheless, to completely prepare yourself for any Microsoft test, I recommend that you begin by taking the Self-Assessment that is included in this book, immediately following this introduction. The Self-Assessment tool will help you evaluate your knowledge base against the requirements for a Microsoft Certified Systems Administrator (MCSA) or Microsoft Certified Systems Engineer (MCSE) certification under both ideal and real circumstances.

Based on what you learn from the Self-Assessment, you might decide to begin your studies with some classroom training, some practice with Windows Server 2003, or some background reading. On the other hand, you might decide to pick up and read one of the many study guides available from Microsoft or third-party vendors on certain topics. We also recommend that you supplement your study program with visits to `www.examcram2.com` to receive additional practice questions, get advice, and track the MCSE and MCSA program.

I also strongly recommend that you install, configure, and play around with Windows Server 2003 and the various services that you'll be tested on because nothing beats hands-on experience and familiarity when it comes to understanding the questions you're likely to encounter on a certification test. Book learning is essential, but without a doubt, hands-on experience is the best teacher of all! Many of the chapters include step-by-step instructions on how to perform various tasks in Windows Server 2003 to assist you in getting familiar with the product. A CD also accompanies the book and contains the PrepLogic Practice Tests, Preview Edition exam-simulation software. The Preview Edition exhibits most of the full functionality of the Premium Edition, but it offers questions sufficient for only one practice exam. To get the complete set of practice questions and exam functionality, visit `www.preplogic.com`.

Taking a Certification Exam

After you've prepared for your exam, you need to register with a testing center. Each computer-based MCP exam costs $125; if you don't pass, you can retest for an additional $125 for each additional try. In the United States and Canada, tests are administered by Prometric and by VUE. Here's how you can contact them:

> ➤ *Prometric*—You can sign up for a test through the company's Web site, at `www.prometric.com`. Within the United States and Canada, you can register by phone at 1-800-755-3926. If you live outside this region, you should check the Prometric Web site for the appropriate phone number.

> ➤ *VUE*—You can sign up for a test or get the phone numbers for local testing centers through the Web at `www.vue.com/ms`.

To sign up for a test, you must possess a valid credit card or contact either Prometric or VUE for mailing instructions to send a check (in the United States). Only when payment is verified or your check has cleared can you actually register for the test.

To schedule an exam, you need to call the number or visit either of the Web pages at least one day in advance. To cancel or reschedule an exam, you must call before 7 p.m. Pacific Standard Time the day before the scheduled test time (or you might be charged, even if you don't show up to take the test). When you want to schedule a test, you should have the following information ready:

➤ Your name, organization, and mailing address.

➤ Your Microsoft test ID. (Inside the United States, this usually means your Social Security number; citizens of other nations should call ahead to find out what type of identification number is required to register for a test.)

➤ The name and number of the exam you want to take.

➤ A method of payment. (As mentioned previously, a credit card is the most convenient method, but alternate means can be arranged in advance, if necessary.)

After you sign up for a test, you are told when and where the test is scheduled. You should try to arrive at least 15 minutes early. You must supply two forms of identification—one of which must be a photo ID—and sign a nondisclosure agreement to be admitted into the testing room.

All Microsoft exams are completely closed book. In fact, you are not permitted to take anything with you into the testing area, but you are given a blank sheet of paper and a pen (or, in some cases, an erasable plastic sheet and an erasable pen). We suggest that you immediately write down on that sheet of paper all the information you've memorized for the test. In *Exam Cram 2* books, this information appears on a tear-out sheet inside the front cover of each book. You are given some time to compose yourself, record this information, and take a sample orientation exam before you begin the real thing. I suggest that you take the orientation test before taking your first exam, but because all the certification exams are more or less identical in layout, behavior, and controls, you probably don't need to do this more than once.

When you complete a Microsoft certification exam, the software tells you immediately whether you've passed or failed. If you need to retake an exam, you have to schedule a new test with Prometric or VUE and pay another $125.

The first time you fail a test, you can retake the test as soon as the next day. However, if you fail a second time, you must wait 14 days before retaking that test. The 14-day waiting period remains in effect for all retakes after the second failure.

Tracking MCP Status

As soon as you pass any Microsoft exam, you attain MCP status. Microsoft generates transcripts that indicate which exams you have passed. You can view a copy of your transcript at any time by going to the MCP secured site and selecting Transcript Tool. This tool enables you to print a copy of your current transcript and confirm your certification status.

After you pass the necessary set of exams, you are certified. Official certification is normally granted after three to six weeks, so you shouldn't expect to get your credentials overnight. The package for official certification that arrives includes a Welcome Kit that contains a number of elements (see Microsoft's Web site for other benefits of specific certifications):

➤ A certificate that is suitable for framing, along with a wallet card and lapel pin.

➤ A license to use the applicable logo, which means you can use the logo in advertisements, promotions, and documents, and on letterhead, business cards, and so on. Along with the license comes a logo sheet, which includes camera-ready artwork. (Note that before you use any of the artwork, you must sign and return a licensing agreement that indicates you'll abide by its terms and conditions.)

➤ A subscription to *Microsoft Certified Professional Magazine*, which provides ongoing data about testing and certification activities, requirements, and changes to the program.

Many people believe that the benefits of MCP certification go well beyond the perks that Microsoft provides to newly anointed members of this elite group. We're starting to see more job listings that request or require applicants to have MCP, MCSA, and other certifications, and many individuals who complete Microsoft certification programs can qualify for increases in pay or responsibility. As an official recognition of hard work and broad knowledge, one of the MCP credentials is a badge of honor in many IT organizations.

How to Prepare for an Exam

Preparing for any MCSE- or MCSA-related test (including Exam 70-291) requires that you obtain and study materials designed to provide comprehensive information about the product and its capabilities that will appear on the specific exam for which you are preparing. The following list of materials can help you study and prepare:

> ➤ The Windows Server 2003 product CD. One of the best resources you can use when preparing for an exam is the help files included with the operating system. They usually cover different aspects of all the technologies included with the operating system.

> ➤ The exam-preparation materials, practice tests, and self-assessment exams on the Microsoft Training & Certification page, at www.microsoft.com/traincert. The Exam Resources link offers examples of the new question types found on the MCSA and MCSE exams. You should find the materials, download them, and use them!

> ➤ The exam-preparation advice, practice tests, questions of the day, and discussion groups on the www.examcram2.com e-learning and certification destination Web site.

In addition, you might find any or all of the following materials useful in your quest for Windows Server 2003 expertise:

> ➤ *Microsoft training kits*—Microsoft Press offers a training kit that specifically targets Exam 70-291. For more information, visit www.microsoft.com/mspress/books/5433.asp. This training kit contains information that you will find useful in preparing for the test.

> ➤ *Microsoft TechNet*—This monthly publication provides information on the latest technologies and topics, some of which pertain to the exam topics covered in Exam 70-291.

> ➤ *Study guides*—Several publishers, including Que Publishing, offer certification titles. Que Publishing offers the following:

>> ➤ *The* Exam Cram 2 *series*—These books give you information about the material you need to know to pass the tests.

>> ➤ *The* MCSE Training Guide *series*—These books provide a greater level of detail than the *Exam Cram 2* books and are designed to teach you everything you need to know about the subject covered by an exam. Each book comes with a CD-ROM that contains interactive practice exams in a variety of testing formats.

> Together, these two series make a perfect pair.

> ➤ *Classroom training*—Microsoft Certified Technical Education Centers (CTECs), online partners, and third-party training companies all offer classroom training on Windows Server 2003. These companies aim to help you prepare to pass Exam 70-291 (or other exams). Although such

training runs upward of $350 per day in class, most of the individuals lucky enough to partake find this training to be quite worthwhile.

➤ *Other publications*—There's no shortage of materials available about Windows Server 2003. The "Need to Know More?" resource sections at the end of each chapter in this book give you an idea of where we think you should look for further discussion.

This set of required and recommended materials represents an unparalleled collection of sources and resources for Windows Server 2003 and related topics. I hope you'll find that this book belongs in this company.

What This Book Will Not Do

This book will *not* teach you everything you need to know about computers, or even about a given topic. Nor is this book an introduction to computer technology. If you're new to network administration or networking in general and are looking for an initial preparation guide, check out www. examcram2.com, where you will find a whole section dedicated to the MCSE/MCSA certifications. This book reviews what you need to know before you take the test, with the fundamental purpose dedicated to reviewing the information needed on the Microsoft 70-291 certification exam.

This book uses a variety of teaching and memorization techniques to analyze the exam-related topics and to provide you with ways to input, index, and retrieve everything you'll need to know to pass the test. Once again, it is *not* an introduction to networking and network administration, nor does it cover introductory topics as they pertain to Windows Server 2003.

What This Book Is Designed to Do

This book is designed to be read as a pointer to the areas of knowledge you will be tested on. In other words, you might want to read the book one time, just to get an insight into how comprehensive your knowledge of computers is. The book is also designed to be read shortly before you go for the actual test and to give you a distillation of the entire field of implementing, managing, and maintaining a Windows Server 2003 network infrastructure in as few pages as possible. We think you can use this book to get a sense of the underlying context of any topic in the chapters—or to skim read for Exam Alerts, bulleted points, summaries, and topic headings.

The material covered in this book is based on Microsoft's own listing of exam objectives. These are the topics that Microsoft intends to test you on during the exam. The book also covers a number of other topics that you are likely to encounter both on the exam and on the job.

Exam 70-291 makes a basic assumption that you already have a strong background of experience with Windows Server 2003 and its related technologies and terminology. On the other hand, because the platform is so new, no one can be a complete expert. I've tried to demystify the jargon, acronyms, terms, and concepts. Also, wherever I think you're likely to blur past an important concept, I've defined the assumptions and premises behind that concept.

About This Book

The topics in this book have been structured around the objectives outlined by Microsoft for Exam 70-291. This ensures that you are familiar with the topics that you'll encounter on the exam.

Some of the topics covered later in the book might require an understanding of topics covered in earlier chapters. Therefore, it's recommended that you read the book from start to finish for your initial reading. After you've read the book, you can brush up on a certain area by using the index or the table of contents to go straight to the topics and questions that you want to re-examine. I've tried to use the headings and subheadings to provide outline information about each given topic. After you've been certified, I think you'll find this book useful as a tightly focused reference and an essential foundation of Windows Server 2003 reference material.

Chapter Formats

Each *Exam Cram 2* chapter follows a regular structure, along with graphical cues about especially important or useful material. The structure of a typical chapter is as follows:

➤ *Opening hotlists*—Each chapter begins with lists of the terms you'll need to understand and the concepts you'll need to master before you can be fully conversant with the chapter's subject matter. I follow the hotlists with a few introductory paragraphs, setting the stage for the rest of the chapter.

➤ *Topical coverage*—After the opening hotlists, each chapter covers the topics related to the chapter's subject.

➤ *Alerts*—Throughout the topical coverage section, I highlight material most likely to appear on the exam by using a special Exam Alert layout that looks like this:

This is what an Exam Alert looks like. An Exam Alert stresses concepts, terms, software, or activities that will most likely appear in one or more certification exam questions. For that reason, I think any information found offset in Exam Alert format is worthy of unusual attentiveness on your part.

Even if material isn't flagged as an Exam Alert, *all* the content in this book is associated in some way with test-related material. What appears in the chapter content is critical knowledge.

➤ *Notes*—This book is an overall examination of computers. As such, I'll dip into many aspects of Windows Server 2003. Where a body of knowledge is deeper than the scope of the book, I use notes to indicate areas of concern or specialty training.

Cramming for an exam will get you through a test, but it won't make you a competent IT professional. Although you can memorize just the facts you need to become certified, your daily work in the field will rapidly put you in water over your head if you don't know the underlying principles of application development.

➤ *Tips*—I provide tips that will help you to build a better foundation of knowledge or to focus your attention on an important concept that will reappear later in the book. Tips provide a helpful way to remind you of the context surrounding a particular area of a topic under discussion.

You should also read Chapter 1, "Microsoft Certification Exams," for helpful strategies used in taking a test. The introduction to Practice Exam #1 in Chapter 7 contains additional tips on how to figure out the correct response to a question and what to do if you draw a complete blank.

➤ *Practice questions*—This section presents a short list of test questions related to the specific chapter topic. Each question has a following explanation of both correct and incorrect answers. The practice questions highlight the areas we found to be most important on the exam.

➤ *"Need to Know More?"*—Each chapter ends with a listing of additional resources offering more details about the chapter topics.

The bulk of the book follows this chapter structure, but there are a few other elements that we would like to point out:

➤ *Practice exams*—The practice exams, which appear in Chapters 7 and 9 (with answer keys in Chapters 8 and 10), are very close approximations of the types of questions you are likely to see on the current Exam 70-291.

➤ *Glossary*—This is an extensive glossary of important terms used in this book.

➤ *The Cram Sheet*—This appears as a tear-away sheet, inside the front cover of this *Exam Cram 2* book. It is a valuable tool that represents a collection of the most difficult-to-remember facts and numbers we think you should memorize before taking the test. Remember, you can dump this information out of your head onto a piece of paper as soon as you enter the testing room. These are usually facts that we've found require brute-force memorization. You need to remember this information only long enough to write it down when you walk into the test room. Be advised that you will be asked to surrender all personal belongings before you enter the exam room itself.

You might want to look at the Cram Sheet in your car or in the lobby of the testing center just before you walk into the testing room. The Cram Sheet is divided under headings, so you can review the appropriate parts just before each test.

➤ *The CD*—The CD contains the PrepLogic Practice Tests, Preview Edition exam-simulation software. The Preview Edition exhibits most of the full functionality of the Premium Edition, but it offers questions sufficient for only one practice exam. To get the complete set of practice questions and exam functionality, visit www.preplogic.com.

Contacting the Author

I've tried to create a real-world tool that you can use to prepare for and pass the 70-291 MCSE/MCSA certification exam. I'm interested in any feedback you would care to share about the book, especially if you have ideas about how I can improve it for future test takers. I'll consider everything you say carefully and will respond to all reasonable suggestions and comments. You can reach me via email at dhuggins@skyweb.ca.

Let me know if you found this book to be helpful in your preparation efforts. I'd also like to know how you felt about your chances of passing the exam *before* you read the book and then *after* you read the book. Of course, I'd love to hear that you passed the exam—and even if you just want to share your triumph, I'd be happy to hear from you.

Thanks for choosing me as your personal trainer, and enjoy the book. I would wish you luck on the exam, but I know that if you read through all the chapters and work with the product, you won't need luck—you'll pass the test on the strength of real knowledge!

Self-Assessment

I included a Self-Assessment in this *Exam Cram 2* book to help you evaluate your readiness to tackle Microsoft certifications. This should also help you understand what you need to know to master the topic of this book—namely, Exam 70-291 "Implementing, Managing, and Maintaining a Windows Server 2003 Network Infrastructure." But before you tackle this Self-Assessment, let's address concerns you might face when pursuing an MCSE (Microsoft Certified Systems Engineer) or MCSA (Microsoft Certified Systems Administrator) certification for the Windows Server 2003 and what an ideal MCSE candidate might look like.

MCSEs in the Real World

In this section, I describe an ideal MCSE candidate, knowing full well that only a few real candidates will meet this ideal. In fact, my description of that ideal candidate might seem downright scary. But take heart: Although the requirements to obtain an MCSE might seem formidable, they are by no means impossible to meet. However, be keenly aware that it does take time, involves some expense, and requires real effort to get through the process.

More than 200,000 MCSEs are already certified, so it's obviously an attainable goal. You can get all the real-world motivation you need from knowing that many others have gone before; you will be able to follow in their footsteps. If you're willing to tackle the process seriously and do what it takes to obtain the necessary experience and knowledge, you can take—and pass—all the certification tests involved in obtaining an MCSE. In fact, we've designed *Exam Cram 2* to make it as easy on you as possible to prepare for these exams. But prepare you must!

The same, of course, is true for other Microsoft certifications, including these:

➤ *MCSA (Microsoft Certified Systems Administrator)*—This is the brand-new certification that Microsoft has provided for Microsoft professionals who will administer networks rather than design them. This certification includes three core exams and a single elective.

➤ *MCSD (Microsoft Certified Solutions Developer)*—This is aimed at software developers and requires one specific exam, two more exams on client and distributed topics, plus a fourth elective exam drawn from a different but limited pool of options.

➤ *MCAD (Microsoft Certified Application Developer)*—This is aimed at software developers functioning at a departmental level with one to two years of applications-development experience. The MCAD certification requires two specific exams, plus a third elective exam drawn from a limited pool of options. The 70-306 exam is a core exam for the MCAD credential.

➤ *MCDBA (Microsoft Certified Database Administrator)*—This is aimed at database administrators and developers who work with Microsoft SQL Server. The MCDBA certification requires three core exams and one elective exam.

The Ideal MCSE Candidate

Just to give you some idea of what an ideal MCSE candidate is like, here are some relevant statistics about the background and experience that such an individual might have. Don't worry if you don't meet these qualifications or don't come that close—this is a far-from-ideal world, and where you fall short is simply where you'll have more work to do.

➤ Academic or professional training in network theory, concepts, and operations. This includes everything from networking media and transmission techniques through network operating systems, services, and applications.

➤ Three-plus years of professional networking experience, including experience with Ethernet, token ring, modems, and other networking media. This must include installation, configuration, upgrade, and troubleshooting experience.

➤ Two-plus years in a networked environment that includes hands-on experience with Windows Server 2003, Windows XP, Windows 2000 Server, Windows 2000 Professional, Windows NT Server, Windows NT Workstation, and Windows 95 or Windows 98. A solid understanding of each system's architecture, installation, configuration, maintenance, and troubleshooting is also essential.

➤ Knowledge of the various methods for installing Windows Server 2003, including manual and unattended installations.

➤ A thorough understanding of key networking protocols, addressing, and name resolution, including TCP/IP, IPX/SPX, and NetBEUI.

➤ A thorough understanding of NetBIOS naming, browsing, and file and print services.

➤ Familiarity with key Windows Server 2003 TCP/IP–based services, including HTTP (Web servers), DHCP, WINS, and DNS, plus familiarity with one or more of the following: Internet Information Server (IIS), Index Server, and ISA Server.

➤ An understanding of how to implement different connectivity models, such as remote access, IP routing, Internet Connection Sharing (ICS), Network Address Translation (NAT), and virtual private networks (VPNs).

➤ An understanding of how to implement security for key network data in a Windows Server 2003 environment.

➤ Working knowledge of NetWare 3.*x* and 4.*x*, including IPX/SPX frame formats; NetWare file, print, and directory services; and both Novell and Microsoft client software. Working knowledge of Microsoft's Client Service for NetWare (CSNW), Gateway Service for NetWare (GSNW), the NetWare Migration Tool (NWCONV), and the NetWare Client for Windows (NT, 95, and 98) is essential.

Fundamentally, this boils down to a Bachelor's degree in computer science, plus three years of experience working in a position involving network design, installation, configuration, and maintenance. We believe that well under half of all certification candidates meet these requirements and that, in fact, most meet less than half of these requirements—at least, when they begin the certification process. But because all 200,000 people who already have been certified have survived this ordeal, you can survive it, too—especially if you heed what our Self-Assessment can tell you about what you already know and what you need to learn.

Put Yourself to the Test

The following series of questions and observations is designed to help you figure out how much work you must do to pursue Microsoft certification and what kinds of resources you should consult on your quest. Be absolutely honest in your answers; otherwise, you'll end up wasting money on exams you're not yet ready to take. There are no right or wrong answers, only steps along the path to certification. Only you can decide where you really belong in the broad spectrum of aspiring candidates.

Two things should be clear from the outset, however:

➤ Even a modest background in computer science and programming will be helpful.

➤ Hands-on experience with Microsoft products and technologies is an essential ingredient to Microsoft certification success.

Educational Background

Following are questions related to your education:

1. Have you ever taken any computer-related classes? [Yes or No]

   If Yes, proceed to Question 2; if No, proceed to Question 4.

2. Have you taken any classes on computer operating systems? [Yes or No]

   If Yes, you will probably be able to handle Microsoft's architecture and system component discussions. If you're rusty, brush up on basic operating system concepts and general computer security topics.

   If No, consider some basic reading in this area. We strongly recommend a good general operating systems book, such as *Operating System Concepts, 6th Edition*, by Abraham Silberschatz, Peter Baer Galvin, and Greg Gagne (John Wiley & Sons, 2001). If this title doesn't appeal to you, check out reviews for other, similar titles at your favorite online bookstore.

3. Have you taken any networking concepts or technology classes? [Yes or No]

   If Yes, you will probably be able to handle Microsoft's networking terminology, concepts, and technologies (brace yourself for frequent departures from normal usage). If you're rusty, brush up on basic networking concepts and terminology, especially networking media, transmission types, the OSI Reference Model, and networking technologies such as Ethernet, token ring, FDDI, and WAN links. Skip to the next section, "Hands-On Experience."

   If No, you might want to read one or two books in this topic area. The two best books that we know of are *Computer Networks, 4th Edition*, by Andrew S. Tanenbaum (Prentice-Hall, 2002, ISBN 0-13-066102-3) and

Computer Networks and Internets, 3rd Edition, by Douglas E. Comer (Prentice-Hall, 2001, ISBN 0-130-91449-5).

4. Have you read operating system or network publications? [Yes or No]

If No, consult the recommended reading for both topics. A strong background will help you prepare for the Microsoft exams better than just about anything else.

Hands-On Experience

The most important key to success on all of the Microsoft tests is hands-on experience, especially with Windows Server 2003, plus the many add-on services and BackOffice components around which so many of the Microsoft certification exams revolve. If we leave you with only one realization after taking this Self-Assessment, it should be that there's no substitute for time spent installing, configuring, and using the various Microsoft products upon which you'll be tested repeatedly and in depth.

5. Have you installed, configured, and worked with Windows Server 2003 Server? [Yes or No]

If Yes, make sure you are familiar with not only installing and configuring the operating system, but also using the different services included. When studying for Exam 70-291, you should pay close attention to the TCP/IP interfaces, utilities, and services. Some of the other services that you need to be very familiar with are DNS, DHCP, WINS, RRAS, and Certificate Services. The exam requires in-depth knowledge and a fair amount of experience with each one.

 You can download objectives, practice exams, and other data about Microsoft exams from the Training and Certification page at **www.microsoft.com/train_cert/**. Use the Find an Exam link to obtain specific exam information.

If you haven't worked with Windows Server 2003, TCP/IP, and IIS (or whatever product you choose for your final elective), you must obtain one or two machines and a copy of Windows Server 2003. Then learn the operating system. Do the same for TCP/IP and whatever other software components you'll be tested on.

In fact, we recommend that you obtain two computers, each with a network interface, and set up a two-node network on which to practice.

With decent Windows Server 2003–capable computers selling for about $500 to $600 apiece these days, this shouldn't be too much of a financial hardship. You might have to scrounge to come up with the necessary software, but if you scour the Microsoft Web site, you can usually find low-cost options to obtain evaluation copies of most of the software that you'll need.

For any and all of these Microsoft exams, the Resource Kits for the topics involved are a good study resource. You can purchase soft-cover Resource Kits from Microsoft Press (search for them at **http://mspress.microsoft.com/**), but they also appear on the TechNet CDs (**www.microsoft.com/technet**). We believe that Resource Kits are among the best preparation tools available, along with the *Exam Cram 2* series of books.

6. For any specific Microsoft product that is not itself an operating system (for example, FrontPage 2000, SQL Server, and so on), have you installed, configured, used, and upgraded this software? [Yes or No]

If the answer is Yes, skip to the "Testing Your Exam-Readiness" section. If it's No, you must get some experience. Read on for suggestions on how to do this.

Experience is a must with any Microsoft product exam, whether it is something as simple as FrontPage 2000 or as challenging as Exchange Server 2000 or SQL Server 7.0. For trial copies of other software, search Microsoft's Web site using the name of the product as your search term. Also search for bundles such as BackOffice or Small Business Server.

If you have the funds or your employer will pay your way, consider taking a class at a Certified Training and Education Center (CTEC) or at an Authorized Academic Training Partner (AATP). In addition to classroom exposure to the topic of your choice, you get a copy of the software that is the focus of your course, along with a trial version of whatever operating system it needs, with the training materials for that class.

Before you even think about taking any Microsoft exam, make sure you've spent enough time with the related software to understand how it can be installed and configured (depending on the exam, this could be an operating system or specific services and applications), how to maintain such an installation, and how to troubleshoot that software when things go wrong. This will help you in the exam and in real life!

Testing Your Exam-Readiness

Whether you attend a formal class on a specific topic to get ready for an exam or use written materials to study on your own, some preparation for the Microsoft certification exams is essential. At $125 a try, pass or fail, you want to do everything you can to pass on your first try. That's where studying comes in.

We have included two practice exams in this book (Chapters 7 and 9), so if you don't score that well on the first, you can study more and then tackle the second.

For any given subject, consider taking a class if you've tackled self-study materials, taken the test, and failed anyway. The opportunity to interact with an instructor and fellow students can make all the difference in the world, if you can afford that privilege. For information about Microsoft classes, visit the Training and Certification page at www.microsoft.com/education/partners/ctec.asp for Microsoft Certified Education Centers.

If you can't afford to take a class, visit the Training page at www.microsoft.com/traincert/training/find/default.asp anyway—it also includes pointers to free practice exams and to Microsoft Certified Professional Approved Study Guides and other self-study tools. Even if you can't afford to spend much at all, you should still invest in some low-cost practice exams from commercial vendors.

7. Have you taken a practice exam on your chosen test subject? [Yes or No]

If Yes and you scored 70% or better, you're probably ready to tackle the real thing. If your score isn't above that threshold, keep at it until you break that barrier.

If No, obtain all the free and low-budget practice tests you can find, and get to work. Keep at it until you can break the passing threshold comfortably.

When it comes to assessing your test readiness, there is no better way than to take a good-quality practice exam and pass with a score of 70% or better. When I'm preparing myself, I shoot for 80% or more, just to leave room for the fact that you might encounter a question or two on the exam that makes little sense due to its wording.

Assessing Readiness for the 70-291 Exam

In addition to following the general exam-readiness information in the previous section, you can do several things to prepare for Exam 70-291. I suggest that you join an active Microsoft mailing list, obtain a Microsoft TechNet subscription, and regularly visit the Windows Server 2003 Web site for new information (see www.microsoft.com/windowsserver2003/default.mspx).

Microsoft exam mavens also recommend checking the Microsoft Knowledge Base (integrated into the TechNet CD-ROM, or on the Microsoft Web site at http://support.microsoft.com/support/) for "meaningful technical support issues" that relate to your exam's topics. Although I'm not sure exactly what the quoted phrase means, I have noticed some overlap between technical support questions on particular products and troubleshooting questions on the exams for those products.

What's Next?

After you've assessed your readiness, undertaken the right background studies, obtained the hands-on experience that will help you understand the products and technologies at work, and reviewed the many sources of information to help you prepare for a test, you'll be ready to take a round of practice tests. When your scores come back positive enough to get you through the exam, you're ready to go after the real thing. If you follow our assessment regime, you'll not only know what you need to study, but you'll also know when you're ready to make a test date at Prometric (www.prometric.com) or VUE (www.vue.com). Good luck!

Microsoft Certification Exams

Terms you'll need to understand:

✓ Case study
✓ Multiple-choice question format
✓ Build-list-and-reorder question format
✓ Create-a-tree question format
✓ Drag-and-connect question format
✓ Select-and-place question format
✓ Hot area question format
✓ Active screen question format
✓ Fixed-length test
✓ Simulation
✓ Adaptive test
✓ Short-form test

Techniques you'll need to master:

✓ Assessing your exam-readiness
✓ Answering Microsoft's various question types
✓ Altering your test strategy depending on the exam format
✓ Practicing to make perfect
✓ Making the best use of the testing software
✓ Budgeting your time
✓ Guessing as a last resort

Exam taking is not something that most people look forward to, no matter how well prepared they may be. In most cases, familiarity helps offset test anxiety. In plain English, this means you probably won't be as nervous when you take your fourth or fifth Microsoft certification exam as you'll be when you take your first one.

Whether it's your first exam or your tenth, understanding the details of taking the new exams (how much time to spend on questions, the environment you'll be in, and so on) and the new exam software will help you concentrate on the material rather than on the setting. Likewise, mastering a few basic exam-taking skills should help you recognize—and perhaps even outfox—some of the tricks and snares you're bound to find in some exam questions.

Besides explaining the exam environment and software, this chapter describes some proven exam-taking strategies that you should be able to use to your advantage. Taking the time to read through the information and recommendations presented in this chapter will bring you one step closer to achieving success on a Microsoft exam.

Assessing Exam-Readiness

We strongly recommend that you read through and take the self-assessment included with this book (it appears just before this chapter). This will help you compare your knowledge base to the requirements for obtaining the Microsoft Certified Systems Engineer (MCSE) certification, and it will help you identify parts of your background or experience that may be in need of improvement, enhancement, or further learning. If you get the right set of basics under your belt, obtaining Microsoft certification will be that much easier.

After you've gone through the self-assessment, you can remedy those topical areas where your background or experience may not measure up to those of an ideal certification candidate. But you can also tackle subject matter for individual tests at the same time, so you can continue making progress while you're catching up in some areas.

After you've worked through an *Exam Cram 2* series book, have read the supplementary materials, and have taken the practice test, you'll have a pretty clear idea of when you should be ready to take the real exam. Although we strongly recommend that you keep practicing until your scores top the 75% mark, 80% would be a good goal, to give yourself some margin for error in a real exam situation (where stress will play more of a role than when you practice). After you hit that point, you should be ready to challenge the exam.

But if you get through the practice exam in this book without attaining that score, you should keep taking practice tests and studying the materials until you get there. You'll find more pointers on how to study and prepare in the self-assessment. At this point, let's talk about the exam itself.

What to Expect at the Testing Center

When you arrive at the testing center where you scheduled your exam, you need to sign in with an exam coordinator. He or she will ask you to show two forms of identification, one of which must be a photo ID. After you sign in and when your time slot arrives, you will be asked to deposit any books, bags, or other items you brought with you. Then you will be escorted into a closed room.

All exams are completely closed book. In fact, you are not permitted to take anything with you into the testing area, but you are furnished with a blank sheet of paper and a pen or, in some cases, an erasable plastic sheet and an erasable pen. Before the exam, be sure to carefully review this book's Cram Sheet, located in the very front of the book. You should memorize as much of the important material as you can so that you can write that information on the blank sheet as soon as you are seated in front of the computer. You can refer to that piece of paper anytime you like during the test, but you have to surrender the sheet when you leave the room.

You are given some time to compose yourself, to record important information, and to take a sample exam before you begin the real thing. We suggest that you take the sample test before taking your first exam, but because all exams are more or less identical in layout, behavior, and controls, you probably don't need to do this more than once.

Typically, the testing room is furnished with anywhere from one to six computers, and each workstation is separated from the others by dividers designed to keep you from seeing what's happening on someone else's computer. Most testing rooms feature a wall with a large picture window. This permits the exam coordinator to monitor the room, to prevent exam takers from talking to one another and to observe anything out of the ordinary that might go on. The exam coordinator will have preloaded the appropriate Microsoft certification exam—for this book, that's Exam 70-291, "Implementing, Managing, and Maintaining a Windows Server 2003 Network Infrastructure"—and you are permitted to start as soon as you're seated in front of the computer.

All Microsoft certification exams allow a certain maximum amount of testing time (this time is indicated on the exam by an onscreen timer clock, so you can check the time remaining whenever you like). All Microsoft certification exams are computer generated. In addition to multiple-choice questions, most exams contain select–and-place (drag-and-drop), create-a-tree (categorization and prioritization), drag-and-connect, and build-list-and-reorder (list prioritization) types of questions. Although this might sound quite simple, the questions are constructed not only to check your mastery of basic facts and figures about a Windows Server 2003 network infrastructure, but also to require you to evaluate one or more sets of circumstances or requirements. Often you are asked to give more than one answer to a question. Likewise, you might be asked to select the best or most effective solution to a problem from a range of choices, all of which are technically correct. Taking the exam is quite an adventure, and it involves real thinking. This book shows you what to expect and how to deal with the potential problems, puzzles, and predicaments.

Exam Layout and Design

The format of Microsoft's Windows Server 2003 and Windows 2000 MCSA (Microsoft Certified Systems Administrator) and MCSE series of exams is different from that of its previous exams covering Windows NT 4.0. For the design exams, each exam consists entirely of a series of case studies, and the questions can be any of six types. The MCSE design exams include the following:

➤ 70-219, "Designing a Microsoft Windows 2000 Directory Services Infrastructure"

➤ 70-220, "Designing Security for a Microsoft Windows 2000 Network"

➤ 70-221, "Designing a Microsoft Windows 2000 Network Infrastructure"

➤ 70-226, "Designing Highly Available Web Solutions with Microsoft Windows 2000 Server Technologies"

➤ 70-229, "Designing and Implementing Databases with Microsoft SQL Server 2000 Enterprise Edition"

➤ 70-297, "Designing a Microsoft Windows Server 2003 Active Directory and Network Infrastructure"

➤ 70-298, "Designing Security for a Microsoft Windows Server 2003 Network"

For design exams, each case study or *testlet* presents a detailed problem that you must read and analyze. Figure 1.1 shows an example of what a case study looks like. You must select the different tabs in the case study to view the entire case.

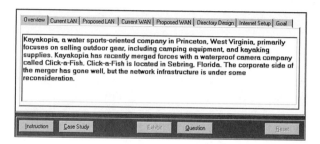

Figure 1.1 The format for case study questions.

Following each case study is a set of questions related to the case study; these questions can be one of six types (which are discussed in the following sections). Careful attention to details provided in the case study is the key to success. You should be prepared to frequently toggle between the case study and the questions as you work. Some of the case studies include diagrams, which are called *exhibits*, which you'll need to examine closely to understand how to answer the questions.

After you complete a case study, you can review all the questions and your answers. However, after you move on to the next case study, you might not be able to return to the previous case study to make any changes.

For the MCSA and MCSE core exams and the upgrade exams, the same six types of questions may appear, but you are not likely to encounter complex multiquestion case studies. The MCSA/MCSE core exams and upgrade exams for the Windows 2000 track and the Windows Server 2003 track include the following:

➤ 70-210, "Installing, Configuring, and Administering Microsoft Windows 2000 Professional"

➤ 70-270, "Installing, Configuring, and Administering Microsoft Windows XP Professional"

➤ 70-215, "Installing, Configuring, and Administering Microsoft Windows 2000 Server"

➤ 70-216, "Implementing and Administering a Microsoft Windows 2000 Network Infrastructure"

➤ 70-217, "Implementing and Administering a Microsoft Windows 2000 Directory Services Infrastructure"

➤ 70-218, "Managing a Microsoft Windows 2000 Network Environment"

➤ 70-290, "Managing and Maintaining a Microsoft Windows Server 2003 Environment"

➤ 70-291, "Implementing, Managing, and Maintaining a Microsoft Windows Server 2003 Network Infrastructure"

➤ 70-292, "Managing and Maintaining a Microsoft Windows Server 2003 Environment for an MCSA Certified on Windows 2000"

➤ 70-293, "Planning and Maintaining a Microsoft Windows Server 2003 Network Infrastructure"

➤ 70-294, "Planning, Implementing, and Maintaining a Microsoft Windows Server 2003 Active Directory Infrastructure"

➤ 70-296, "Planning, Implementing, and Maintaining a Microsoft Windows Server 2003 Environment for an MCSE Certified on Windows 2000"

Traditional Exam Question Formats

Historically, six types of question formats have appeared on Microsoft certification exams. These types of questions continue to appear on current Microsoft tests, and they are discussed in the following sections:

➤ Multiple-choice, single-answer

➤ Multiple-choice, multiple-answer

➤ Build-list-and-reorder (list prioritization)

➤ Create-a-tree

➤ Drag-and-connect

➤ Select-and-place (drag-and-drop)

 You can expect to encounter all the question formats listed previously on the 70-291 exam.

The Single-Answer and Multiple-Answer Multiple-Choice Question Formats

Some exam questions require you to select a single answer, whereas others ask you to select multiple correct answers. The following multiple-choice question requires you to select a single correct answer. Following the question is a brief summary of each potential answer and why it is either right or wrong.

Question 1

> You have three domains connected to an empty root domain under one contiguous domain name: tutu.com. This organization is formed into a forest arrangement, with a secondary domain called frog.com. How many schema masters exist for this arrangement?
>
> ○ A. 1
> ○ B. 2
> ○ C. 3
> ○ D. 4

Answer A is correct because only one schema master is necessary for a forest arrangement. The other answers (answers B, C, and D) are misleading because they try to make you believe that schema masters might be in each domain or perhaps that you should have one for each contiguous namespace domain.

This sample question format corresponds closely to the Microsoft certification exam format. The only difference is that on the exam, the questions are not followed by answers and their explanations. To select an answer, you position the cursor over the radio button next to the answer you want to select. Then you click the mouse button to select the answer.

Let's examine a question in which one or more answers are possible. This type of question provides check boxes rather than option buttons for marking all appropriate selections.

Question 2

> What can you use to seize FSMO roles? (Select all the correct answers.)
>
> ❑ A. The ntdsutil.exe utility
>
> ❑ B. The Replication Monitor
>
> ❑ C. The secedit.exe utility
>
> ❑ D. Active Directory domains and trusts

Answers A and B are correct. You can seize roles from a server that is still running through the Replication Monitor, or, in the case of a server failure, you can seize roles with the ntdsutil.exe utility. The secedit.exe utility is used to force group policies into play; therefore, answer C is incorrect. Active Directory domains and trusts are a combination of truth and fiction; therefore, answer D is incorrect.

For this particular question, two answers are required. Microsoft sometimes gives partial credit for partially correct answers. For question 2, you must mark the check boxes next to answers A and B to obtain credit for a correct answer. Notice that choosing the right answers also means knowing why the other answers are wrong!

The Build-List-and-Reorder Question Format

Questions in the build-list-and-reorder format present two lists of items—one on the left and one on the right. To answer the question, you must move items from the list on the right to the list on the left. The final list must then be reordered into a specific order.

These questions generally sound like this: "From the following list of choices, pick the choices that answer the question. Arrange the list in a certain order." To give you practice with this type of question, some questions of this type are included in this book. Question 3 shows an example of how they appear in this book; for an example of how they appear on the test, see Figure 1.2.

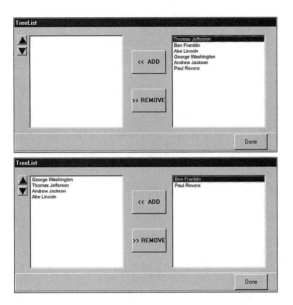

Figure 1.2   The format for build-list-and-reorder questions.

Question 3

From the following list of famous people, choose those that have been elected president of the United States. Arrange the list in the order in which the presidents served.

Thomas Jefferson

Ben Franklin

Abe Lincoln

George Washington

Andrew Jackson

Paul Revere

The correct answer is

George Washington

Thomas Jefferson

Andrew Jackson

Abe Lincoln

On an actual exam, the entire list of famous people would initially appear in the list on the right. You would move the four correct answers to the list on the left and then reorder the list on the left. Notice that the answer to question 3 does not include all items from the initial list. However, that might not always be the case.

To move an item from the right list to the left list on the exam, you first select the item by clicking it, and then you click the Add button (left arrow). After you move an item from one list to the other, you can move the item back by first selecting the item and then clicking the appropriate button (either the Add button or the Remove button). After items have been moved to the left list, you can move an item by selecting the item and clicking the up or down buttons.

The Create-a-Tree Question Format

Questions in the create-a-tree format also present two lists—one on the left side of the screen and one on the right side of the screen. The list on the right consists of individual items, and the list on the left consists of nodes in a tree. To answer the question, you must move items from the list on the right to the appropriate node in the tree.

These questions can best be characterized as simply a matching exercise. Items from the list on the right are placed under the appropriate category in the list on the left. Question 4 shows an example of how they appear in this book; for a sample of how they appear on the test, see Figure 1.3.

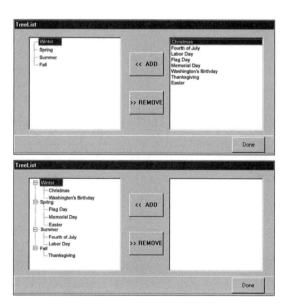

Figure 1.3 The create-a-tree question format.

Question 4

> The calendar year is divided into four seasons:
>
> Winter
>
> Spring
>
> Summer
>
> Fall
>
> Identify the season during which each of the following holidays occurs:
>
> Christmas
>
> Fourth of July
>
> Labor Day
>
> Flag Day
>
> Memorial Day
>
> Washington's Birthday
>
> Thanksgiving
>
> Easter

The correct answer is

➤ Winter

Christmas

Washington's Birthday

➤ Spring

Flag Day

Memorial Day

Easter

➤ Summer

Fourth of July

Labor Day

➤ Fall

Thanksgiving

In this case, all the items in the list are used. However, that might not always be the case.

To move an item from the right list to its appropriate location in the tree, you must first select the appropriate tree node by clicking it. Then you select the item to be moved and click the Add button. If one or more items have been added to a tree node, the node is displayed with a + icon to the left of the node name. You can click this icon to expand the node and view the item(s) that has been added. If any item has been added to the wrong tree node, you can remove it by selecting it and clicking the Remove button.

The Drag-and-Connect Question Format

Questions in the drag-and-connect format present a group of objects and a list of connections. To answer the question, you must move the appropriate connections between the objects.

This type of question is best described using graphics. Question 5 shows an example.

Question 5

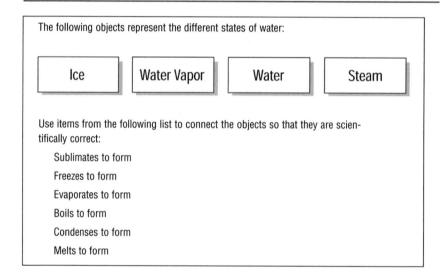

The following objects represent the different states of water:

Ice	Water Vapor	Water	Steam

Use items from the following list to connect the objects so that they are scientifically correct:

Sublimates to form

Freezes to form

Evaporates to form

Boils to form

Condenses to form

Melts to form

The correct answer is

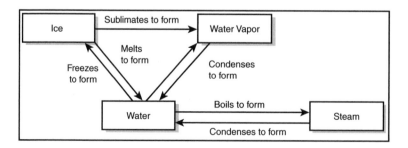

For this type of question, it's not necessary to use every object, and each connection can be used multiple times.

The Select-and-Place Question Format

Questions in the select-and-place (drag-and-drop) format present a diagram with blank boxes and a list of labels that need to be dragged to correctly fill in the blank boxes. To answer such a question, you must move the labels to their appropriate positions on the diagram.

This type of question is best described using graphics. Question 6 shows an example.

Question 6

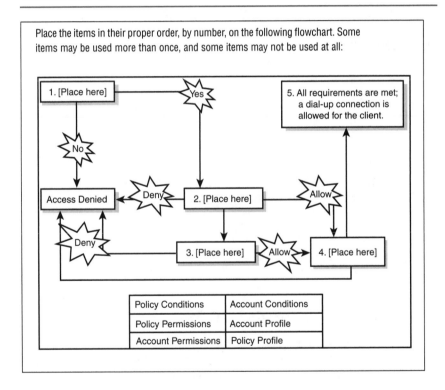

The correct answer is

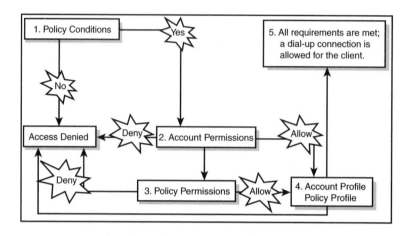

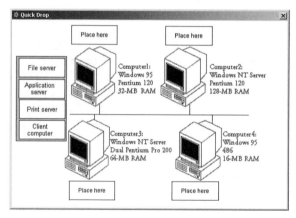

Figure 1.4 A sample select-and-place question.

New Exam Question Formats

Microsoft is introducing several new question types in addition to the more traditional types of questions that are still widely used on all Microsoft exams. These new, innovative question types were highly researched and tested by Microsoft before they were chosen to be included in many of the newer exams for the MCSA/MCSE on Windows 2000 track and the MCSA/MCSE on Windows Server 2003 track. These new question types are as follows:

➤ Hot area questions

➤ Active screen questions

➤ New drag-and-drop type questions

➤ Simulation questions

Hot Area Question Types

Hot area questions ask you to indicate the correct answer by selecting one or more elements within a graphic. For example, you might be asked to select multiple objects within a list, as shown in Figure 1.5.

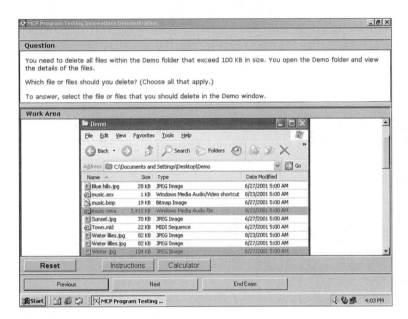

Figure 1.5   Selecting objects within a list box to answer a hot area question.

Active Screen Question Types

Active screen questions ask you to configure a dialog box by modifying one or more elements. These types of questions offer a realistic interface in which you must properly configure various settings, just as you would within the actual software product. For example, you might be asked to select the proper option within a drop-down list box, as shown in Figure 1.6.

New Drag-and-Drop Question Types

New drag-and-drop questions ask you to drag source elements to their appropriate corresponding targets within a work area. These types of questions test your knowledge of specific concepts and their definitions or descriptions. For example, you might be asked to match a description of a computer program to the actual software application, as shown in Figure 1.7.

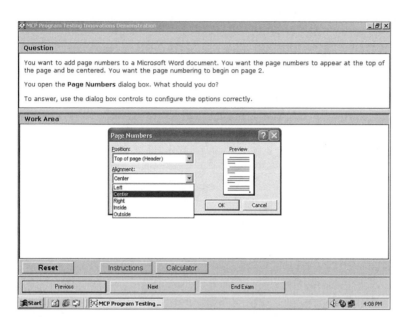

Figure 1.6   Configuring an option from a dialog box's drop-down list box to answer an active screen question.

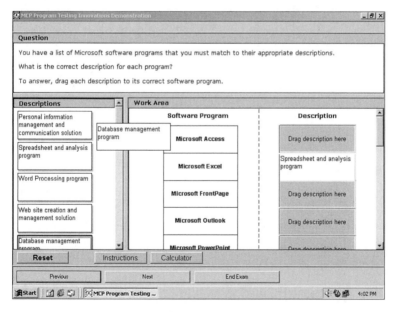

Figure 1.7   Using drag-and-drop to match the correct application description to each software program listed.

Simulation Question Types

Simulation questions ask you to indicate the correct answer by performing specific tasks, such as configuring and installing network adapters or drivers, configuring and controlling access to files, or troubleshooting hardware devices. Many of the tasks that systems administrators and systems engineers perform can be presented more accurately in simulations than in most traditional exam question types (see Figure 1.8).

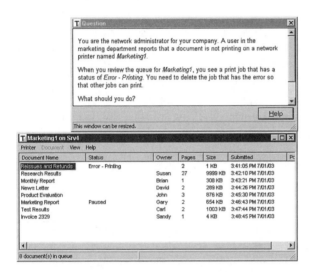

Figure 1.8   Answering a simulation question about how to troubleshoot a network printing problem.

 When in doubt, don't change your first instinct! If you're not sure of the possible answers, always go with your first instinct.

Microsoft's Testing Formats

Currently, Microsoft uses four different testing formats:

➤ Case study

➤ Fixed-length

➤ Adaptive

➤ Short-form

As mentioned earlier, the case study approach is used with Microsoft's design exams. These exams consist of a set of case studies that you must analyze so that you can answer questions related to the case studies. Such exams include one or more case studies (tabbed topic areas), each of which is followed by 4 to 10 questions. The question types for design exams and for the four core exams are multiple-choice, build-list-and-reorder, create-a-tree, drag-and-connect, and select-and-place. Depending on the test topic, some exams are totally case based, whereas others are not.

Other Microsoft exams employ advanced testing capabilities that might not be immediately apparent. Although the questions that appear are primarily multiple-choice, the logic that drives them is more complex than that in older Microsoft tests, which use a fixed sequence of questions, called a *fixed-length test*. Some questions employ a sophisticated user interface, which Microsoft calls a *simulation*, to test your knowledge of the software and systems under consideration in a more or less live environment that behaves just like the real thing. You should review the Microsoft Training and Certification Web pages at www.microsoft.com/traincert for more information.

For some exams, Microsoft has turned to a well-known technique called *adaptive testing* to establish a test taker's level of knowledge and product competence. Adaptive exams look the same as fixed-length exams, but they discover the level of difficulty at which an individual test taker can correctly answer questions. Test takers with differing levels of knowledge or ability therefore see different sets of questions; individuals with high levels of knowledge or ability are presented with a smaller set of more difficult questions, whereas individuals with lower levels of knowledge are presented with a larger set of easier questions. Two individuals may answer the same percentage of questions correctly, but the test taker with a higher knowledge or ability level will score higher because his or her questions are worth more. Also, the lower-level test taker will probably answer more questions than his or her more-knowledgeable colleague. This explains why adaptive tests use ranges of values to define the number of questions and the amount of time it takes to complete the test.

Adaptive tests work by evaluating the test taker's most recent answer. A correct answer leads to a more difficult question, and the test software's estimate of the test taker's knowledge and ability level is raised. An incorrect answer leads to a less difficult question, and the test software's estimate of the test taker's knowledge and ability level is lowered. This process continues until the test targets the test taker's true ability level. The exam ends when the test taker's level of accuracy meets a statistically acceptable value (in other words, when his or her performance demonstrates an acceptable level of knowledge and ability) or when the maximum number of items has been presented (in which case the test taker is almost certain to fail).

Microsoft has also introduced a short-form test for its most popular tests. This test delivers 25 to 30 questions to its takers, giving them exactly 60 minutes to complete the exam. This type of exam is similar to a fixed-length test, in that it allows readers to jump ahead or return to earlier questions and to cycle through the questions until the test is done. Microsoft does not use adaptive logic in short-form tests, but it claims that statistical analysis of the question pool is such that the 25 to 30 questions delivered during a short-form exam conclusively measure a test taker's knowledge of the subject matter in much the same way as an adaptive test. You can think of the short-form test as a kind of greatest-hits version of an adaptive exam on the same topic—that is, the most important questions are covered.

NOTE
Microsoft certification exams may use either the adaptive-question format or the more traditional fixed-length question format. Historically, Microsoft tests have been primarily fixed-length format, but the company seems to be moving in the direction of publishing more adaptive-question format exams.

Because you won't know which form the Microsoft exam may be, you should be prepared for an adaptive exam instead of a fixed-length or a short-form exam. The penalties for answering incorrectly are built in to the test itself on an adaptive exam, whereas the layout remains the same for a fixed-length or short-form test, no matter how many questions you answer incorrectly.

TIP
The biggest difference between adaptive tests and fixed-length or short-form tests is that you can mark and revisit questions on fixed-length and short-form tests after you've read them. On an adaptive test, you must answer the question when it is presented, and you cannot go back to that question later.

Strategies for Different Testing Formats

Before you choose a test-taking strategy, you must determine what type of test it is—case study, fixed-length, short-form, or adaptive:

➤ Case study tests consist of a tabbed window that allows you to navigate easily through the sections of the case.

➤ Fixed-length tests consist of 50 to 70 questions, with a check box for each question. You can return to these questions if you want.

➤ Short-form tests have 25 to 30 questions, with a check box for each question. You can return to these questions if you want.

➤ Adaptive tests are identified in the introductory material of the test. Questions have no check boxes and can be visited (and answered) only once. You do not have the option of reviewing any questions after you have answered them all.

You'll be able to tell for sure whether you are taking an adaptive, fixed-length, or short-form test by the first question. Fixed-length and short-form tests include a check box that allows you to mark the question for later review. Adaptive test questions include no such check box and can be visited (and answered) only once.

Case Study Exam Strategy

Most test takers find that the case study type of test used for the design exams (including exams 70-219, 70-220, 70-221, and 70-226, among others) is the most difficult to master. When it comes to studying for a case study test, your best bet is to approach each case study as a standalone test. The biggest challenge you're likely to encounter with this type of test is that you might feel that you won't have enough time to get through all the cases that are presented.

Each case study provides a lot of material that you need to read and study before you can effectively answer the questions that follow. The trick to taking a case study exam is to first scan the case study to get the highlights. You should make sure that you read the overview section of the case so that you understand the context of the problem at hand. Then you should quickly move on to scanning the questions.

As you are scanning the questions, you should make mental notes to yourself so that you'll remember which sections of the case study you should focus on. Some case studies may provide a fair amount of extra information that you don't really need to answer the questions. The goal with this scanning approach is to avoid having to study and analyze material that is not completely relevant.

When studying a case, read the tabbed information carefully. It is important to answer each and every question. You will be able to toggle back and forth from case to questions, and from question to question within a case testlet. However, after you leave the case and move on, you might not be able to return to it. We suggest that you take notes while reading useful information to help you when you tackle the test questions. It's hard to go wrong with this strategy when taking any kind of Microsoft certification test.

The Fixed-Length and Short-Form Exam Strategies

A well-known principle when taking fixed-length or short-form exams is first to read through the entire exam from start to finish. Answer only those questions that you feel absolutely sure you know. On subsequent passes, you can dive into more complex questions more deeply, knowing how many such questions you have left and the amount of time remaining.

 There's at least one potential benefit to reading the exam completely before answering the trickier questions: Sometimes information supplied in later questions sheds more light on earlier questions. At other times, information you read in later questions may jog your memory about facts, figures, or behavior and help you answer earlier questions. Either way, you'll come out ahead if you answer only those questions on the first pass that you're absolutely confident about.

Fortunately, the Microsoft exam software for fixed-length and short-form tests makes the multiple-visit approach easy to implement. At the top-left corner of each question is a check box that permits you to mark that question for a later visit.

Here are some question-handling strategies that apply to fixed-length and short-form tests. Use them if you have the chance:

➤ When returning to a question after your initial read-through, read every word again; otherwise, your mind can miss important details. Sometimes revisiting a question after turning your attention elsewhere lets you see something you missed, but the strong tendency is to see what you've seen before. Try to avoid that tendency at all costs.

➤ If you return to a question more than twice, try to articulate to yourself what you don't understand about the question, why answers don't appear to make sense, or what appears to be missing. If you chew on the subject a while, your subconscious may provide the missing details, or you may notice a trick that points to the right answer.

As you work your way through the exam, another counter that Microsoft provides will come in handy—the number of questions completed and questions outstanding. For fixed-length and short-form tests, it's wise to budget your time by making sure that you've completed one quarter of the questions one quarter of the way through the exam period, and three quarters of the questions three quarters of the way through.

If you're not finished when only five minutes remain, use that time to guess your way through any remaining questions. Remember, guessing is potentially more valuable than not answering. Blank answers are always wrong, but a guess may turn out to be right. If you don't have a clue about any of the remaining questions, pick answers at random or choose all A's, B's, and so on. Questions left unanswered are counted as answered incorrectly, so a guess is better than nothing at all.

 At the very end of your exam period, you're better off guessing than leaving questions unanswered.

The Adaptive Exam Strategy

If there's one principle that applies to taking an adaptive test, it could be summed up as "Get it right the first time." You cannot elect to skip a question and move on to the next one when taking an adaptive test because the testing software uses your answer to the current question to select the question it presents next. You also cannot return to a question after you've moved on because the software gives you only one chance to answer the question. However, you can take notes, and sometimes information supplied in earlier questions sheds more light on later questions.

Also, when you answer a question correctly, you are presented with a more difficult question next, to help the software gauge your level of skill and ability. When you answer a question incorrectly, you are presented with a less difficult question, and the software lowers its current estimate of your skill and ability. This continues until the program settles into a reasonably accurate estimate of what you know and can do; it takes you, on average, somewhere between 15 and 30 questions to complete the test.

The good news is that if you know your stuff, you are likely to finish most adaptive tests in 30 minutes or so. The bad news is that you must really, really know your stuff to do your best on an adaptive test. That's because some questions are so convoluted, complex, or hard to follow that you're bound to miss one or two, at a minimum, even if you do know your stuff. So the more you know, the better you'll do on an adaptive test, even accounting for the occasionally weird or unfathomable questions that appear on these exams.

Because you can't always tell in advance whether a test is a fixed-length, short-form, or adaptive exam, you should prepare for the exam as if it were adaptive. That way, you will be prepared to pass no matter what kind of test you take. But if you do take a fixed-length or short-form test, you need to remember the tips from the preceding sections. These tips should help you perform even better on a fixed-length or short-form exam than on an adaptive test. When studying for the 70-291 exam, be prepared to encounter any of these three test formats.

If you encounter a question on an adaptive test that you can't answer, you must guess an answer immediately. Because of how the software works, however, you might suffer for your guess on the next question if you guess right because you get a more difficult question next!

Question-Handling Strategies

For questions that have only one right answer, usually two or three of the answers will be obviously incorrect, and two of the answers will be plausible. Unless the answer leaps out at you (if it does, reread the question to look for a trick—sometimes those are the ones you're most likely to get wrong), begin the process of answering by eliminating those answers that are most obviously wrong.

At least one answer out of the possible choices for a question can usually be eliminated immediately because it matches one of these conditions:

➤ The answer does not apply to the situation.

➤ The answer describes a nonexistent issue, an invalid option, or an imaginary state.

After you eliminate all answers that are obviously wrong, you can apply your retained knowledge to eliminate further answers. You should look for items that sound correct but refer to actions, commands, or features that are not present or not available in the situation that the question describes.

If you're still faced with a blind guess among two or more potentially correct answers, reread the question. Try to picture how each of the possible remaining answers would alter the situation. Be especially sensitive to terminology; sometimes the choice of words (*remove* instead of *disable*) can make the difference between a right answer and a wrong one.

You should guess at an answer only after you've exhausted your ability to eliminate answers and are still unclear about which of the remaining possibilities is correct. An unanswered question offers you no points, but guessing gives you at least some chance of getting a question right; just don't be too hasty when making a blind guess.

If you're taking a fixed-length or a short-form test, you can wait until the last round of reviewing marked questions (just as you're about to run out of time or unanswered questions) before you start making guesses. You will usually have the same option within each case study testlet (but once you leave a testlet, you may not be allowed to return to it). If you're taking an adaptive test, you'll have to guess to move on to the next question if you can't figure out an answer some other way. Either way, guessing should be your technique of last resort!

Numerous questions assume that the default behavior of a particular utility is in effect. If you know the defaults and understand what they mean, this knowledge will help you cut through many of the trickier questions. Simple final actions may be critical as well. If a utility must be restarted before proposed changes take effect, a correct answer may require this step as well.

Mastering the Inner Game

In the final analysis, knowledge breeds confidence, and confidence breeds success. If you study the materials in this book carefully and review all the practice questions at the end of each chapter, you should become aware of the areas in which you need additional learning and study.

After you've worked your way through the book, take the practice exams in the back of the book. Taking these tests provides a reality check and helps you identify areas to study further. Make sure you follow up and review materials related to the questions you miss on the practice exams before scheduling a real exam. Don't schedule your exam appointment until after you've thoroughly studied the material and feel comfortable with the whole scope of the practice exams. You should score 80% or better on the practice exams before proceeding to the real thing (otherwise, obtain some additional practice tests so that you can keep trying until you hit this magic number).

If you take a practice exam and don't get at least 70% to 80% of the questions correct, keep practicing. Microsoft provides links to practice exam providers and also self-assessment exams at **www.microsoft.com/traincert/mcpexams/prepare/**.

Armed with the information in this book and with the determination to augment your knowledge, you should be able to pass the certification exam. However, you need to work at it, or you'll spend the exam fee more than once before you finally pass. If you prepare seriously, you should do well.

The next section covers other sources that you can use to prepare for Microsoft certification exams.

Additional Resources

A good source of information about Microsoft Certification Exams comes from Microsoft itself. Because its products and technologies—and the exams that go with them—change frequently, the best place to go for exam-related information is online.

If you haven't already visited the Microsoft Training and Certification Web site, you should do so right now. Microsoft's Training and Certification home page resides at www.microsoft.com/traincert (see Figure 1.9).

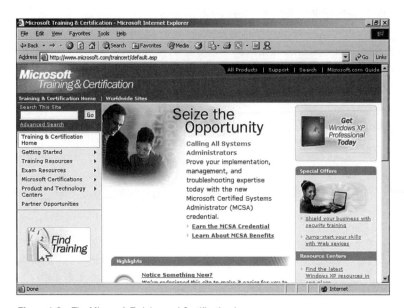

Figure 1.9   The Microsoft Training and Certification home page.

Coping with Change on the Web

Sooner or later, all the information we've shared with you about the Microsoft Certified Professional pages and the other Web-based resources mentioned throughout the rest of this book will go stale or be replaced by newer information. In some cases, the URLs you find here may lead you to their replacements; in other cases, the URLs will go nowhere, leaving you with the dreaded "404 File not found" error message. When that happens, don't give up.

There's always a way to find what you want on the Web if you're willing to invest some time and energy. Most large or complex Web sites—and Microsoft's qualifies on both counts—offer search engines. On all of Microsoft's Web pages, a Search button appears at the top edge of the page. As long as you can get to Microsoft's site (it should stay at **www.microsoft.com** for a long time), you can use the Search button to find what you need.

The more focused you can make a search request, the more likely it is that the results will include information you can use. For example, you can search for this string to produce a lot of data about the subject in general:

"training and certification"

However, if you're looking for the preparation guide for Exam 70-291, "Implementing, Managing, and Maintaining a Windows Server 2003 Network Infrastructure," you'll be more likely to get there quickly if you use a search string similar to the following:

"Exam 70-291" AND "preparation guide"

Likewise, if you want to find the Training and Certification downloads, you should try a search string such as this:

"training and certification" AND "download page"

Finally, you should feel free to use general search tools—such as **www.google.com**, **www.altavista.com**, and **www.excite.com**—to look for related information. Although Microsoft offers great information about its certification exams online, there are plenty of third-party sources of information and assistance that need not follow Microsoft's party line. Therefore, if you can't find something where the book says it lives, you should intensify your search.

Managing IP Addressing

Terms you'll need to understand:

✓ Dynamic Host Control Protocol (DHCP)
✓ Transmission Control Protocol/Internet Protocol (TCP/IP)
✓ Scope
✓ DHCP database
✓ Lease
✓ DHCP clients

Techniques you'll need to master:

✓ Configuring TCP/IP on a server computer
✓ Managing a DHCP server
✓ Managing DHCP clients
✓ Managing the DHCP database
✓ Configuring and managing DHCP scope options
✓ Troubleshooting TCP/IP

One of the requirements of Active Directory is the *Transmission Control Protocol/Internet Protocol (TCP/IP)* suite. For computers on a TCP/IP network to communicate, each computer must be assigned a unique IP address. In some cases, it might make sense to configure each workstation with a static IP address or to use automatic private IP addressing. However, statically configuring IP addresses can add a lot of administrative overhead. Not only can it become time consuming, but it also increases the possibility of a workstation being configured with incorrect parameters. Imagine having to visit 10,000 workstations and type in 10,000 IP addresses without making a single error. The *Dynamic Host Configuration Protocol (DHCP)* service can be implemented to centralize the administration and assignment of IP addresses. DHCP automates and centralizes many of the tasks associated with IP addressing.

This chapter discusses how to configure TCP/IP on a server computer and how to implement a DHCP server, including the installation process, the authorization of the server, and the configuration of DHCP scopes. This chapter also looks at some of the management tasks associated with running DHCP.

Configuring TCP/IP on a Server Computer

IP addresses can be assigned automatically or statically. Using DHCP or Automatic Private IP Addressing (APIPA), IP addresses can be assigned automatically. In some instances, however, it is necessary to statically configure IP addresses. This is often the case with servers on the network. Some of the components that you might install on a server require that the server be configured with a static IP address. For example, during the installation of Active Directory or the Domain Name System (DNS), a message appears informing you that the server should be configured with a static IP address.

Automatic Private IP Addressing (APIPA) is not normally used as a method of assigning IP addresses. It is limited in use because it does not automatically configure additional parameters such as a default gateway or DNS servers. It is designed to be used in single-segment networks (networks that are not routed). It is also useful if a DHCP server is unavailable. *DHCP clients* can assign themselves an IP address in the range of 169.254.0.1 to 169.254.255.254. APIPA enables clients to communicate with other computers on the same network segment until an IP address can be obtained from a DHCP server, allowing the machine to fully participate on the network.

DHCP IP Address Assignments

If you plan to use DHCP to assign IP addresses to clients, you can leave the default client configuration for TCP/IP as is. During the installation of Windows Server 2003, the default configuration is to obtain an IP address automatically. This is also the case with Windows 2000 and Windows XP clients.

Static IP Addressing

To statically configure IP address parameters, you need to edit the properties of the TCP/IP for the network connection.

To statically configure TCP/IP, follow these steps:

1. From the Windows Server 2003 desktop, right-click My Network Places and select Properties from the menu.

2. From the Network Connections window, right-click the network connection that you want to configure a static IP address for, and click Properties.

3. Select Internet Protocol (TCP/IP) and click the Properties button.

4. Select the Use the Following IP Address option (see Figure 2.1). Enter a unique IP address, the subnet mask, the IP address of the default gateway, and the IP address of the primary and secondary DNS servers. Click OK.

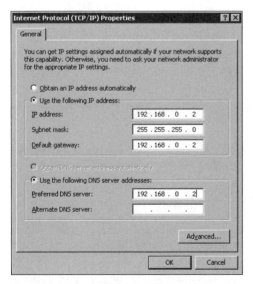

Figure 2.1   You can statically configure IP address parameters from the General tab of the TCP/IP Properties dialog box.

Configuring Advanced Settings

Aside from configuring a static IP address, you can configure a number of advanced settings for TCP/IP. Clicking the Advanced button shown in Figure 2.1 brings up the Advanced TCP/IP Settings window (see Figure 2.2).

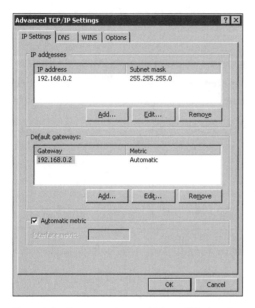

Figure 2.2 You can configure additional TCP/IP settings via the Advanced TCP/IP Settings dialog box.

From the IP Settings tab shown in Figure 2.2, you can configure additional IP addresses and gateways for the network connection. Additional IP addresses for the interface might need to be configured if the computer is connected to a single network subnet and requires multiple IP addresses to communicate on the network, or if the computer needs to communicate with multiple subnets. Similarly, you can configure multiple default gateways to be used by the connection.

The metric is used to assign a numeric value for the gateway that is used in routing. The default setting of Automatic Metric assigns a metric value to the gateway based on interface speed. Deselecting the Automatic Metric option enables you to manually configure this value. The gateway with the lowest value is favored.

Selecting the DNS tab shown in Figure 2.3 enables you to configure advanced DNS settings for the network connection if multiple DNS servers are in use on your network. Additional DNS servers can be configured, along with the order in which they are used for name resolution.

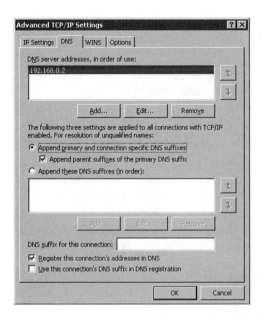

Figure 2.3   You can configure DNS settings from the DNS tab of the Advanced TCP/IP Settings dialog box.

You can also select from the following three options to configure name resolution:

➤ *Append Primary and Connection-Specific DNS Suffixes*—This option specifies that name resolution for unqualified names is limited to the primary DNS suffix as well as connection-specific suffixes.

➤ *Append Parent Suffix of the Primary DNS Suffix*—This option specifies whether the parent suffix of the primary DNS suffix is used for name resolution.

➤ *Append These DNS Suffixes*—When this option is selected, the primary and connection-specific suffixes are not used for unqualified name resolution. Instead, unqualified name resolution is limited to the domain suffixes listed in the Append These DNS Suffixes list.

From the bottom of the DNS tab, you can configure the DNS suffix for the connection as well as specify whether the IP address and the connection's DNS suffix should be automatically registered with a DNS server.

Using the WINS tab shown in Figure 2.4, you can configure the IP addresses of the WINS servers on the network and specify the order in which they will be used for NetBIOS name resolution. You also can enable LMHOSTS for name resolution.

NOTE

DNS is the primary namespace used in a Windows Server 2003 environment. NetBIOS is also supported for backward compatibility. Windows Internet Name Service (WINS) is used to centralize the process of registering and resolving NetBIOS names to IP addresses. LMHOSTS files are another method of resolving NetBIOS names to IP addresses. An LMHOSTS file is a text file that maps NetBIOS names to IP addresses; it must be manually configured and updated.

The three options at the bottom of the dialog box enable you to configure additional NetBIOS settings. The first option, Default, should be selected if the NetBIOS settings are assigned through a DHCP server. The remaining two options allow you to enable or disable NetBIOS if IP configuration is performed manually. For example, if the network does not have any pre–Windows 2000 clients and all names are registered with a DNS server, NetBIOS over TCP/IP can be disabled. On the other hand, this option should be enabled if there are legacy clients on the network.

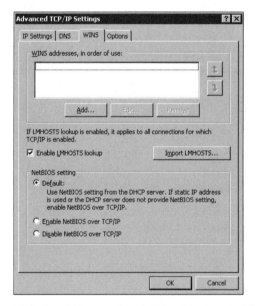

Figure 2.4 You can configure WINS settings from the WINS tab of the Advanced TCP/IP Settings dialog box.

The Options tab allows you to enable TCP/IP filtering to control the type of TCP/IP traffic that reaches your computer. Clicking the Properties button on the Options tab brings up the TCP/IP filtering window (see Figure 2.5), where you can enable filtering to specify the type of traffic that is permitted based on Transmission Control Protocol (TCP) and User Datagram Protocol (UDP) ports (ports are the endpoints for the logical connections), as well as specific IPs.

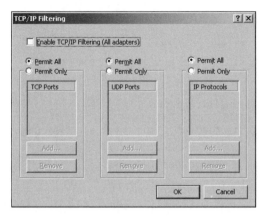

Figure 2.5 You can configure TCP/IP filtering by clicking the Properties button on the Options tab of the Advanced TCP/IP Settings dialog box and adjusting settings on the TCP/IP Filtering dialog box.

Managing DHCP

Every device with a network interface card on an IP network requires a unique IP address and a corresponding subnet mask. The previous section outlined how to manually configure an IP address on Windows Server 2003. The process is very similar for other clients, such as Windows 2000 and Windows XP. Manual assignment is one method for assigning IP addresses, although it might not be suitable for many network environments.

To illustrate how difficult it could be to manually assign IP addresses, imagine having a large network with 5,000 or more users. It is possible to visit each workstation and manually configure IP addresses, but the work does not stop there. Any changes that must be made to IP parameters, such as the addition of a DNS server, will again require you to visit a number of workstations, if not all of them, to reconfigure the parameters. The more efficient solution is to implement a DHCP server to centralize administration and automate IP address assignment.

To implement this solution on Windows Server 2003 (or another platform such as Windows 2000 Server), the DHCP service must be running and configured. The service can be installed on a domain controller, a member server, or a server that is a member of a workgroup.

Before a DHCP server can be fully functional on a network, the following steps must be completed:

➤ The server that will be assigned the role of DHCP server must be configured with a static IP address.

➤ The DHCP server component must be installed.

➤ The DHCP server must be configured with a range of IP addresses (also known as a *scope*) to be *leased* to DHCP clients. Each DHCP server requires at least one scope, and the scope must be activated.

➤ The DHCP server must be authorized within Active Directory.

After all of these steps have been performed, your DHCP server will be capable of leasing IP addresses to DHCP clients. The process of leasing an IP address occurs in the following four phases:

 Acronyms are always a great way to remember information. An easy way to remember the four phases of the IP address lease process is DORA: discover, offer, request, acknowledge.

1. *Discover*—The DHCP client broadcasts a DHCP discover message on the network containing its MAC address and NetBIOS name. If no DHCP servers respond to the request, the client continues to broadcast up to 4 times at 2, 4, 8, and 16 seconds. If a response is not received during this time, the client continues to broadcast every 5 minutes.

2. *Offer*—Each DHCP server on the network that receives the request responds with a DHCP offer message. An offered IP address is included in the message.

3. *Request*—If multiple DHCP servers respond, the client selects the first offer it receives and broadcasts a DHCP request for the IP address. The message is broadcast on the network because the client has not yet been assigned an IP address; it has only been offered one.

4. *Acknowledge*—The DHCP server responds with a DHCPACK (acknowledgment) granting the client's request to use the IP address. The DHCPACK also contains information about any DHCP options that have been configured on the server (such as the IP address of the DNS server).

Remember that if a DHCP server is unavailable, the DHCP client continues to broadcast the DHCP discover message until a DHCP server responds. However, the client assigns itself an IP address in the range of 169.254.0.0 to 169.254.255.255 during this time. This is known as Automatic Private IP Addressing (APIPA). The client can communicate on the network, but only with other clients on the same subnet that also are using an IP address in this range. If clients are running Windows XP, you can use the Alternate Configuration tab from the Internet Protocol (TCP/IP) window to manually configure the automatically assigned IP address and other parameters that should be used if the DHCP server is unavailable.

Installing DHCP

To automate the process of assigning IP addresses to network clients, the DHCP Server service must be installed on at least one server. The service can be installed in a number of ways. You can opt to install it during the installation of Windows Server 2003, or you can install it later using the Configure Your Server Wizard or through the Add or Remove Programs applet within the Control Panel.

To install DHCP using the Configure Your Server Wizard, perform the following steps:

1. Click Start and click Manage Your Server.

2. Within the Manage Your Server window, select Add or Remove a Role. This launches the Configure Your Server Wizard. Click Next after reviewing the list of preliminary steps that should be completed.

3. Select DHCP server from the list of server roles (see Figure 2.6). Click Next.

4. A summary of selections appears listing the tasks that will be performed. Click Next.

5. After the service has been installed, the New Scope Wizard launches automatically. At this point, you can click Next to configure a scope for the DHCP server or click Cancel. The scope can then be configured later through the DHCP console. The concepts of DHCP scopes are discussed in the following section. Click Finish.

 Before a DHCP server is fully functional on a network, it must be configured with at least one scope and must be activated. A scope is a range, or pool, of IP addresses that can be leased to DHCP clients by the server when requested. The DHCP server must also be authorized within Active Directory.

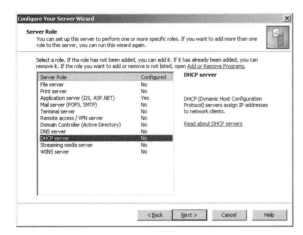

Figure 2.6 You can select a server role through the Configure Your Server Wizard.

To install DHCP using the Add or Remove Programs applet, follow these steps:

1. Click Start, point to Control Panel, and click Add or Remove Programs.

2. Click Add/Remove Windows Components.

3. Click Networking Services in the Components list and click the Details button.

4. Select Dynamic Host Configuration Protocol (DHCP) from the list of Networking Services (see Figure 2.7). Click OK. Click Next to continue.

5. Click Finish.

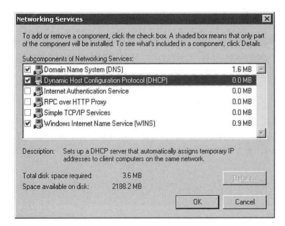

Figure 2.7 You can install DHCP through the Add or Remove Programs applet in the Control Panel.

Authorizing a DHCP Server

The authorization of DHCP servers was a feature introduced in Windows 2000 and is included with Windows Server 2003. Before a DHCP server can lease IP addresses to clients on a network, it must be authorized to do so. This prevents a DHCP server with incorrect information from being introduced on the network. For example, a DHCP server with incorrect scope information can't lease providing DHCP clients with incorrect IP parameters. DHCP servers are authorized through the DHCP management console; this process must be performed by a user who is a member of the Enterprise Admins group.

To authorize a DHCP in Active Directory, follow these steps:

1. Click Start, point to Administrative Tools, and select DHCP.

2. Within the DHCP management console, right-click the DHCP server and click Authorize. Any server not yet authorized appears with a red arrow beside it.

3. After the server has been successfully authorized within Active Directory, it appears with a green arrow beside it.

If a DHCP server needs to be removed from the network—for example, if it has been replaced by another one—you will want to "unauthorize" the server so that it no longer has the capability to lease IP addresses to clients. To do so, right-click the DHCP server within the DHCP console and select the Unauthorize option. Click Yes to confirm your actions. The DHCP server then is removed from Active Directory.

Creating Scopes

For a DHCP server to provide clients with IP addresses, the server must be configured with a scope. A scope is a range, or pool, of IP addresses that can be leased to DHCP clients on a given subnet. (If the DHCP server services multiple subnets, each with DHCP clients, you must create multiple scopes.)

In addition to IP addresses, a scope can include optional parameters that can be assigned to DHCP clients, including the IP address of DNS servers, WINS servers, and routers. The optional parameters are discussed in the "Managing DHCP Scope Options" section later in this chapter.

Before creating scopes, you should keep the following guidelines in mind:

➤ All DHCP servers on the network require a scope to be active.

➤ Any IP addresses within the scope that should not be leased to DHCP clients must be excluded from the scope. This eliminates the possibility of duplicate IP addresses.

➤ A DHCP server can be configured with multiple scopes.

➤ DHCP servers do not share scope information, meaning that one DHCP server will not know the IP addresses being leased by another DHCP server. With this in mind, make sure the IP addresses in each scope do not overlap, again to eliminate the possibility of duplicate IP addresses.

Chances are, you will run into scenarios that include multiple DHCP servers. You can provide redundancy on the network for DHCP servers without the possibility of duplicate IP addresses. To accomplish this, use the "80/20 rule." That is, 80% of the IP addresses for the local subnet are added to a scope on the local DHCP server, and the remaining 20% of the IP addresses are added to a scope for the same subnet on another DHCP server. In other words, 80% of the IP addresses are from the local subnet, and 20% are from a remote subnet. Because both servers have IP addresses available for the same subnet, clients can always obtain an IP address if one of the servers becomes unavailable (until the scope runs out of available addresses).

After the DHCP component has been installed, you can create scopes from within the DHCP management console. A scope can also be configured when installing DHCP using the Configure Your Server Wizard, as you saw earlier in the chapter. Each scope created consists of the following information:

➤ A range of IP addresses that can be leased to clients.

➤ A subnet mask that determines the subnet for the IP address.

➤ A scope name that appears in the DHCP management console.

➤ The lease duration, which determines when a DHCP client must renew its IP address.

➤ Optional parameters, also known as scope options, that need to be assigned to clients, such as the IP address of the DNS server, default gateway, and WINS server.

➤ Client reservations. If a client requires the same IP address at all times, a client reservation can be configured to ensure that it always leases the same IP address.

To create a new scope using the DHCP management console, perform the following steps:

1. Click Start, point to Administrative Tools, and click DHCP.

2. Within the DHCP management console, right-click your DHCP server and click the New Scope option. This launches the New Scope Wizard. Click Next to continue.

3. Type in a name and description for the scope that will make it easily identifiable within the management console. Click Next.

4. Enter the range of IP addresses for the scope (see Figure 2.8). Verify the length and subnet mask.

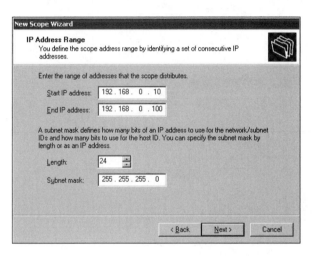

Figure 2.8   The first step in configuring a scope is entering the range of IP addresses to use.

5. Configure any IP addresses that should be excluded from the scope (see Figure 2.9), and then click the Add button. Click Next.

6. Next, configure the lease duration for the scope (see Figure 2.10). The lease duration determines the length of time a client can use an IP address before it must be renewed. The default value is 8 days. Click Next.

7. At this point, you can configure additional parameters to assign to DHCP clients. Select No, I Will Configure These Options Later. Click Next. The scope options are discussed later in the chapter.

8. Click Finish.

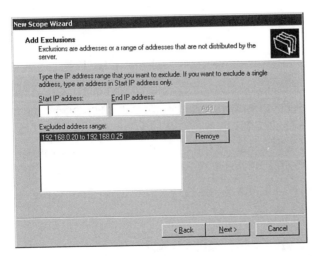

Figure 2.9 You can exclude addresses from the scope via the Add Exclusions screen.

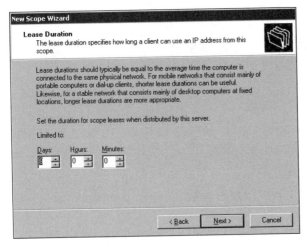

Figure 2.10 You can configure the lease duration for a scope in days, hours, and minutes.

The new scope now appears under the DHCP server within the management console. Before the DHCP server can lease IP addresses from the scope, however, it must be activated. To do so, right-click the new scope and click Activate.

Superscopes

Aside from a regular scope, you can create a second type of scope known as a *superscope*. In a multinetted environment (one that has multiple logical IP subnets defined on a single physical network), superscopes allow a DHCP server to assign leases to clients on multiple subnets.

For example, a physical network is divided into two subnets, Subnet A and Subnet B, connected by a router. Subnet B contains two multinets. A single DHCP server is located on Subnet A. The DHCP server contains a single scope with a range of IP addresses to lease to clients on Subnet A. To have the DHCP assign IP addresses to clients on Subnet B, you can create a superscope and add to it the IP address ranges for the multinets on Subnet B. The scope configuration on the DHCP server could be similar to the following:

Subnet A:

Scope 1: 192.168.1.2 to 192.168.1.254

Subnet B:

Superscope for Subnet B:

Scope 2: 192.168.2.2 to 192.168.2.254

Scope 3: 192.168.3.2 to 192.168.3.254

One of the biggest advantages of creating superscopes is to ease the administration in a multinetted environment. It can be difficult in terms of administration to identify which scopes go with which networks. Creating superscopes and grouping scopes in some logical manner can make them easier to administer. For example, you might group all the scopes from a single floor in a large office building into a superscope.

To create a new superscope within the DHCP management console, perform the following steps:

1. Right-click the DHCP server from within the DHCP management console and select the New Superscope option from the menu. This launches the New Superscope Wizard. Click Next.

2. Type in a descriptive name for the superscope (something that makes it easy to identify). This is the name that will appear within the DHCP management console. Click Next.

3. From the list of available scopes, select the ones to include in the superscope (see Figure 2.11). Keep in mind that you can add only active scopes. Click Next.

4. Click Finish.

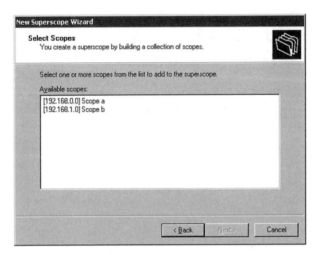

Figure 2.11 You can create a superscope through the DHCP management console.

Multicast Scopes

Multicasting is the process of sending a message to a group of recipients, as opposed to *unicasting*, in which a message is sent to a specific recipient.

Normally, DHCP is used to assign each DHCP client a single unique IP address from a range of IP addresses configured in a scope. Windows Server 2003 extends the functionality to enable you to create multicast scopes so that messages destined to a multicast IP address can be sent to all clients in a multicast group.

Multicast scopes are supported through a protocol known as the Multicast Address Dynamic Client Allocation Protocol (MADCAP). MADCAP controls how the DHCP servers dynamically assign IP addresses on a TCP/IP network.

The multicast server (in this case, the DHCP server) is configured with a group of Class D IP addresses (in the range of 224.0.0.0 to 239.255.255.255) that can be assigned to multicast clients. The server is also responsible for maintaining the group membership list and updating the list as members join and leave a group.

To create a multicast scope, perform the following steps:

1. Within the DHCP management console, right-click the DHCP server and choose the New Multicast Scope option. This launches the New Multicast Scope Wizard. Click Next.

2. Type in a name and description for the scope. Click Next.

3. Specify a range of IP addresses and a TTL (see Figure 2.12). Click Next.

4. Type in any IP addresses that you want to exclude from the range. Click Next.

5. Specify a lease duration that defines how long a client can lease a multicast address from the scope. The default is 30 days. Click Next.

6. Click Yes to activate the scope. Click Next.

7. Click Finish.

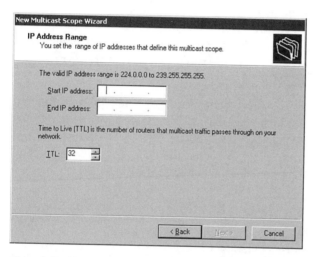

Figure 2.12   You can configure a multicast scope by specifying a range of Class D IP addresses.

Configuring DHCP for DNS Integration

Pre–Windows 2000 operating systems use NetBIOS names to identify clients and servers on the network and the different services they are running. These names can be resolved to IP addresses using a WINS server or an LMHOSTS file. Because the WINS database is dynamic, meaning that clients dynamically register their NetBIOS name and IP addresses, integrating DHCP and WINS on a network is simple. The DNS database is static on a Windows NT network, so implementing DHCP and DNS requires the use of a WINS Server.

Windows 2000 and Windows Server 2003 primarily use DNS. DNS is required to locate clients, servers, and services on the network. Traditionally, administrators had to manually enter host records into the DNS database. To overcome this and allow DHCP and DNS to be integrated on a network without the use of WINS, Windows 2000, Windows XP, and Windows Server 2003 workstations configured as DHCP clients can be automatically registered in the DNS database. These clients can automatically update their own A records (the records mapping their hostnames to their IP addresses), and the DHCP server updates the PTR records (the records that map the IP address to the hostname for reverse lookups). You can change the default behavior by configuring the properties of the DHCP server (as you will see later in the chapter).

DHCP Clients

The workstation platform determines how the client interacts with the DHCP and DNS servers. Clients running Windows 2000 and later can send update requests directly to a DNS server to update their own pointer and address records, or the client can request that the DHCP server make the update on its behalf.

Clients running platforms earlier than Windows 2000 do not support dynamic DNS updates and cannot interact directly with a DNS server. In this case, when a pre–Windows 2000 client or a non-Microsoft client receives an IP address from a DHCP server, the DHCP server can be configured to perform the DNS updates on behalf of these clients.

Be sure you know which clients support dynamic DNS and how to configure DHCP for those clients that cannot update their own records. Remember that, by default, Windows 2000 and Windows XP clients register their own A records, and the DHCP server registers their PTR records.

Configuring DHCP/DNS Integration

To configure DHCP for DNS integration, right-click the DHCP server within the management console and choose Properties. If you select the DNS tab, you'll see a window similar to the one shown in Figure 2.13.

Here are the settings that can be configured for DHCP integration with DNS:

➤ *Enable DNS Dynamic Updates According to the Settings Below*—This option is selected by default. Deselecting this option means that the DHCP server will not perform any dynamic updates.

➤ *Dynamically Update DNS A and PTR Records Only If Requested by the DHCP Clients*—This option is selected by default. Selecting this option means that the DHCP server will perform the updates if requested to do so by the client.

➤ *Always Dynamically Update DNS A and PTR Records*—Selecting this option means that the DHCP server always updates DNS A and PTR records on behalf of DHCP clients.

➤ *Discard A and PTR Records When the Lease Is Deleted*—This option specifies whether the DHCP server should discard the records when a DHCP client lease expires.

➤ *Dynamically Update DNS A and PTR Records for DHCP Clients That Do Not Request Updates (for example, clients running Windows NT 4.0)*—Select this option if there are clients on the network that do not support dynamic updates, such as clients running Windows NT 4.0. In such cases, the DHCP server performs the updates on behalf of the client.

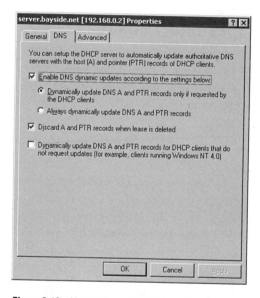

Figure 2.13   You configure DHCP integration with DNS via the DHCP management console.

If you select the Advanced tab, you have the option of configuring the dynamic update registration credentials that can be used by the DHCP server when updating the DNS records. One of the reasons for doing this is to protect against unsecure updates to the DNS database. After you've created a dedicated user account, you can select the Credentials button and type in the username and password. These are the credentials that the DHCP server uses when registering names on behalf of DHCP clients.

Dynamic update credentials must be configured in the following situations:

➤ If the DHCP service is running on a domain controller. Because the DHCP server inherits the power of the domain controller, it has the capability to delete and update any records within the DNS database. By configuring dynamic update credentials, you can limit the power of the DHCP server.

➤ If the DHCP server has been configured to perform dynamic updates on behalf of DHCP clients.

➤ If the zone for which the DHCP server will be performing updates is configured only for secure updates.

Managing DHCP Clients and Leases

Each DHCP scope is configured with a lease duration. This specifies how long a DHCP client can use an IP address before it must be renewed by a DHCP server. By default, this value is set to 8 days. However, you might want to change this depending on the number of IP addresses available as compared to the number of DHCP clients.

The lease duration can be customized to meet the requirements of your network. If the number of IP addresses exceeds the number of DHCP clients on the network, you can configure a longer lease duration. However, if the number of IP addresses available in the scope is comparable to the number of DHCP-enabled clients, you should configure a shorter lease duration. Also, if your network consists of a number of mobile users who move between subnets, consider creating a shorter lease time. By shortening the lease duration, you might also see a slight increase in network traffic because IP addresses are being renewed at a more frequent interval.

As you saw earlier in the chapter, the lease duration for a scope can be configured when the scope is created. You can also change the lease duration at any time afterward through the DHCP management console. Simply right-click the scope, click Properties, and edit the lease duration (see Figure 2.14).

The renewal process between a DHCP client and a DHCP server begins after 50% of the configured lease duration expires. At this time, the client attempts to contact the DHCP server. A DHCPRequest message is broadcast by the client requesting to renew the IP address with which it's currently configured. If the DHCP server is available, it responds with a DHCPACK, granting the client's request to renew the IP address.

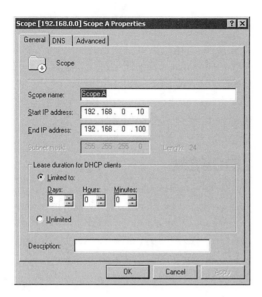

Figure 2.14   You can reconfigure the lease duration for an active scope via its Properties page.

If the client does not receive a response from the DHCP server, it again attempts to renew the IP address when 87.5% of the lease duration expires. Again, if the server is available, the request is granted. If not, the client continues to use the IP address until the lease duration expires. When it does, the IP address lease process described earlier in the chapter must be repeated.

Viewing Lease Information

As a DHCP server leases an IP address to DHCP clients, the management console provides administrators with an easy way of viewing lease information. The Active Leases container listed under the DHCP server lists all the IP addresses currently leased to clients. From here, you can also delete or cancel a lease, forcing a client to acquire a new IP address. To do so, right-click any of the active leases within the Active Leases container and click Delete.

Verifying, Renewing, and Releasing IP Addresses

The IPCONFIG command-line utility can be used to verify IP parameters as well as release and renew an IP address that has been assigned by a DHCP server.

The IPCONFIG /ALL command can be used to view detailed information about the IP parameters of a TCP/IP host. It returns information such as the IP address assigned to the client, the subnet mask, the optional parameters (including the IP address of any DNS servers), and the DHCP server from which the client is leasing the IP address.

Although a client eventually releases and renews the IP address that it has been assigned from a DHCP server on its own, this can be done manually as well. Using the IPCONFIG /RELEASE command followed by the IPCONFIG /RENEW command manually releases and renews a DHCP client lease.

Managing a DHCP Database

The *DHCP database* stores information about client leases. There is no limit to the number of entries that a single database can hold. Little management is associated with maintaining the database. For example, Windows Server 2003 automatically compacts the database to reclaim unused space, although it can also be performed manually by an administrator. The following sections look at some of the management tasks that an administrator might need or want to perform manually.

Backing Up and Restoring a DHCP Database

Backups are an integral part of most administrators' jobs. If you are using DHCP on a network, the DHCP database should also be included in the backup routine, in case the database becomes corrupt or fails.

The DHCP database is automatically backed up every 60 minutes by default. You can also perform manual backups using the Backup option within the DHCP management console or by using the Windows Backup program (NTBackup.exe).

 The default interval at which the database is automatically backed up can be changed by editing the value of the **BackupInterval** entry found under the **HKEY_LOCAL_MACHINE\SYSTEM\Currentcontrolset\services\DHCPServer\ Parameters** Registry key.

During an automatic or manual backup of the DHCP database, the following information is backed up:

➤ Client reservations

➤ Any configured scopes, including superscopes and multicast scopes

➤ DHCP options

➤ IP address leases

➤ Any Registry information pertaining to the configuration of DHCP

To back up the DHCP database using the management console, perform the following steps:

1. Click Start, point to Administrative Tools, and click DHCP.

2. Select the DHCP server that you want to back up. From the Action menu, click Backup.

3. Browse to the folder where the backed-up files should be placed (see Figure 2.15). The default location is `<systemroot>\system32\DHCP\Backup`. Click OK.

Figure 2.15   You can choose a location for the DHCP backup files via the management console.

 NOTE   When you back up the DHCP database using the Backup option within the management console, you must back up to a local drive. To back up to a nonlocal drive, you must use the Windows Backup program.

If the DHCP database needs to be restored, you can do so through the management console using the Restore option. To do so, select the appropriate server within the DHCP console and choose Restore from the Action menu. Browse to the location containing the database backup. After you click OK, a message appears informing you that the service must be stopped and restarted for the operation to complete. Click Yes to restore the database.

Moving the DHCP Database

You can move the DHCP database from one DHCP server to another using the Backup and Restore options within the DHCP management console. To move the database, begin by performing a backup using the process outlined in the previous section. When the backup is complete, stop the DHCP service using the Services applet in the Control Panel. This ensures that the DHCP server does not continue to lease IP addresses to clients after the second server starts leasing the same addresses. The folder containing the backup of the database can then be copied to the destination DHCP server. You can use the Restore option to restore the database on the new DHCP server.

 To back up and restore the DHCP database, you must be a member of the DHCP Administrators group, the Backup Operators group, or the Administrators group. To move the database, you must belong to the appropriate groups on both servers.

Managing DHCP Scope Options

After a scope has been created, you can configure several DHCP options. The options can be configured at one of the following four levels:

➤ Server

➤ Scope

➤ Class

➤ Client

Options configured at the server level are applied to all DHCP clients, regardless of the subnet on which they reside. Any options that should be applied to all DHCP clients should be configured at this level. For example, to configure all clients on the network to use the same DNS server, you can configure the option at the server level. Keep in mind that when you are configuring scope options, any options configured at the scope or client levels override those configured at the server level. To configure server-level options, right-click the Server Options container listed under the DHCP server and select Set Predefined Options from the menu.

If you want to configure DHCP options so that they apply only to DHCP clients on a specific subnet, configure the options at the scope level. For example, the IP address of the default gateway for a subnet should be configured at the scope level. Configuring scope-level options can be done by right-clicking the Scope Options container and selecting Configure Options from the menu.

Finally, if you want to apply DHCP options to only a specific DHCP client, you can configure the options at the client level. You can configure options at this level only for clients that have a client reservation, meaning that they are DHCP clients but always lease the same IP address. Any option that you configure at this level overrides any configured at the server and scope levels. To configure a client-level option, right-click the client reservation and select Configure Options.

Windows Server 2003 also allows DHCP options to be applied to groups of users or workstations with similar needs. User-class options can be used to assign options to DHCP clients that have common needs for similar DHCP options configurations. For example, a user class can be used to configure options for mobile users. Vendor-class options can be used to assign DHCP options on the basis of vendor information. For example, specific options can be assigned to clients running a specific version of Windows.

Be sure you are familiar with the order in which scope options are applied. The order is: server, scope, class, and then client.

Now that you're familiar with how DHCP options can be applied, let's take a look the different DHCP options that can be assigned to clients.

As previously mentioned, a DHCP server can assign parameters other than just an IP address and subnet mask to a DHCP client. A number of different options can be configured, some of which are shown in Figure 2.16. To access the Server Options dialog box, highlight Server Options in the left pane of the DHCP management console and select Configure Options from the Action menu.

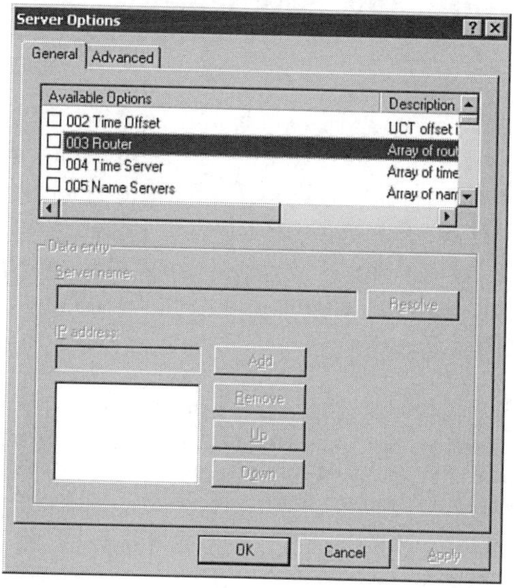

Figure 2.16   DHCP options.

The following list provides a description of the commonly used DHCP options:

➤ *006 DNS Servers*—Specifies the IP address of the DNS servers available to clients on the network.

➤ *015 DNS Domain Name*—Specifies the DNS domain name used for client resolutions.

➤ *003 Router*—Specifies the IP address of the router or default gateway.

➤ *044 WINS/NBNS Servers*—Specifies the IP address of the WINS servers on the network available to clients.

➤ *046 WINS/NBT Node Type*—Specifies the name resolution type. The available options include 1 = B-node (broadcast), 2 = P-node (peer), 4 = M-node (mixed), and 8 = H-node (hybrid).

➤ *240 Classless Static Routes*—Specifies a list of static routes, including the destination network IP address, the subnet mask, and the router that is responsible for forwarding messages to that network.

Most of the options outlined in the preceding list can also be configured locally on the client. By doing so, any options configured on the DHCP server will be overwritten by those configured locally. If you are using DHCP, however, it would not make sense to configure the options locally as well, especially in terms of administrative overhead.

Managing Reservations and Reserved Clients

In some instances, a workstation on the network requires a permanent IP address, but you still want that workstation to be a DHCP client. With a client reservation, the workstation can still be DHCP enabled, but the DHCP server always assigns the client the same IP address. In terms of administration, the client network configuration settings remain the same, IP addressing remains centralized, and the clients can still be assigned optional parameters through the DHCP server.

 If multiple DHCP servers are configured with a range of IP addresses that cover the range of the reserved addresses, the client reservation must be duplicated on all DHCP servers. If not, the client might end up receiving an incorrect IP address (one other than the preferred address that has been reserved for the client on the first DHCP server).

Creating a client reservation is a relatively simple process. Within the DHCP management console, right-click the Reservations container listed under your DHCP server and click the New Reservation option. In the New Reservation dialog box, type in a descriptive name, the IP address to be reserved, and the MAC address of the client that will be assigned the IP address. Then click the Add button and the Close button. The reservation appears in the Reservations container in the DHCP management console.

Each client reservation that is created has a set of properties that can be used to change or configure the reservation. Any client reservations that have been configured appear under the Reservations container. To edit a client reservation, right-click the reservation and select Properties. From the properties window, you can use the General tab to change the information that was provided when the reservation was first configured. The only value that cannot be changed is the IP address. You can configure dynamic updates for the DHCP client via the DNS tab.

Troubleshooting TCP/IP Addressing

TCP/IP is one of the protocols that requires a certain amount of configuration either on individual clients or centrally on a server. Many issues can arise related to such things as incorrect IP parameters on a client or a nonresponsive DHCP server. To successfully implement TCP/IP and DHCP on a network, it's important to have a general understanding of some of the common issues that can arise, as well as how to troubleshoot them. The following section discusses some of the more common problems that might be encountered on a TCP/IP network.

Diagnosing and Resolving Issues Related to Automatic Private IP Addressing

Automatic Private IP Addressing (APIPA) was introduced in Windows 98. It is enabled by default and is supported by the following clients:

➤ Windows 98

➤ Windows Me

➤ Windows 2000 (all platforms)

➤ Windows XP

➤ Windows Server 2003

Clients that support this feature can assign themselves an IP address in the following situations:

➤ When a DHCP client cannot contact a DHCP server or there is no DHCP server on the network

➤ When a DHCP client's attempt to renew its IP address leased from a DHCP server fails

In both cases, the client assigns itself an IP address in the range of 169.254.0.1 to 169.254.255.254. You can use the IPCONFIG command-line utility to verify that APIPA is enabled and that an IP address within the specific range has been assigned. Remember that APIPA is enabled by default. However, this feature can be disabled through the Registry. Remember, the APIPA settings on XP clients can also be manually adjusted in the network properties to match the addresses used on the local subnet. If you decide to do this, you need to make sure that the address used on the APIPA Settings dialog box is excluded from the DHCP scope, to avoid IP address conflicts.

If your network consists of multiple subnets, clients using APIPA can communicate only with hosts on their local subnet. APIPA does not include optional parameters. Clients assign themselves only an IP address and a subnet mask. Without the IP address of the default gateway and DNS server, communication outside of the local subnet will fail.

Diagnosing and Resolving Issues Related to Incorrect TCP/IP Configuration

A number of command-line utilities can be used to test and diagnose incorrect TCP/IP configurations. To do so, click Start, All Programs, Accessories, Command Prompt, and type `ipconfig` (using the /all parameter brings up more detailed configuration information).

The following list outlines some of the common parameters that can be used with the `ipconfig` command:

➤ /all—Displays detailed IP configuration information

➤ /release—Releases the IP address for the specified adapter

➤ /renew—Renews the IP address for the specified adapter

➤ /flushDNS—Purges the entries in the DNS cache

➤ /registerDNS—Refreshes all leased IP addresses and re-registers DNS names

➤ /displayDNS—Displays the contents of the DNS cache

The PING command-line utility is useful in verifying connectivity with another TCP/IP host. Connectivity on the network is verified by sending Internet Control Message Protocol (ICMP) echo requests and replies. When the PING command is issued, the source computer sends echo requests messages to another TCP/IP host. If reachable, the remote host then responds with four echo replies. The PING command is also issued at the command prompt along with the TCP/IP address or domain name of the other TCP/IP host, as follows:

```
C:> PING 124.120.105.110
C:> PING www.bayside.net
```

To determine whether TCP/IP is initialized on the local computer, issue the **PING** command and specify the loopback address of **127.0.0.1**.

The general steps for troubleshooting TCP/IP using the PING command are as follows:

1. PING the loopback address of 127.0.0.1 to ensure that TCP/IP is initialized on the local computer.

2. If successful, PING the IP address assigned to the local computer.

3. Next PING the IP address of the default gateway. If this fails, verify that the IP address of the default gateway is correct and that the gateway is operational.

4. Next PING the IP address of a host on a remote network. If this is unsuccessful, verify that the remote host is operational, verify the IP address of the remote host, and verify that all routers and gateways between the local computer and remote computer are operational.

A quick way of verifying TCP/IP connectivity is to complete step 4 from the preceding list. If you can successfully **PING** the IP address of a remote host, steps 1 through 3 will be successful.

Two other utilities that can be used for TCP/IP troubleshooting are tracert and pathping. The tracert command determines the route that is taken to a specific destination. You might want to use the tracert command if you are not able to successfully PING the IP address of a remote host. The results of the tracert command indicate whether there is a problem with a router or gateway between the local computer and the remote destination. The pathping command is basically a combination of the PING and tracert commands. When the command is issued, packets are sent to each router between the local computer and a remote computer. The results determine which routers and gateways could be causing problems on the network.

Diagnosing and Resolving Issues Related to DHCP Authorization

As mentioned earlier in the chapter, a DHCP server must be authorized within Active Directory before it can begin leasing IP addresses to clients. Again, the purpose of this is to eliminate the possibility that a DHCP server is mistakenly or maliciously introduced onto a network, especially if it has been misconfigured.

Authorizing a DHCP server is a relatively simple process. If you are unable to authorize a DHCP server, verify that the user account you are logged on has the required permissions. Only members of the Enterprise Admins group are permitted to perform this operation.

Multiple DHCP servers can exist on a network. However, you might encounter problems if you have a DHCP server configured as a standalone server and a DHCP server configured as a member server on the same subnet. When the standalone server detects the second DHCP server, it attempts to verify with a domain controller that it is authorized. Because the standalone server is not a member of the domain, it will fail to contact a domain controller and stop servicing DHCP client requests. To resolve the problem, the authorized DHCP server must be removed from the subnet.

Verifying DHCP Reservation Configuration

As previously mentioned, client reservations are created so that certain DHCP clients can always be assigned the same IP address from a DHCP server. When you create the reservation, you specify the IP address to be leased and the MAC address of the DHCP client. If you find that a client for which a reservation has been configured is receiving a different IP address than intended, verify the configuration of the client reservation. To do so, right-click the appropriate client reservation within the Reservations container in the DHCP console and click Properties. From the Properties window, verify that you have correctly entered the MAC address of the DHCP client.

Keep in mind that DHCP servers do not share information. If there are multiple DHCP servers on the network, the client reservation must be configured on each one. This way, if one DHCP server is unavailable, the client can still be assigned the same IP address from another DHCP server.

Examining the System Event Log and DHCP Server Audit Log to Find Related Events

Log files can provide administrators with valuable information when it comes to troubleshooting. You can use the system log within the Event Viewer to monitor and troubleshoot DHCP-related events. When an event occurs, such as the DHCP Server service being restarted, it is written to the log file and provides useful information, including a description of the event and when it occurred.

Windows Server 2003 also supports auditing logging of the DHCP service. By default, the audit logs are stored in the `%system%\system32\DHCP` directory. Audit logging for a DHCP server can be enabled by right-clicking the appropriate DHCP server within the management console and selecting Properties. Using the General tab, auditing logging can be enabled or disabled. The default location of the audit logs can be changed by clicking the Advanced tab and editing the Audit log file path.

As events occur, they are written to a log file. Entries in the log contain an event ID, the date and time that the event occurred, as well as the IP address, hostname, and MAC address of the workstation that generated the event. Some of the common audit codes are as follows:

➤ *00*—The log was started.

➤ *01*—The log was stopped.

➤ *02*—The log was temporarily paused due to low disk space.

➤ *10*—A new IP address was leased to a client.

➤ *11*—A client renewed an existing lease.

➤ *12*—A client released an IP address.

➤ *13*—An IP address was found in use on the network.

➤ *14*—A client cannot lease an IP address because the address pool is exhausted.

➤ *15*—A lease request was denied.

➤ *30*—A DNS dynamic update request occurred.

➤ *31*—The DNS dynamic update failed.

➤ *32*—The DNS dynamic update was successful.

➤ *55*—The DHCP server was authorized to start on the network.

➤ *56*—The DHCP server was not authorized to start on the network.

Diagnosing and Resolving Issues Related to Configuration of DHCP Server and Scope Options

Scope options can be configured at different levels. The level at which scope options are configured determines which DHCP clients are affected. For example, configuring an option at the server level affects all clients, regardless of the IP subnet on which they reside.

One of the most common problems that can occur with DHCP options is that clients end up being assigned incorrect parameters. In such cases, you must verify the level at which the option has been configured. For example, configuring the router option at the server level when the network consists of multiple subnets results in some DHCP clients being configured with an incorrect gateway. In this case, the option needs to be configured at the scope level instead of the server level.

Verifying Database Integrity

The Reconcile All Scopes option is useful when you need to fix any inconsistencies in the DHCP database, such as when not all IP address leases are being reflected in the DHCP database. Information in the database is compared with information stored in the Registry.

Selecting the Reconcile All Scopes option opens the Reconcile All Scopes dialog box. Click the Verify button to check the database for inconsistencies. Any errors are displayed.

Exam Prep Questions

Question 1

> A DHCP server is running on your network. The range of IP addresses within the scope far exceeds the number of DHCP clients on the network. However, you notice that the number of IP address lease requests is very high. Where should you begin looking to determine why this is occurring?
>
> ○ A. Check the Event Viewer for any DHCP-related messages.
> ○ B. Verify that the lease duration isn't configured with a low value.
> ○ C. Run System Monitor to view the performance of the server.
> ○ D. Run Network Monitor to capture DHCP-related traffic.

Answer B is correct. The first thing that should be verified is that a shorter lease duration has not been configured. Because the number of IP addresses exceeds the number of DHCP clients, the lease duration can be increased. After that has been verified, you can begin using the other tools to troubleshoot the problem if it continues. Therefore answers A, C, and D are incorrect. After you have verified that the lease duration is properly configured, you can choose to follow up using one of the other options.

Question 2

> Your network consists of two subnets: SubnetA and SubnetB. Each has its own DHCP server. You configure the scope on DHCP1 for SubnetA. Users are leasing an IP address but report that they cannot access any resources outside of their own subnet. How can you most easily solve the problem?
>
> ○ A. Activate the scope on DHCP1.
> ○ B. Configure the default gateway on each workstation.
> ○ C. Configure the 003 router option on DHCP1.
> ○ D. Configure the 006 DNS server option on DHCP1.

Answer C is correct. If clients have not been configured with the IP address of the default gateway, they cannot access resources outside of their local subnet. Answer A is incorrect because the clients are already successfully leasing IP addresses from the server. Answer B would solve the problem but would not be the easiest solution; therefore, it is also incorrect. Answer D is incorrect because configuring the DNS server option allows clients to resolve hostnames but doesn't give them access outside of the local subnet.

Question 3

You recently installed the DHCP Server service on one of your member servers in the domain. You notice that the DHCP service is constantly being shut down and the server cannot lease IP addresses to DHCP clients. What is causing the problem to occur?

○ A. The DHCP server has not been configured with a scope.

○ B. The scope on the DHCP server has not been activated.

○ C. The DHCP server has not been authorized within Active Directory.

○ D. There is a DHCP server on the network with a duplicate scope.

Answer C is correct. If a DHCP server has not been authorized within Active Directory, it is considered to be a rogue server and the service will continue to shut down until it is authorized by a member of the Enterprise Admins group. Answers A, B, and D are incorrect because none of these problems would cause the DHCP service to shut down.

Question 4

A DHCP server is used to assign IP addresses to clients and member servers on the network. Three of the member servers host print devices. How can you ensure that these print servers lease the same IP address from the DHCP server?

○ A. Exclude the IP addresses from the scope.

○ B. Create a separate scope for each of the print servers.

○ C. Create a client reservation for each print server.

○ D. Configure the DHCP options for the scope.

Answer C is correct. By creating a client reservation for each of the member servers, you ensure that they will always lease the same IP address from the DHCP server. Therefore, answers A, B, and D are incorrect.

Question 5

> You have recently deployed a DHCP server to centralize the administration of all IP addresses on the network. Before this, they were all statically configured. All users are successfully leasing IP addresses, but they now report that they can no longer print to the network interface printers. Upon examining the printers' properties, you notice they have been assigned incorrect IP addresses. What should you have done?
>
> ○ A. Defined separate scopes for each of the print devices
>
> ○ B. Created client reservations for the print devices
>
> ○ C. Excluded the IP addresses of the print devices from the scope
>
> ○ D. Created client exclusions for the print devices

Answer B is correct. To ensure that the IP address of the network interface printers did not change when the DHCP server was placed on the network, client reservation should have been defined. Answer A is incorrect because defining additional scopes does not address the problem. Answer C is incorrect because excluding the IP addresses means that the DHCP server will never offer them to DHCP clients. Answer D is incorrect because there is no such option in DHCP called a client exclusion.

Question 6

> Your network consists of multiple subnets connected by routers. You have finished installing a Windows Server 2003 DHCP server. You create the necessary scopes and configure the 003 router option to assign all clients the IP address of their local router. All clients successfully lease an IP address. However, you soon discover that users on Subnet A are the only ones capable of communicating outside their local subnet. What could be causing the problem?
>
> ○ A. All the scopes have not yet been activated.
>
> ○ B. The DHCP option is configured at the server level.
>
> ○ C. The DHCP server has not yet been authorized.
>
> ○ D. The 003 router option must first be activated.

Answer B is correct. Each subnet will have its own gateway, so the 003 router option should be configured at the scope level instead of the server level. Answers A and C are incorrect because all clients are successfully leasing IP addresses. Answer D is incorrect because DHCP options do not have to be activated.

Question 7

> Several DHCP servers are being deployed in different domains throughout the forest. To which group must you belong to authorize the DHCP servers?
>
> ○ A. DNSUpdateProxy
>
> ○ B. Enterprise Admins
>
> ○ C. Domain Admins
>
> ○ D. Administrators

Answer B is correct. To authorize DHCP servers throughout the forest, the user account that you log on with must be a member of the Enterprise Admins group. Therefore, answers A, C, and D are incorrect.

Question 8

> You are a junior network administrator. One of your tasks is to maintain a newly installed DHCP server. The scopes have not yet been created. The senior administrator documents all the required scopes and asks you to create them on the server. You notice that several DHCP options are to be configured, but it is not specified what type of scope options to configure. You are trying to recall how scope options are applied. Which of the following correctly lists the order in which they are applied to clients?
>
> ○ A. Server, scope, class, client
>
> ○ B. Server, class, scope, client
>
> ○ C. Server, scope, client, class
>
> ○ D. Scope, server, client, class

Answer A is correct. The correct order in which DHCP options are applied is server, scope, class, and then client. Therefore, answers B, C, and D are incorrect.

Question 9

Your network consists of three Unix servers that provide name-resolution services. The servers are all configured with static IP addresses. How can you ensure that the DHCP server does not assign these three IP addresses to any DHCP clients on the network?

- ○ A. Configure client reservations for the three Unix servers.
- ○ B. Exclude the three IP addresses from the scope.
- ○ C. Place the Unix servers on a separate subnet.
- ○ D. Create a superscope for the three IP addresses.

Answer B is correct. To ensure that the IP addresses of the Unix servers are not leased to any DHCP clients, exclude the three IP addresses from the scope. Answer A is incorrect because client reservations are configured for the DHCP clients that need to lease the same IP address. Answer C is incorrect because placing the Unix servers on a different subnet will have no impact on the IP addresses leased by the DHCP server. Answer D is incorrect because superscopes are created to support multinetted environments.

Question 10

Two DHCP servers are configured on a network with two subnets. How can you configure the scopes so that the DHCP servers can provide fault tolerance for one another?

- ○ A. Configure replication to occur between the two DHCP servers.
- ○ B. Nothing needs to be done because DHCP servers on the same network share scope information, to provide fault tolerance.
- ○ C. Configure each server with a range of IP addresses for both subnets.
- ○ D. Configure all clients with the IP address of both DHCP servers.

Answer C is correct. By configuring each DHCP server with a range of IP addresses from the remote subnet, you can provide some level of fault tolerance. Each server should be configured with 80% of the IP address for the local subnet and 20% of the IP address for the remote subnet, to avoid IP address conflicts. Answers A and B are incorrect because DHCP servers do not replicate, nor do they share scope information. Answer D is incorrect because clients are not configured with the IP address of DHCP servers.

Need to Know More?

 Search the online version of TechNet and the Windows Server 2003 Resource Kit using keywords such as "DHCP," "IP addresses," and "Dynamic Updates."

 Alcott, Neall. *DHCP for Windows 2000*. Sebastopol, California: O'Reilly & Associates, Inc., 2001.

 Microsoft Corporation. *Implementing, Managing, and Maintaining a Microsoft Windows Server 2003 Network Infrastructure*. Seattle, Washington: Microsoft Press, 2003.

Managing Name Resolution

. . . .

Terms you'll need to understand:

✓ Hostnames
✓ Domain Name System (DNS)
✓ Recursive and iterative queries
✓ Primary, secondary, and stub zones
✓ Dynamic update
✓ Delegation
✓ Caching-only server
✓ Root name server
✓ Resource records

Techniques you'll need to master:

✓ Installing and configuring the DNS Server service
✓ Configuring zones
✓ Understanding a caching-only server
✓ Understanding DNS zone types
✓ Managing zones and resource records
✓ Implementing a delegated zone for DNS
✓ Monitoring a DNS server

Each machine on a computer network is assigned a unique network address. Computers communicate with each other across networks by connecting to these network addresses. These numbers, also known as Internet Protocol (IP) addresses, consist of four groups of numbers, or octets, and can be difficult for people to remember. To solve this dilemma, a system was developed whereby people can use "friendly" names that are then translated automatically into IP addresses that computers use to locate each other and to communicate. These friendly names are called *hostnames*, and each machine is assigned one. Groups of these hosts form a *domain*. The software that translates these names to network addresses is called the *Domain Name System (DNS)*.

Before the advent of DNS, HOSTS files were used for name resolution, but as the Internet quickly grew in size and popularity, HOSTS files became impossible to maintain and keep current. When the Internet community realized there was a need for a more manageable, scalable, and efficient name-resolution system, DNS was created. Since that time, DNS servers have been used on the Internet almost exclusively.

Before the introduction of Windows 2000, Network Basic Input/Output System (NetBIOS) names were used to identify computers, services, and other resources on Windows-based machines. In the early days of Windows networks, LMHOSTS files were used for NetBIOS name resolution. Later, these names were often resolved to IP addresses using a NetBIOS Name Server (NBNS). Microsoft's version of the NBNS was called Windows Internet Naming Service (WINS). With Windows 2000 and now Windows Server 2003, hostnames are used instead of NetBIOS names. In a Windows Server 2003 domain, DNS is used to resolve hostnames and locate resources such as network services.

This chapter introduces the Windows Server 2003 implementation of DNS. You'll learn how to install and configure a DNS server, as well as how to maintain and monitor it. Having a thorough understanding of the topics presented here is important to both the exam and on-the-job success.

Installing and Configuring the DNS Server Service

At one time or another, most of us have typed a universal resource locator (URL) to get to one of our favorite Web sites. Before you can view the Web site stored on a Web server, that URL you typed must be resolved to an IP address, and this is where DNS servers come into play.

You might have also heard the term *fully qualified domain name (FQDN)*. An FQDN contains both the hostname and a domain name. It uniquely identifies a host within a DNS hierarchy. For example, `www.bayside.net` is an FQDN. Every FQDN is broken down into different levels, each separated by a period. In the preceding example, .net is the top-level domain and bayside is the second-level domain. The top-level domain normally identifies the type of organization, such as a government organization (gov) or an educational organization (edu). The second-level domain indicates a specific domain within that top-level namespace, whereas the third level might indicate a specific host within that domain. In all cases, DNS servers are used to resolve FQDNs to IP addresses.

DNS can use two different processes to resolve queries: recursive and iterative. With a *recursive query*, the DNS client requires the DNS server to respond with the IP address of the request or an error message that the requested name does not exist. The DNS server cannot refer the client to another DNS server if it cannot map the request to an IP address. When a DNS server receives a recursive request, it queries other DNS servers until it finds the information or until the query fails.

With an *iterative query*, the DNS server uses zone information and its cache to return the best possible answer to the client. If the DNS server does not have the requested information, it can refer the client to another DNS server.

For example, when a DNS client enters `www.bayside.net` into a browser, the following process occurs:

1. A DNS request is sent to the local DNS server. This can be a DNS server on the client's local network or a DNS server at the client's Internet service provider (ISP).

2. Before forwarding the request to a root server, the DNS server checks its local cache to determine whether the name has recently been resolved. If there is an entry in the local cache, the IP address is returned to the client.

3. If no entry exists in the cache for the hostname, the request is sent by the DNS server to a *root name server*.

4. The root name server refers the DNS server to a name server responsible for the first-level domain within the hostname. For example, the root name server would refer the request to the bayside.net DNS server.

5. The original DNS server is referred to second-level DNS servers, and then third-level DNS servers, until one of them can resolve the hostname to an IP address and return the results back to the client.

Now that you have a general idea what happens when a DNS client attempts to connect to another computer using a hostname, let's take a look at the types of roles that can be assigned to Windows Server 2003 DNS.

Implementing Windows 2003 DNS Server Roles

You can configure a DNS server in one of three possible roles. The role the server plays depends on the configuration of *zone files* and how they are maintained. The zone files contain configuration information for the zone as well as the resource records.

 A zone file contains the *resource records* for a portion of the DNS namespace. Resource records map hostnames to IP addresses. Both of these topics are covered later in this chapter, in the section "Creating Resource Records."

The three possible DNS server configuration roles are as follows:

➤ Caching-only server

➤ Primary server

➤ Secondary server

Keep in mind when you are planning DNS server roles that a single DNS server can perform multiple roles. For example, a DNS server can be the primary server for one zone and at the same time be a secondary server for another DNS zone.

Caching-only Server

All DNS servers maintain a `cache.dns` file that contains a list of all Internet root servers. Any time a DNS server resolves a hostname to an IP address, the information is added to the cache file. The next time a DNS client needs to resolve that hostname, the information can be retrieved from the cache instead of the Internet.

Caching-only servers do not contain any zone information, which is the main difference between them and primary and secondary DNS servers. The main purpose of a caching-only server (other than providing name resolution) is to build the cache file as names are resolved. They resolve hostnames, cache the information, and return the results to the client. Because these servers hold no zone information, either hostnames are resolved from the cache or else another DNS server is required to resolve them.

Caching-only servers are useful when you need to reduce network traffic. Again, because there is no zone information, no zone transfer traffic is generated (meaning that no information is replicated between DNS servers). Hostname traffic is also reduced as the cache file is built up because names can be resolved locally using the contents of the local DNS server's cache

It's important to understand when caching-only servers should be implemented. Caching-only servers are useful when there are remote locations that have slow WAN links. Configuring a caching-only server in these locations can reduce WAN traffic that would normally be generated between primary and secondary DNS servers, and can speed up hostname resolution after the cache file has been established.

Primary Server

A primary DNS server hosts the working (writable) copy of a zone file. If you need to make changes to the zone file, it must be done from the server that is designated as the primary server for that zone. For those of you who are familiar with Windows NT 4.0, this is similar to how the primary domain controller (PDC) maintains the working copy of the directory database. After a server has been configured as a primary DNS server for a zone, it is said to be authoritative for that domain. Also, a single DNS server can be the primary DNS server for multiple *zones*.

Secondary Server

A secondary server gets all its zone information from a master DNS server. The secondary DNS server hosts a read-only copy of the zone file, which it gets from the primary server or another secondary DNS server. Through a process known as a *zone transfer*, the master DNS server sends a copy of the zone file to the secondary server.

Pre–Windows 2000 implementations of DNS supported only full transfers, in which an update to the zone file resulted in the entire zone database being transferred to the secondary servers. Windows Server 2003 (as well as Windows 2000 DNS) supports incremental zone transfers, so the secondary servers can synchronize their zone files by pulling only the changes. This results in less network traffic.

For example, if Server2 is configured as a secondary server for bayside.net, Server2 would get all of its zone information from Server1, the primary DNS server for the zone. Any changes that need to be made to the zone file would have to be done on Server1. The changes would then be copied to Server2. As already mentioned, a DNS server can be both a primary and a secondary server at the same time. Using this example, Server2 could also be configured as the primary server for riverside.net, and, to provide fault tolerance for the zone file, Server1 could be configured as a secondary server for this zone.

Secondary DNS servers provide the following benefits:

➤ *Fault tolerance*—Because the secondary server has a copy of the zone file, name resolution can continue if the primary DNS server becomes unavailable.

➤ *Reduction in name-resolution traffic*—Secondary servers can be placed in remote locations with a large number of users. Clients can then resolve hostnames locally instead of having to contact a primary DNS using a WAN link.

➤ *Load balancing*—Name-resolution services for a zone can be provided by the secondary server as well, thereby reducing the load placed on the primary DNS server.

Installing DNS

DNS can be installed in several ways. It can be added during the installation of Windows Server 2003, after installation using the Configure Your Server Wizard, or through the Add or Remove Programs applet in the Control Panel. DNS can also be installed when promoting a server to a domain controller using the DCPROMO command.

The only real requirement for installing DNS is Windows Server 2003 Server. It cannot be installed on a computer running Windows XP. Also, if you are using Dynamic Host Configuration Protocol (DHCP) on the network to assign IP addresses, it's generally a good idea to configure the DNS server with a static IP address that is outside the range of addresses included in the DHCP scope.

To install the DNS Server service using the Add or Remove Programs applet within the Control Panel, perform the following steps:

1. Click Start, point to Control Panel, and click Add or Remove Programs.

2. Click Add/Remove Windows Components.

3. Highlight Networking Services from the Components list and click the Details button.

4. From the list of components, select Domain Name System (DNS). Click OK and then click Next.

5. After the necessary files are copied, click Finish.

6. Close the Add or Remove Programs applet.

Configuring DNS Server Options

When DNS is installed, the DNS management console is added to the Administrative Tools menu. From the management console, you can manage all aspects of a DNS server, from configuring zones to performing management tasks.

A number of options can be configured for a DNS server. By right-clicking the DNS server within the management console and selecting the Properties option, the Properties window for the server is displayed (see Figure 3.1).

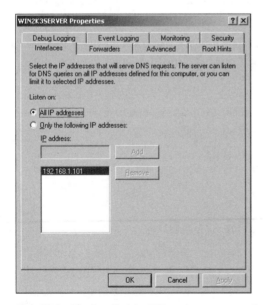

Figure 3.1 After installing the DNS service, you can configure DNS server options through the server's Properties dialog box.

The available tabs from the DNS server Properties sheet and their uses are summarized as follows:

➤ *Interfaces*—Using this tab, you can configure the interfaces on which the DNS server will listen for DNS queries.

➤ *Forwarders*—From this tab, you can configure where a DNS server can forward DNS queries that it cannot resolve.

➤ *Advanced*—This tab allows you to configure advanced options, determine the method of name checking, determine the location from which zone data is loaded, and enable automatic scavenging of stale records.

➤ *Root Hints*—This tab enables you to configure root name servers that the DNS server can use and refer to when resolving queries.

➤ *Debug Logging*—From this property tab, you can enable debugging. When this option is enabled, packets sent and received by the DNS server are recorded in a log file. You can also configure the type of information to record in the file.

➤ *Event Logging*—The Event Logging tab enables you to configure the type of events that should be written to the DNS event log. You can log errors, warnings, and all events. You can also turn off logging by selecting No Events.

➤ *Monitoring*—The Monitoring tab can be used to test and verify the configuration by manually sending queries against the server. You can perform a simple query that uses the DNS client on the local server to query the DNS service to return the best possible answer. You can also perform a recursive query in which the local DNS server can query other DNS servers to resolve the query.

➤ *Security*—This tab enables you to assign permissions to users and groups for the DNS server.

Configuring DNS Zone Options

After you have installed the DNS Server service, your next step is to create and configure zones (unless the DNS server is not authoritative for any zones).

A *zone* is basically an administrative entity. A zone is nothing more than a portion of the DNS database that is administered as a single unit. A zone can contain a single domain or span multiple domains. The DNS server that is authoritative for a zone is ultimately responsible for resolving any requests for that particular zone. The zone file maintains all of the configuration information for the zone and contains the resource records for the domains in the zone.

Each new zone consists of a forward lookup zone and an optional reverse lookup zone. A *forward lookup zone* maps hostnames to IP addresses. When a client needs the IP address for a hostname, the information is retrieved from the forward lookup zone. A *reverse lookup zone* does the opposite. It allows for reverse queries, or mapping of an IP address back to a hostname. Reverse queries are often used when troubleshooting with the NSLookup command.

Zone Types

Windows Server 2003 supports four types of zones:

➤ *Standard primary zone*—This type of zone maintains the master writable copy of the zone in a text file. An update to the zone must be performed from the primary zone.

➤ *Standard secondary zone*—This zone type stores a copy of an existing zone in a read-only text file. To create a secondary zone, the primary zone must already exist, and you must specify a master name server. This is the server from which the zone information is copied.

➤ *Active Directory–integrated zone*—This zone type stores zone information within Active Directory. This enables you to take advantage of additional features, such as secure *dynamic updates* and replication. Active Directory–integrated zones can be configured on Windows Server 2003 domain controllers running DNS. Each domain controller maintains a writable copy of the zone information, which is stored in the Active Directory database.

➤ *Stub zone*—This type of zone is new in Windows Server 2003. A stub zone maintains only a list of authoritative name servers for a particular zone. The purpose of a stub zone is to ensure that DNS servers hosting a parent zone are aware of authoritative DNS servers for its child zones. One of the advantages of stub zones is that they create a dynamic relationship between the parent and child. Compared to delegation, which points to a single IP address, stub zones allow much more flexibility for the administrator because changes in the child zone are automatically reflected in the stub without making changes to the configuration.

Windows Server 2003 now includes a fourth type of DNS zone known as a stub zone. Because this is a new feature of Windows Server 2003, be prepared to encounter exam questions related to this topic.

Creating Zones

After the DNS service is installed, you can manage it using the DNS management console. From this management console, you can begin configuring a DNS server by creating zones. To create a new zone, follow these steps:

1. Click Start, point to Administrative Tools, and click DNS. This opens the DNS management console.

2. Right-click the DNS server and click New Zone. The New Zone Wizard opens. Click Next.

3. Select the type of zone you want to create: primary zone, secondary zone, or stub zone. You also have the option of storing the zone within Active Directory, if it is available. (The option to store information within Active Directory is available only if Active Directory is installed on the local machine.) Click Next.

4. Select the type of zone you want to create: a forward lookup zone or a reverse lookup zone. Click Next.

5. If you select a forward lookup zone, the Zone Name page appears. Type the name for the zone, such as bayside.net. Click Next.

6. If you selected to create a reverse lookup zone, type the network ID (see Figure 3.2). This is used to create the in-addra.arpa domain, with subdomains named using the network ID of the IP address. DNS uses the reverse lookup zone for performing address to name translations. For example, a network ID of 192.168.1 would be translated into 1.168.192.in-addra.arpa. Click Next.

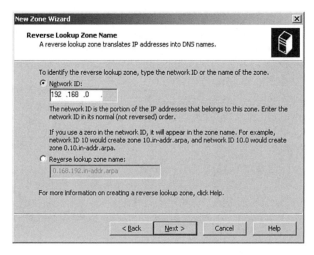

Figure 3.2 If you are creating a reverse lookup zone, you must supply the network ID.

7. In the Zone File screen, select whether to create a new zone file or to use an existing one (see Figure 3.3). This option appears when creating a forward or reverse lookup zone. Click Next.

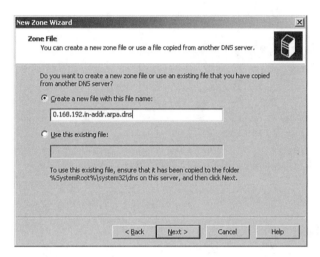

Figure 3.3   You must provide a filename for the zone file or select an existing file.

8. Specify how the DNS zone will receive updates from DNS client computers. Three options are available, as shown in Figure 3.4. If the zone is Active Directory integrated, you can allow secure updates only. You can allow both nonsecure and secure updates, or you can turn off dynamic updates so that the resource records must be manually updated. Dynamic updates are covered in more detail later in the chapter in the section "Dynamic Updates."

9. Click Finish.

Creating Resource Records

After a zone has been created, it can be populated with resource records. Remember, if your clients are all running Windows Server 2003, Windows XP, or Windows 2000 and the zone is configured for dynamic updates, the clients can add and update their own resource records. You can also manually add resource records to a zone file through the DNS management console. A number of resource records can be created. To view all of the resource records supported by Windows Server 2003 DNS, right-click a zone and select Other New Records (see Figure 3.5).

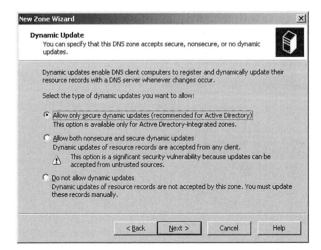

Figure 3.4 You must configure how the DNS zone will receive dynamic updates.

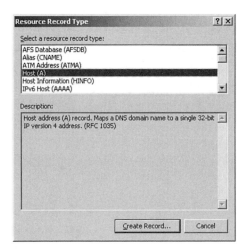

Figure 3.5 The next step in zone creation is populating the zone with DNS resource records.

The following list summarizes some of the more common resource records you might encounter:

➤ *Host Address (A) record*—Maps a DNS name to an IP address.

➤ *Mail Exchanger (MX) record*—Routes messages to a specified mail exchanger for a specified DNS domain name.

➤ *Pointer (PTR) record*—Points to a location in the DNS namespace. PTR records are normally used for reverse lookups.

➤ *Alias (CNAME) record*—Specifies another DNS domain name for a name that is already referenced in another resource record.

As already mentioned, resource records can be created using the DNS management console. To create a new host record, simply right-click the zone in which you want to create the record and select the New Host (A) option. In the New Host dialog box, type the name and IP address for the host. To automatically create a pointer record, select the Create Associated Pointer (PTR) Record check box (see Figure 3.6).

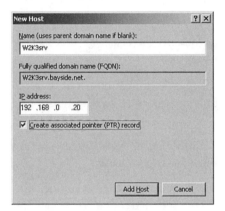

Figure 3.6   You can add a new host record via the DNS management console.

To create additional resource records, simply select the type of record you want to create and fill in the required information.

The **NSLookup** command can be used to determine the hostname associated with a specific IP address. To use the **NSLookup** command, PTR records must exist.

Configuring DNS Simple Forwarding

DNS servers often must communicate with DNS servers outside of the local network. A *forwarder* is an entry that is used when a DNS server receives DNS queries that it cannot resolve locally. It then forwards those requests to external DNS servers for resolution.

By configuring forwarders, you can specify which DNS servers are responsible for handling external traffic. Otherwise, all DNS servers can send queries outside of the local network, possibly exposing DNS information to untrusted hosts on the Internet. Configuring forwarding adds another level of security to the network because only servers identified as forwarders are permitted to forward queries outside the local network.

Additionally, if all DNS servers were allowed to forward queries outside the network, the result could be a large amount of unnecessary network traffic. This can become an important issue if the Internet connection is slow, costly, or already heavily utilized. Because a forwarder receives queries from local DNS servers, it builds up a large amount of cache information. This means that many of the queries received by the forwarder can be resolved from the cache instead of forwarding the requests outside the local network. This is obviously more efficient in terms of network traffic.

When a DNS server configured to use forwarding receives a DNS query from a DNS client, the following process occurs:

1. When a DNS server receives a DNS query, it first attempts to resolve the request using its zone information and information within its local cache.

2. If the request cannot be resolved locally, the DNS server sends a recursive query to the DNS server designated as the forwarder.

3. The forwarder attempts to resolve the query. If the forwarder does not respond, the DNS server attempts to resolve the request by contacting the appropriate DNS server, as specified in the root hints. (Root hints list authoritative root servers for the Internet.)

A DNS server can be configured to send all queries that it cannot resolve locally to a forwarder, and you can also configure conditional forwarders. With conditional forwarders, DNS servers are configured to forward requests to different servers based on the DNS name within the query. When configuring conditional forwarding, you must specify the following information:

➤ The domain name for which queries will be forwarded

➤ The IP address of the DNS server for which unresolved queries for a specified domain should be forwarded

To configure DNS forwarders, follow these steps:

1. Within the DNS management console, right-click the DNS server and click Properties.

2. From the Properties window for the DNS server, click the Forwarders tab.

3. Under DNS Name, select a domain name. To add a new domain name, click the Add button.

4. Under the Selected Domain's Forwarder IP Address list, type the IP address of the forwarder and click Add.

Managing DNS

After DNS is installed, it can be managed using the DNS management console. Management tasks include configuring zone settings, creating and managing resource records, and monitoring the status and performance of DNS. The following sections discuss some of the common management tasks associated with DNS.

Managing DNS Zone Settings

After a zone has been successfully added to your DNS server, you can configure it via the zone's Properties dialog box. To do so, right-click the zone from within the DNS management console and click Properties. The Properties dialog box for the zone displays six tabs, as shown in Figure 3.7. If Active Directory is not installed, only five tabs are available (the Security tab is not present).

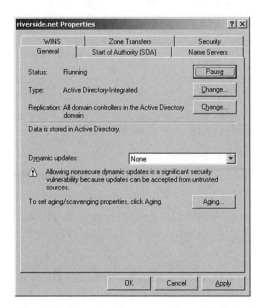

Figure 3.7   You can configure a zone through its Properties dialog box.

The following list summarizes each of the tabs for a DNS zone's properties:

➤ *General*—View the status of the zone, change the type of zone, change the zone filename, change the replication scope for a zone, and configure dynamic updates. You can also set the aging and scavenging properties for the zone.

➤ *Start of Authority (SOA)*—Configure the zone transfer information and the email address of the zone administrator. The serial number is used to determine whether a zone transfer is required. Each time a change is made this number is incremented by 1. By using the Increment button, you can increase the value, thereby forcing a zone transfer.

➤ *Name Servers*—Specify the list of secondary servers that should be notified when changes to the zone file occur.

➤ *WINS*—Enable the DNS server to query the list of WINS servers for name resolution.

➤ *Zone Transfers*—Configure which secondary servers can receive zone transfers. You can specify any server, only those listed on the Name Servers tab, or the ones configured from this property sheet. Clicking the Notify button enables you to configure which secondary servers will be notified of changes.

➤ *Security*—If the zone is Active Directory integrated, the Security tab is available and can be used to configure permissions to the zone file. This is where you can control who can perform dynamic updates.

Changing Zone Types

Using the General tab from the Zone Properties dialog box, you can change the current zone type (see Figure 3.8). To do so, click the Change button beside the zone type. You have the option of changing a primary or secondary zone to an Active Directory–integrated zone or changing an Active Directory–integrated zone to a primary zone or secondary zone.

Before you attempt to change the zone type, be aware of the following points:

➤ The option to store zone information within Active Directory is available only when the DNS server is also configured as a domain controller.

➤ If you convert to a secondary zone or a stub zone, you must specify the IP address of the server from which the zone information will be retrieved.

➤ Changing a secondary zone to a primary zone affects such things as dynamic updates, the use of the DNS Notify option, and zone transfers.

➤ When the option to store information within Active Directory is cleared, zone information is deleted from Active Directory and copied into a text file on the local DNS server in the %systemeroot%/system32/DNS folder.

➤ Because the purpose of a stub zone is to maintain information about only authoritative name servers for the zone, it is not recommended that a stub zone be converted to a primary zone because primary zones can contain a number of other records rather than just those for authoritative name servers.

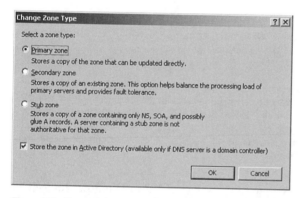

Figure 3.8   You can change the zone type via a zone's Properties dialog box.

Dynamic Updates

Windows 2003 Server, Windows XP, and Windows 2000 clients can interact directly with a DNS server. With dynamic updates, clients can automatically register their own resource records with a DNS server and update them as changes occur. Resource records are the entries within the DNS server database files. Each resource record contains information about a specific machine, such as the IP address or specific network services running. The type of information within a resource record depends upon the type of resource record that is created. For example, an A (address) record contains the IP address associated with a specific computer; it's used to map a hostname to an IP address.

Dynamic updates greatly reduce the administration associated with maintaining resource records. Dynamic updates eliminate the need for administrators to manually update these records. In terms of DHCP, with a short lease duration configured, the IP address assigned to DNS clients can change frequently. If dynamic updates are not enabled, an administrator can end up spending a lot of time updating zone information. In addition, there is always the chance for human error when done manually.

Dynamic updates provide the following advantages:

➤ DHCP servers can dynamically register records for clients. This is particularly important because DHCP servers can perform updates on behalf of clients that do not support dynamic updates, such as Windows 95, 98, or NT4 clients.

➤ The administrative overhead is reduced because A records and PTR records can be dynamically updated by Windows DNS clients that support this option.

➤ The SRV records required to locate domain controllers can be dynamically registered.

 To implement dynamic updates on a network with pre–Windows 2000 clients, a DHCP server and a DNS server are required on the network. The DHCP and DNS servers must be running Windows Server 2003 or Windows 2000 because Windows NT 4.0 DNS servers don't support dynamic updates. A DHCP server is required to perform dynamic updates on behalf of clients that do not support this feature, such as Windows 95 clients.

By default, any Windows Server 2003, Windows XP, or Windows 2000 client can update its own records with the DNS server. The DHCP client service attempts to update records with the DNS server when any of the following events occur:

➤ The workstation is rebooted.

➤ The client records are manually refreshed using the `ipconfig /registerDNS` command.

➤ A statically configured IP address is modified.

➤ The IP address leased from a DHCP server changes or is renewed. An IP address can be manually renewed using the `ipconfig /renew` option.

Let's take a look at an example of what happens when a Windows XP DNS client performs a dynamic update. Assume that you change a bayside.net workstation's computer name from computer1 to computer2. Upon changing the computer name, you are required to restart before the changes take effect. When the workstation restarts, the following process occurs:

1. The DHCP client service sends a query to an authoritative DNS server for the domain using the new DNS domain name of the workstation.

2. The DNS server that is authoritative for the workstation's domain responds to the request with information about the primary DNS server for the domain.

3. The client sends a dynamic update request to the primary DNS server.

4. The update request is processed by the primary DNS server. The old host and pointer records are removed and replaced with the updated ones.

5. The master name server randomly notifies any secondary servers that a change to the zone file has occurred.

6. Secondary servers request the zone transfer update to the zone file according to the frequency configured on the zone's Start of Authority tab.

Dynamic updates are configured on a per-zone basis. To configure a zone for dynamic update, right-click the zone within the DNS management console and click Properties. In the Properties dialog box, ensure that the General tab is selected. To enable dynamic updates, select one of the following options:

➤ *None*—Select this option to disable dynamic updates for the zone. Doing so means that the zone file must be manually updated.

➤ *Nonsecure and Secure*—Select this option to allow nonsecure updates (anyone can perform the update) as well as secure updates (only certain users can perform the update).

➤ *Secure Only*—Select this option to enable dynamic updates for those users and groups authorized to do so because they have accounts in Active Directory and have been granted permission to update their records. This option is available only for zones that store information within Active Directory. You can use the Security tab from the zone's Properties window to configure who can perform dynamic updates.

When configuring dynamic updates, remember that the zone must be standard primary (information is stored locally in files) or Active Directory integrated (information is stored on all DCs). Also, to use secure updates, the zone must be Active Directory integrated. This feature is not supported by standard primary zones.

Secure Updates

Windows Server 2003 supports secure dynamic updates for zones that store information within Active Directory. With secure updates, only those clients authorized within the domain are permitted to update resource records. This means that the DNS server accepts updates only from clients that have accounts within Active Directory. Any computers that do not have accounts are not permitted to register any records, thereby eliminating the chance that unknown computers will register with the DNS server. Secure updates for a zone can be configured by selecting the Secure Only option.

The benefit of selecting this option is obviously an increase in security. The resource records and zone files can be modified only by users who have been authorized to do so. This also provides administrators with a finer granularity of control because they can edit the access control list (ACL) for the zone and specify which users and groups can perform dynamic updates. You edit the ACL for a zone by right-clicking the zone, selecting Properties, and choosing the Security tab.

Zone Transfers

Secondary servers get their zone information from a master name server. The master name server is the source of the zone file; it can be a primary server or another secondary server. If the master name server is a secondary server, it must first get the updated zone file from the primary server. The process of replicating a zone file to a secondary server is referred to as a *zone transfer*. Zone transfers occur between a secondary server and a master name server in the following situations:

➤ When the master name server notifies the secondary server that changes have been made to the zone file. When the secondary server receives notification, it requests a zone transfer. If multiple secondary servers exist, they are notified at random so that the master name server is not overburdened with zone transfer requests.

➤ When the refresh interval expires and the secondary server contacts the primary name server to check for changes to the zone file.

➤ When the DNS server service is started on a secondary server.

➤ When a zone transfer is manually initiated through the DNS management console on a secondary server.

Windows Server 2003 DNS (as well as Windows 2000 DNS) supports two types of zone transfers. Pre–Windows 2000 implementations of DNS supported a *full zone transfer (AXFR)* only, in which the entire zone file is replicated to the secondary server. This type of zone transfer is supported by most implementations of DNS. If the secondary server's zone file is not current, which means that changes were made, the entire zone file is replicated. The second type of zone transfer is known as an *incremental zone transfer (IXFR)*, in which only the changes made to a zone file are replicated to the secondary server, thereby reducing the amount of network traffic. Frequency of zone transfers is configured on the Start of Authority tab.

The following list summarizes the configurable options for zone transfers:

➤ *Serial Number*—Lists the number used to determine whether the zone file has changed. Each time a change is made, this number is incremented by 1. You can force a zone transfer by manually increasing this number.

➤ *Primary Server*—Lists the hostname of the primary DNS server for the zone.

➤ *Responsible Person*—Lists the e-mail address of the person responsible for administering the zone.

➤ *Refresh Interval*—Determines how often the secondary server polls the primary server for updates. Consider increasing this value for slow network connections.

➤ *Retry Interval*—Specifies how often the secondary server attempts to contact the primary server if the server does not respond.

➤ *Expires After*—Specifies when zone file information should expire if the secondary server fails to refresh the information. If a zone expires, zone data is considered to be potentially outdated and is discarded. Secondary master servers do not use zone data from an expired zone.

➤ *Minimum (Default) TTL*—Specifies how long records from the zone should be cached on other servers.

➤ *TTL for this Record*—Specifies how long DNS servers are allowed to store a record from the zone in their cache before it expires.

When zone information is stored within Active Directory, zone updates are replicated differently than in a standard primary/secondary scenario. DNS notification is no longer needed, and configuring a notify list is unnecessary. Instead, the DNS servers that store information within Active Directory poll Active Directory at 15-minute intervals to check for updates.

Zone Delegation

Delegation is the process of designating a portion of the DNS namespace for another zone. It gives administrators a way of dividing a namespace among multiple zones. For example, an administrator might place the bayside.net domain in one zone and place the sales.bayside.net subdomain in another delegated zone. The bayside.net zone would contain all the records for the sales subdomain if it is not delegated. Through delegating, the bayside.net zone contains only information for bayside.net, as well as records to the authoritative name servers for the sales.bayside.net zone. The host entries for any machines in sales.bayside.net are contained only on the delegated server.

In any case, when deciding whether to delegate, keep the following points in mind:

➤ Zone delegation allows you to delegate management of part of the DNS namespace to other departments or locations.

➤ Zone delegation allows you to distribute a large DNS database across multiple servers for load balancing, faster name resolution, and increased performance.

➤ Zone delegation allows you to extend the namespace for business expansion, that is, it is scalable with business needs.

To facilitate the delegation of zones, you need the appropriate delegation records that point to authoritative name servers for the new zone(s).

You can use the following procedure to delegate a zone:

1. From within the DNS management console, right-click the domain you want to delegate and select New Delegation. The New Delegation Wizard opens. Click Next.

2. Type a name for the delegated domain in the Delegated Domain text box. Click Next.

3. Specify the name servers that will host the delegated domain by clicking the Add button. The New Resource Record screen appears, allowing you to specify the name and IP address of the name servers. Click OK. Click Next.

4. Click Finish.

Managing DNS Record Settings

After resource records have been created, they can be managed through the management console. Tasks associated with resource records include modifying the resource records, deleting existing records, and configuring security.

Modifying Resource Records

If you have manually created resource records within a zone, at some point you might need to modify them, such as change the IP address associated with a particular hostname. This won't be an issue if you are using dynamic updates because DNS clients (running the appropriate platform) can update this information on their own.

You can modify a resource record within the DNS management console by selecting the appropriate zone, right-clicking the resource record, and clicking Properties (see Figure 3.9). For example, you can change the hostname, domain name, and IP address of a Host (A) record.

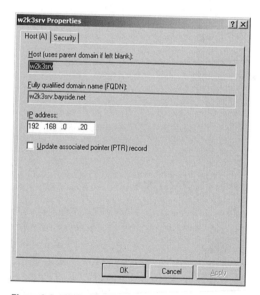

Figure 3.9   You can modify the properties of a resource record through the management console.

Deleting Resource Records

You can delete resource records within a zone file at any time. For example, if you manually create resource records for a server and remove it from the network, you will want to delete the records from the zone file. Deleting a record is a simple process. Simply right-click the record within the zone and click the Delete option. Click Yes to confirm your actions.

Modifying Security for Records

Each record has an associated ACL that can be edited. Doing so enables you to specify which users and groups are permitted to securely update the record and change their permissions. You can modify the security by opening the Properties window for a record and selecting the Security tab (see Figure 3.10).

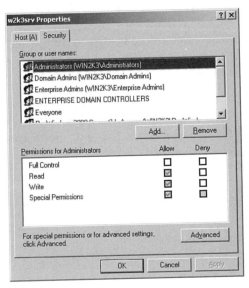

Figure 3.10   You modify security for a record on its Security tab.

Managing DNS Server Options

Most management tasks performed on a DNS server are done through the DNS management console. When you highlight your DNS server within the DNS management console and click the Action menu, you see a number of options that can be used to manage different aspects of DNS. Some of the options available are summarized as follows:

➤ *Set Aging/Scavenging for All Zones*—Use this option to configure refresh intervals for resource records. This enables you to refresh resource records on a set schedule. Refreshing periodically keeps bad records, such as invalid URLs, out of the database.

➤ *Scavenge Stale Resource Records*—Use this option to manually scavenge stale resource records. Stale resource records can accumulate within a zone over a period of time. For example, if a computer registers its own resource record and is shut down improperly, the record might not be

removed from the zone file. Scavenging stale resource records can eliminate any problems, such as outdated information.

➤ *Update Server Data Files*—Use this option to write all changes to the
zone file stored within Active Directory to a zone file on the disk.

➤ *Clear Cache*—Use this option to clear the contents of the name server's
cache.

➤ *Launch NSLookup*—Use this option to open the command prompt from
which you can use the NSLookup command.

Monitoring DNS

You should monitor your DNS servers on a regular basis. Obviously, in large
enterprise environments, you will want to monitor DNS servers more
frequently than for small businesses. Because DNS servers play such an
important role for a Windows Server 2003 domain, it's important that solid
performance is maintained.

System Monitor

The tool most often used to monitor how services are performing is the
System Monitor tool, located within the Performance console. When you
install DNS, several counters are added specifically for monitoring this service (see Figure 3.11).

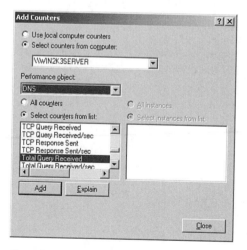

Figure 3.11   DNS-specific counters are added to the System Monitor tool for monitoring DNS
activity.

The following list outlines some of the common DNS performance counters:

➤ *Caching Memory*—Monitors the total caching memory used by the DNS server

➤ *Dynamic Update Received/Sec*—Determines the number of dynamic update requests received by the server per second

➤ *Dynamic Update Requests*—Counts the total number of dynamic updates received by the server

➤ *Recursive Queries*—Monitors the total number of recursive queries received by the server

➤ *Total Queries Received*—Calculates the total number of queries received by the server

Event Viewer

If logging is enabled, DNS-related events can be written to the DNS Server log. As already mentioned, logging can be enabled using the Event Logging tab from the DNS server's Properties window. By default, all DNS-related events are written to the log. You can choose to log errors only or to log both errors and warnings. By selecting the No Events option, you can disable event logging.

You can use the Event Viewer, located on the Administrative Tools menu, to view events. When the Event Viewer is open, click the DNS Server entry. Any DNS-related events are displayed within the right pane (see Figure 3.12). To view more detailed information about an event, double-click the event within the right pane. The Properties window for the event displays information such as the date and time the event occurred, the type of event, the user and computer under which the event occurred, and an event ID. A basic description of the event is also provided.

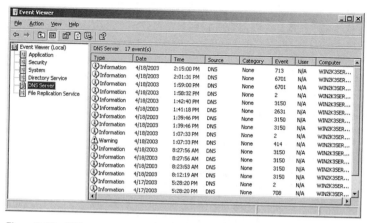

Figure 3.12   DNS events are logged in the Event Viewer's DNS log.

Replication Monitor

As mentioned earlier in the chapter, zone information can be stored within Active Directory if DNS is installed on a domain controller. This also means that zone updates can be included in Active Directory replication.

Using a tool called Replication Monitor, you can monitor the status of Active Directory replication between domain controllers. If zone information is stored within Active Directory, this also enables you to monitor replication between DNS servers.

Replication Monitor is not installed by default. It can be added by browsing to the i386\Support\Tools directory on the Windows Server 2003 CD and running setup. After it is installed, it can be launched from the command prompt using the Replmon command.

Exam Prep Questions

Question 1

> Two DNS servers are currently configured on the Windows Server 2003 network and are connected by high-speed links. Both servers are configured with identical hardware. Currently, one server is configured as a primary server and the other is configured as a secondary server. Both DNS servers are upgraded to domain controllers. You want to store the zone information within Active Directory and perform updates on either server. How should you proceed?
>
> ○ A. In the Properties dialog box for the DNS server, select the General tab and click the Change button beside the zone type. Select the option to store the zone in Active Directory.
>
> ○ B. In the Properties dialog box for the zone, select the Zone Type tab and click the Change button. Select the Active Directory–Integrated option.
>
> ○ C. In the Properties dialog box for the zone, select the General tab and click the Change button beside the zone type. Select the option to store the zone in Active Directory.
>
> ○ D. In the Properties dialog box for the DNS server, select the Zone Type tab and click the Change button. Select the Active Directory–Integrated option.

Answer C is correct. To change the zone type, right-click the zone within the DNS management console and click Properties. In the Properties dialog box, make sure the General tab is selected and click the Change button beside the zone type. Select the option to store the zone within Active Directory. Answer A is incorrect because the zone type is configured at the zone level. Answers B and D are incorrect because there is no Zone Type tab available in either the server's Properties dialog box or the zone's Properties dialog box. There is also no option known as Active Directory Integrated.

Question 2

> You have just finished installing a DNS server on a Windows Server 2003 member server in the bayside.net domain. You need to add a record into the zone file for the mail server on the domain. Which type of resource record should be created?
>
> ○ A. PTR
>
> ○ B. A
>
> ○ C. CNAME
>
> ○ D. MX

Answer D is correct. Mail servers are identified within a zone file using Mail Exchanger (MX) records. Answer A is incorrect because PTR records are used to associate an IP address with its hostname. Answer B is incorrect because A records are used to map hostnames to IP addresses. Answer C is incorrect because CNAME records are used to assign alias names to those names that are already referenced in another record.

Question 3

A DNS server has been installed on a member server within a Windows Server 2003 domain. You want to provide fault tolerance for your zone so that name resolution can still continue if the DNS server goes offline. You plan to add another DNS server to the domain. In what type of role should the new DNS server be configured?

- O A. Secondary server
- O B. Master name server
- O C. Caching-only server
- O D. Backup name server

Answer A is correct. The new server should be configured as a secondary server. It will then maintain a copy of the DNS zone file. If the original DNS server goes offline, name resolution can still occur. Answer B is incorrect because master name servers are the source of the zone file for secondary servers. Answer C is incorrect because caching-only servers do not hold any zone information. Answer D is incorrect because there is no such DNS server role called a backup name server.

Question 4

Bayside has seven offices located in different parts of the United States. One central office hosts the primary DNS server. All office locations have their own DNS servers configured as secondary servers. The offices are currently connected with slow links, with no plans to upgrade them. The annual budget allows for the addition of a second DNS server at each of the locations. However, you do not want any more traffic generated from zone transfers on the WAN or the local networks. What type of DNS servers should you configure?

- O A. Standard primary servers
- O B. Standard secondary servers
- O C. Master name servers
- O D. Caching-only servers

Answer D is correct. By configuring caching-only servers within each location, you can decrease the name resolution response time for users. Because the caching-only servers do not maintain any zone information, no traffic is generated from zone transfers. Therefore, answers A, B, and C are incorrect.

Question 5

> Sean is trying to determine the hostname associated with the IP address of 192.168.0.20 using the **NSLookup** command from Wrk02, but he is unsuccessful. He knows the IP address is associated with Wrk01. He can successfully resolve other hostnames on the network using this command. What could be causing the problem?
>
> ○ A. There is no A record for Wrk01.
> ○ B. There is no A record for Wrk02.
> ○ C. There is no PTR record for Wrk01.
> ○ D. There is no PTR record for Wrk02.

Answer C is correct. If the hostname cannot be resolved using the NSLookup command, adding a PTR to the zone file will allow you to resolve the IP address to a hostname. Answer B is incorrect because Wrk02 is not the hostname being resolved. Answers A and B are incorrect because A records are used to map hostnames to IP addresses, not vice versa.

Question 6

> You want to clear the contents of the cache on your DNS server. How can you most easily accomplish this?
>
> ○ A. Uninstall the DNS server service.
> ○ B. Delete the **cache.dns** file.
> ○ C. Use the Clear Cache option from the DNS server's Property window.
> ○ D. Use the Clear Cache option from the Action menu.

Answer D is correct. Using the Clear Cache option from the Action menu within the DNS management console allows you to delete the contents of the cache file. Although uninstalling the service would clear the contents of the cache, it's not the easiest way to perform the task; therefore, answer A is incorrect. Answer B is incorrect because deleting the file will completely remove it. Answer C is incorrect because there is no Clear Cache option available from the server's property window.

Question 7

> All of the DNS servers on your network are also configured as domain controllers. Zone information is stored within Active Directory. You want to verify that replication between DNS servers is occurring as it should. Which tool can you use to verify this?
>
> ○ A. System Monitor
>
> ○ B. Replication Monitor
>
> ○ C. DNS management console
>
> ○ D. DNS Monitor

Answer B is correct. If the support tools have been installed, you can use Replication Monitor to ensure that replication between DNS servers is occurring on a regular basis. Answer A is incorrect because System Monitor is used to monitor the real-time performance of a DNS server. Answer C is incorrect because the DNS management console is used to configure and manage a DNS server but cannot be used to monitor DNS replication. Answer D is incorrect because there is no such tool known as DNS Monitor.

Question 8

> You are trying to configure secure updates on your DNS server. When you open the Properties window for the zone, you do not see the Secure Only option. What could be causing the problem?
>
> ○ A. You are not logged on as the administrator.
>
> ○ B. You do not have permission to dynamically update the zone database.
>
> ○ C. Active Directory is not installed.
>
> ○ D. The zone is configured as a primary zone.

Answer C is correct. The Secure Only option is available only if Active Directory is installed on the DNS server. Answer A is incorrect because this would not make the Secure Updates option unavailable. Answer B is incorrect because dynamic updates are performed when a computer or server updates resource records. Answer D is incorrect because primary and stub zones can be configured for secure updates.

Question 9

> You have delegated the sales.bayside.net zone to another DNS server on the network. You want to ensure that the name server for bayside.net is notified anytime a new authoritative name server is added to the sales.bayside.net zone. What should you do?
>
> ○ A. Using the Name Servers tab from the sales.bayside.net zone, configure the DNS server to notify the DNS server in the parent domain of any changes.
>
> ○ B. Configure a stub zone on the DNS server within the parent domain.
>
> ○ C. Configure a DNS server within the bayside.net zone to be a secondary server to the sales.bayside.net zone.
>
> ○ D. Configure all zones to store information within Active Directory.

Answer B is correct. By configuring an authoritative DNS server within bayside.net to host a stub zone for the sales.bayside.net zone, any updates made to the authoritative name server resource records will be updated within the parent zone as well. None of the other options provided remedies this scenario effectively; therefore, answers A, B, and D are incorrect.

Question 10

> Your corporate office contains the primary DNS server. One of the branch locations has a large number of users, so you install a secondary server to decrease name resolution response time. Because the link between the remote office and the corporate office is slow, you want to increase the interval at which the secondary server will poll the primary server for updates. How can you do this?
>
> ○ A. In the Properties dialog box for the DNS server, select the Zone Transfers tab and increase the refresh interval.
>
> ○ B. In the Properties dialog box for the zone, select the Start of Authority (SOA) tab and increase the refresh interval.
>
> ○ C. In the Properties dialog box for the zone, select the Start of Authority (SOA) tab and increase the retry interval.
>
> ○ D. In the Properties dialog box for the zone, select the General tab and increase the retry interval.

Answer B is correct. To increase the rate at which the secondary server polls for updates, select the Start of Authority (SOA) tab from the zone's Properties dialog box and increase the refresh interval. Answer A is incorrect because the interval at which a secondary server polls for updates is configured at the zone level. Answer C is incorrect because the retry interval defines how often the secondary server continues to poll if the server does not respond. Answer D is incorrect because you must configure the refresh interval, and it must be done from the Start of Authority (SOA) tab.

Need to Know More?

 Search the online version of TechNet and the Windows Server 2003 Resource Kit using keywords such as "DNS," "zones," and "dynamic updates."

Maintaining Network Security

Terms you'll need to understand:

✓ IP Security Monitor
✓ Automatic Updates Services
✓ Software Update Services (SUS)
✓ Event Viewer
✓ Network Monitor
✓ IPSec
✓ Secure baseline
✓ Security configuration and analysis
✓ Security templates

Techniques you'll need to master:

✓ Implementing security baseline settings
✓ Auditing security settings using security templates
✓ Installing and configuring Software Update Services
✓ Monitoring network protocol security
✓ Troubleshooting network protocol security

Although the current configuration of a server might be secure, performing day-to-day administrative tasks or failing to update the server with new patches can leave a server vulnerable. It's extremely important that organizations implement and follow standard network administration procedures to ensure that the required level of security is met and maintained. This chapter looks at some of the common network administration procedures that should be followed to ensure that security is maintained.

Implementing Security Baseline Settings

One of the first steps you need to take to implement standard network administration procedures is to establish a baseline. What exactly is a secure baseline? The idea or concept behind a secure baseline or secure build is to implement a common standard security configuration that is used throughout an organization for installing any operating system, whether it is for a client or server platform. The baseline establishes a set of rules or recommendations that outline the minimum acceptable security configuration for new installations. Certainly no common baseline can be implemented across all organizations—needs undoubtedly vary from organization to organization. Each organization must assess its own needs and security requirements when establishing a secure baseline.

A secure baseline or build involves installing the operating system, applying service packs and hot fixes, and configuring various operating system settings, as well as documenting each step of the process so that it can be repeated. You must determine what procedures need to be performed on the computer and then establish documentation outlining the secure baseline and how to manage deployment. Remember, the purpose here is to increase security. The secure baseline therefore needs to be implemented consistently throughout an organization.

The first step in adding a new server to the network is to install the base operating system. Because the initial installation of an operating system is often vulnerable to attacks, precautions must be taken after installation to ensure that the system is not compromised. Service packs and hot fixes exist that eliminate many of the known security issues associated with the base installation of an operating system. Until those updates are installed, the server might be left vulnerable to attacks.

To perform a secure baseline installation of an operating system, it is recommended that the server be disconnected from the network until the necessary service packs and hot fixes have been added. Keep in mind that because the server will not be connected to the network, you must have the service packs and hot fixes available locally.

Preparing the Development and Test Environment

One of the steps that should be taken to ensure server security during installation is to disconnect the server from the production network until the service packs and hot fixes have been applied. Ideally, an organization will have a development and test environment that is separate from the production network where installations can be performed securely.

The goal of a development and test environment is to provide a way for administrators to securely test server installations and configurations (as well as the installation of different services and applications). The test and development environment should mirror the actual production environment as closely as possible.

Applying Service Packs and Hot Fixes

Soon after an operating system is released, Microsoft normally releases a service pack. Service packs allow a vendor to easily distribute updates to an operating system. Users can simply access the vendor's Web site and download the service pack for installation. In terms of security and monitoring the updates that are installed, you can use a technology called Software Update Services (SUS), which is discussed later in the chapter. Service packs are intended to fix known issues with an operating system, keep the product up-to-date, and introduce new features. Service packs can include any of the following:

➤ Updates to the operating system

➤ New administrative tools

➤ Drivers

➤ Additional components

It is not uncommon for several service packs to be released over time for a single operating system. Keep in mind when using service packs that they are cumulative, so any new service packs contain all the fixes in the previous service packs, along with new updates.

Most organizations opt to keep up-to-date and install the latest service packs on their servers after they have been assessed in a test environment. Because service packs often contain fixes for known security issues for an operating system, applying the latest service pack is an important step in creating a secure baseline installation for servers.

Between the releases of service packs, Microsoft releases hot fixes, which are used to temporarily patch a specific problem with an operating system. One of the issues associated with installing hot fixes is that they are developed and released rather quickly and, therefore, are not tested thoroughly. So, installing the hot fix can, in turn, have a negative impact. It is important to evaluate the hot fixes released by Microsoft to determine whether they are necessary. If a particular vulnerability does not apply to your server, the patch should not be applied.

When service packs and hot fixes are deployed, they should first be deployed within a test environment so that you can evaluate the impact on the server before installing it in the production environment.

You can use the Hfnetchk.exe utility to determine the hot fixes that might be required for your server. When the command-line utility is run, it scans the system to determine the operating system, service packs, and programs installed. It then determines the security patches available for your system based on the components running. Hfnetchk.exe displays the hot fixes that should be installed to bring the system up-to-date.

You can run HFNetChk from Windows NT 4.0, Windows 2000, or Windows XP systems, and it will scan either the local system or remote systems for patches available for the following products:

➤ Windows NT 4.0, Windows 2000, and Windows XP

➤ Internet Information Server 4.0 and 5.0

➤ SQL Server 7.0 and 2000 (including Microsoft Data Engine)

➤ Internet Explorer 5.01 and later

The system requirements to run the utility include these:

➤ Windows NT 4.0, Windows 2000, or Windows XP

➤ Internet Explorer 5.0 or later (an XML parser is required and one is included with Internet Explorer 5.0)

Securing the Operating System

After the operating system has been installed and the necessary service packs and hot fixes have been added, a number of configuration changes can be made to the operating system to make it more secure. This is often referred to as operating system *hardening*. Again, the changes that are made to harden the server should be documented and made standard for all servers throughout an organization. Some of the steps that should be included with securing the operating system are as follows:

➤ Install antivirus software. All servers (and workstations) should run antivirus software.

➤ During the installation of Windows Server 2003, you must select the type of file system to use. If you did not choose NTFS during the installation, you should convert any partitions from FAT to NTFS. You can do so using the convert command without losing any data. Because NTFS offers security features that FAT does not, such as file-level security, ensure that this is the file system being used on network servers.

➤ Configure a strong password for the Administrator account. During the installation of Windows Server 2003, you are prompted to create a password for the Administrator account. Keep in mind that Windows Server 2003 does not allow you to create noncomplex passwords.

➤ Disable unnecessary services. In Windows Server 2003, many of the services enabled in previous versions are now disabled by default. You can use the Services applet within the Control Panel to further restrict which services will be running.

➤ Remove or disable any unnecessary protocols, such as IPX/SPX. By default, when Windows Server 2003 is installed, the only protocol added is TCP/IP (unless you perform a custom network setup). If any other protocols are inadvertently installed and are not required, they should be removed.

➤ Any unnecessary user accounts should be disabled or deleted. Accounts that are considered inactive should be disabled, and those that are no longer needed should be removed entirely.

➤ Configure the various security settings within the local or domain security policy. This includes a password policy, an account lockout policy, a Kerberos policy, and an audit policy. You can use the *Guide to Securing Microsoft Windows 2000 Group Policy: Security Configuration Tool Set*, published by the National Security Agency, as a basis for configuring security settings. You can find a copy of the guide at http://nsa1.www.conxion. com/win2k/.

Keeping the System Secure

When your organization has a secure baseline installation that is followed by all administrators when installing new servers and workstations, what happens after the installation? What about after the service packs and updates have been applied? Or after you've taken the time to harden the operating system? To ensure that the level of security is maintained, some standardized methods must be put in place outlining how to maintain the security of servers. There is no point in taking the time to perform a secure baseline installation if the security configuration is not documented and maintained afterward. To ensure that the required level of security is maintained, follow these guidelines:

➤ Check for operating system updates on a regular basis. Because software updates are often released quite frequently, you should check for updates on a regular basis to determine whether any are applicable to your server configuration. You can also automate this process by using the Windows Update feature. Again, before deploying updates, you should test them within a controlled environment.

➤ Keep antivirus signature files updated. Again, many vendors have an automatic update option, so this can be done automatically.

➤ View the information in the audit log on a regular basis.

➤ Use the Security Baseline Analyzer to ensure that the minimum security requirements continue to be met. The Security Baseline Analyzer enables you to analyze the current security settings on a computer and compare them to those within a database to find discrepancies that might occur over time.

Implementing the Principle of Least Privilege

Implementing the principle of least privilege adds another level of security to your network. The principle of least privilege is based on the idea that a user who is logged on should have only the minimum privileges required to perform a task. This minimizes the amount of damage that can occur if the user becomes compromised. This means that even network administrators should be logged on with user accounts that have restrictive permissions when performing routine tasks. These users can perform administrative tasks under the context of another user account with additional privileges either by logging off and logging on under that account or by using the Runas command.

Auditing Security Settings Using Security Templates

Windows Server 2003 makes it simple to deploy security configurations. A security template holds a number of security settings that Microsoft considers to be appropriate for a server, domain controller, or workstation. Windows Server 2003 comes with several predefined sample security templates. Each of the templates contains security settings for different levels of security based on the type of server to which the template is applied. For example, you can apply the highsecdc.inf template to all domain controllers in an environment requiring a high level of security. The templates can be used as is or can be customized to meet the specific security needs of an organization. Security templates can be used to configure the following settings within a local security policy or a group policy:

➤ Account policies

➤ Local policies

➤ Event log

➤ Restricted groups

➤ System services

➤ Registry

➤ File system

Using the Default Security Templates

The predefined security templates included with Windows Server 2003 can be viewed using the Security Templates snap-in. To view the default security templates, perform the following steps:

1. Click Start, Run and type MMC. Press Enter.

2. From the File menu, click Add/Remove Snap-In. From the Add/Remove Snap-In window, click Add.

3. Scroll through the list of available snap-ins. Select Security Templates and click Add (see Figure 4.1). Click Close.

4. Click OK.

5. Within the management console, expand Security Templates and click the default container. The preconfigured security templates are listed in the right pane, as shown in Figure 4.2.

Figure 4.1 Adding the Security Templates snap-in.

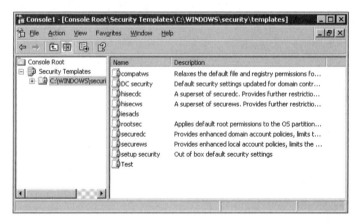

Figure 4.2 Viewing the default security templates included with Windows Server 2003.

By default, the following security templates are stored within the %systemroot%\security\templates directory:

➤ *Setup Security*—This template is created during the installation of Windows Server 2003 and contains the default security settings applied during the installation of the operating system. You should not change the settings within this template because it can be used to reapply default security settings.

➤ *Compatible (compatws.inf)*—This template relaxes security so that members of the Users group can run applications that are not a part of the Designed for Windows Logo Program. The default permission allows only members of this group to run applications that are part of the Windows Logo group. Instead of adding members to the Power Users group, permissions can be relaxed so that members of this group can run the necessary applications.

➤ *Secure (secure*.inf)*—This template modifies security settings that impact the operating system and network protocols such as the password policy, account policy, and various Registry settings. It also removes all members from the Power Users group.

➤ *Highly Secure (hisec*.inf)*—This template increases the security of the parameters defined within the secure template. This template also removes all members from the Power Users group.

The Designed for Windows Logo Program helps customers identify those products that have been tested with the operating system.

Analyzing Security with the Security Configuration and Analysis Tool

Windows Server 2003 includes a tool known as the Security Configuration and Analysis tool. Using this tool, you can analyze the current security state of a server or workstation by comparing the existing settings against a standard template provided with the operating system. By performing a security analysis on a regular basis, administrators can ensure that a server or workstation continues to meet the security requirements of an organization. Over time, discrepancies can occur in the security configuration of a server or workstation. The analysis pinpoints any discrepancies, allowing an administrator to resolve any security conflicts that exist. After an analysis is run, the results are displayed for review.

To analyze the existing security configuration, perform the following steps:

1. Click Start, Run, and type MMC. Press Enter.

2. From the File menu, click Add/Remove Snap-In. From the Add/Remove Snap-In window, click Add.

3. Scroll through the list of available snap-ins. Select Security Configuration and Analysis, and click Add. Click Close and then click OK.

4. Within the management console, right-click Security Configuration and Analysis, and click Open Database.

5. Type a new filename to create a new database, or select an existing database.

6. If you are creating a new database, select an existing template and click Open.

7. Within the Details pane, right-click Security Configuration and Analysis, and click Analyze Computer Now.

8. Specify the path for the error log, or use the default location. Click OK.

9. After the security settings have been analyzed, double-click Security Configuration and Analysis within the Details pane. Any security settings that do not match those within the security template are marked with an X, as shown in Figure 4.3. As you can see in the figure, the values configured on the computer for Minimum Password Age and Minimum Password Length do not match the values defined within the database.

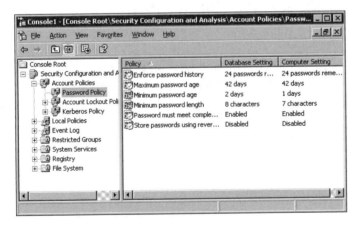

Figure 4.3 Viewing the results of a security analysis.

Applying Security Templates

A security template can be applied in two ways: locally or through a group policy. To apply a security template to a local policy, perform the following steps:

1. Within the Security Configuration and Analysis console, right-click Security Configuration and Analysis, and click Open Database.

2. Type a name for the database and click Open.

3. From the Import Template window, select a template and click Open (see Figure 4.4).

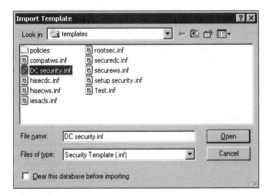

Figure 4.4   Importing a security template into a local policy.

4. Right-click Security Configuration and Analysis, and click Configure Computer Now. The security settings are immediately applied to the local computer.

To import a security template for a domain or Organizational Unit, perform the following steps:

1. Click Start, Administrative Tools, and select Active Directory Users and Computers.

2. Right-click the domain or Organizational Unit for which you want the security settings applied, and click Properties.

3. From the Properties window, select the Group Policy tab (see Figure 4.5).

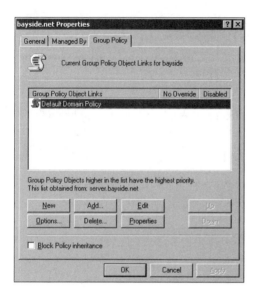

Figure 4.5 Using the Group Policy tab to import a security template.

4. Click Edit to edit an existing group policy, or click New to create a new group policy.

5. In the Group Policy console, under Computer Configuration, expand Windows Settings and right-click Security Settings. Click Import Policy.

6. Select the security template that you want to import and click Open.

 Security settings on a domain controller are automatically refreshed every 5 minutes. Security settings on a workstation or server are automatically refreshed every 90 minutes.

After you make changes to any security settings, you can force an immediate refresh using the gpupdate command. When the command is used on its own, it automatically refreshes any user and computer settings that have changed. Using the command with the /target switch enables you to specify whether computer or user settings are refreshed. Using the /force switch means that all settings are refreshed, regardless of whether they were changed. The gpupdate command replaces the secedit command in Windows 2000. On Windows Server 2003, the secedit command does not work.

Creating Custom Templates

The predefined security templates can be applied as is. However, they can also serve as a starting point for configuring security. Any of the predefined templates can be customized to meet the specific security requirements of an organization.

To customize an existing template, perform the following steps:

1. Open the Security Templates snap-in. Expand the Security Templates container.

2. Click the default path folder. In the right pane, right-click the security template that you want to modify and click Save As.

3. Type a new name for the security template and click Save (see Figure 4.6).

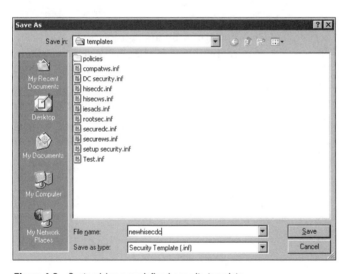

Figure 4.6 Customizing a predefined security template.

The newly created template appears within the right pane. To modify the security settings, double-click the new template. Any of the settings contained within the template can be modified by right-clicking an attribute and selecting Properties. For example, to configure a password history, right-click the Enforce Password History option from within the Password Policies container for a security template, and click Properties. Select the option to Define This Policy Setting in the template and configure a value.

If you do not want to customize one of the existing security templates and would rather define an entirely new template, you can do so again using the Security Templates snap-in. To do so, right-click the default path location within the Security Templates snap-in and click New Template. Type in a name and description for the template, and click OK. The new template is displayed within the right pane, from which you can begin configuring the security settings.

Installing and Configuring a Software Update Infrastructure

One of the challenges most network administrators face is the need to distribute software updates to servers and workstations. In small environments, visiting each computer to perform the installation of an update might take only a few hours. However, in medium to large networks, administrators need a secure, reliable, and efficient way of distributing updates as they are released.

One of the options now available for distributing updates is Software Update Services (SUS). SUS consists of two components: the server and the client. The server (which can be running Windows 2000 or Windows Server 2003) downloads updates from Microsoft and stores them locally. As soon as the updates are posted to the Windows Update site, they are downloaded and the network administrator is notified that they are available. The clients can then download the updates from the server instead of retrieving them from the Windows Update site.

 One of the benefits of using SUS is that updates can be tested before being deployed. This eliminates the possibility that clients will download updates before they have been tested and approved by the network administrator.

Installing and Configuring Software Update Services

Software Update Services (SUS) is installed on a server to centralize the distribution of software updates. Before you install SUS, make sure that the computer meets the hardware and software requirements outlined in the following lists:

➤ Pentium III 700MHZ

➤ 512MB of RAM

➤ 6GB free space to store updates

The minimum configuration is capable of supporting up to 15,000 clients.

The software requirements to run SUS are as follows:

➤ Windows 2000 SP2 or higher, or Windows Server 2003

➤ IIS 5.0 or higher

➤ Internet Explorer 5.5 or higher

Also keep in mind that SUS must be installed on an NTFS partition. The system partition must also be formatted with NTFS. If the computer does not meet the software requirements just outlined, the SUS setup program will not permit you to install the software.

Installing Software Update Services

After you have determined that your computer meets all the requirements, you are ready to begin the installation of SUS. The software can be downloaded for free from Microsoft's Web site.

After SUS has been downloaded, you can run setup using the following steps:

1. Double-click Sus10sp1.exe. This launches the setup program for Software Update Services Service Pack 1. Click Next.

2. Accept the licensing agreement and click Next.

3. Select the type of installation. Performing a typical installation installs SUS with the default settings. Click Next.

4. The next window displays the URL that clients will use to connect to the SUS server. Click Install.

5. Click Finish. The SUS administration Web site opens, from which you can configure your SUS server.

Configuring Software Update Services

If you choose a typical installation, the SUS server is automatically configured with specific default settings:

➤ The SUS server is configured to retrieve software updates from the Microsoft Windows Update servers.

➤ The proxy server configuration is set to automatically detect settings.

➤ Content that is downloaded is stored locally.

➤ All packages are available in all supported languages.

➤ Any approved packages that are later updated are not automatically approved.

➤ Clients locate the server using its NetBIOS name.

If the default settings are sufficient, you do not need to reconfigure the SUS server. If you need to make configuration changes, an SUS server can be configured using the SUS Web administration tools. You can access the administration tools in two ways. You can access the administration site using the following URL: http://<yourservername>/SUSAdmin. You can also access the Web page by clicking Start, Administrative Tools, and selecting Microsoft Software Update Services (see Figure 4.7). To begin configuring the SUS server, click the Set Options link.

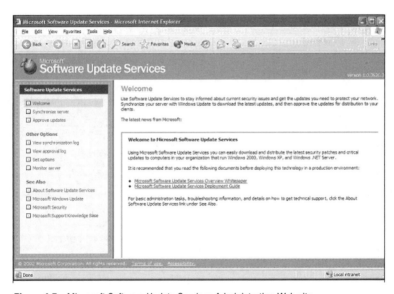

Figure 4.7 Microsoft Software Update Services Administration Web site.

From the Set Options page shown in Figure 4.8, you can configure three different options. Under Select a Proxy Server Configuration, you can specify how the SUS server accesses the Internet.

Choose one of the following options based on your network configuration:

➤ *Do Not Use a Proxy Server to Access the Internet*—Select this option if the SUS server does not use a proxy server to connect to the Internet.

➤ *Use a Proxy Server to Access the Internet*—Select this option if the SUS server accesses the Internet through a proxy server.

➤ *Automatically Detect Proxy Server Settings*—Select this option if your network supports automatic discovery of proxy server settings.

➤ *Use the Following Proxy Server to Access the Internet*—Select this option if the network does not support automatic configuration of proxy settings. Specify the address or port number of the proxy server. You can also specify the user account and password that the SUS server should use if credentials are required.

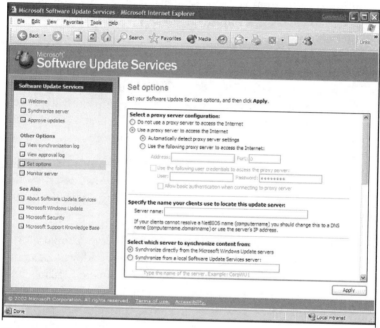

Figure 4.8 The Set Options page.

The next section enables you to specify the name that clients will use to locate the SUS server. You can specify the NetBIOS name of the SUS server, or, if clients on the network do not support NetBIOS, you can specify the DNS name or the IP address.

The final section on the Set Options window enables you to configure the location from which the SUS server will get software updates. An SUS server can retrieve software updates directly from Microsoft, or it can retrieve them from another SUS server. To have the SUS server retrieve updates from Microsoft, select Synchronize Directly from the Microsoft Windows Update Servers. To have the SUS server retrieve updates from another SUS server, select Synchronize from a Local Software Update Services Server and specify the name of the server.

An administrator can also change how the SUS server handles updated content. This enables you to specify what the SUS server should do when software packages that are previously approved are updated. You can select from two options:

➤ Automatically Approve New Versions of Previously Approved Updates.

➤ Do Not Automatically Approve New Versions of Previously Approved Updates. I Will Manually Approve These Later.

If you want to test an update before it is downloaded and installed by clients, you should select the second option (Do Not Automatically Approve New Versions of Previously Approved Updates. I Will Manually Approve These Later). This means that any software packages that you previously approved but that have been updated by Microsoft require approval again by the administrator before clients can install them.

When an SUS server connects to the Microsoft Windows Update site, it can download two types of content. First, it downloads a file that describes the list of packages (Aucatalog1.cab). Second, it downloads the actual software packages.

As an administrator, you can choose whether the SUS server should download the packages or just the catalog file. If the SUS server downloads only the catalog file, any clients that are configured for Automatic Updates first check the list of approved packages from the local SUS server and then connect to the Windows Update servers to download the approved packages. You can also choose to download the packages and store them locally on the SUS server. If the updates are stored locally on the SUS server, any clients configured for Automatic Updates will download the approved software packages directly from the local SUS server. On this screen, you can also specify the locales that will be downloaded by selecting each language that you need to support on the network.

Installing and Configuring Automatic Client Update Settings

For SUS to work, clients need to install a special version of Automatic Update software. When the updated version of Automatic Update is installed, clients can download updates from a server running SUS, and the updates can be installed at a preconfigured interval. The updated version of Automatic Update can run on Windows 2000 and later platforms.

Installing Automatic Client Update

The Automatic Updates client can be installed in a number of ways. You can run the setup locally on each client computer, or you can choose to perform a centralized deployment. Installing the client locally is a very simple process. Simply download the client from Microsoft's Web site and run the WUAU22.msi file. To install the client automatically using Active Directory, perform the following steps:

1. Click Start, point to Administrative Tools, and click Active Directory Users and Computers.

2. Right-click the appropriate Organizational Unit and click Properties.

3. From the Group Policy tab, click Edit to use an existing group policy object, or click New to create a new one.

4. Under Computer Configuration, select Software Settings.

5. Right-click Software Installation, point to New, and click Package.

6. Locate the WUAU22.msi file and click Open.

7. The Deploy Software window appears. Click Assigned and click OK.

Configuring Automatic Client Update Settings

After you've installed the Automatic Updates software, you can configure the settings using the software interface on the client or through a Group Policy Object.

A few steps must be completed before you can configure Automatic Updates via a Group Policy Object. First, you must load the Automatic Updates policy settings template. To do so, open the appropriate Group Policy Object. Under either Computer Settings or User Settings, right-click Administrative Templates and click Add. Type in the name for the Automatic Updates ADM file (WUAU.adm) located in the Windows\inf directory and click Open.

After you have completed these steps, you can begin configuring the Automatic Updates Group Policy Object settings for clients on the network. Table 4.1 summarizes the settings that are available (see Figure 4.9).

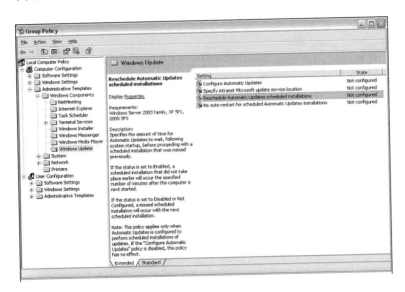

Figure 4.9 Automatic Update group policy settings.

Table 4.1 Automatic Updates Settings	
Group Policy Setting	**Description**
Configure Automatic Updates	Three options are available: **Notify for Download and Notify for Install**—An administrative user (member of the Local Administrators group) is notified before the download and installation of any updates. This means that an administrator must approve any new updates before they are downloaded and installed. **Auto Download and Notify for Install**—Updates are automatically downloaded, and an administrative user is notified before installation. **Auto Download and Schedule the Install**—Updates are automatically downloaded and scheduled for installation.
Specify Intranet Microsoft Update Service Location	With this option, administrators can define the SUS server from which clients will retrieve updates. You can also specify which server clients will send statistics to, such as the successful installation of an update.
Reschedule Automatic Updates Scheduled Installation	If automatic updates are configured to install at a particular time and the scheduled time passes, an administrator can use this option to configure when the installation will occur next.

(continued)

Table 4.1 Automatic Updates Settings *(continued)*	
Group Policy Setting	**Description**
No Autorestart for Scheduled Automatic Updates Installation	This option can be used to prevent Automatic Updates from restarting a computer when a user is logged on.

If an environment does not employ Active Directory, Automatic Updates settings can be configured only by instituting various Registry entries to make the needed changes.

To define which SUS server clients you should use to retrieve updates and send status information to, add the following entries under HKEY_LOCAL_ MACHINE\Software\Policies\Microsoft\Windows\WindowsUpdate:

➤ WUServer—This specifies the location of the server from which updates will be downloaded. The SUS server is identified by HTTP name, such as http://SUSserver.

➤ WUStatusServer—This specifies the location of the server to which the client will send status information. Again, the server is identified by HTTP name.

To configure other settings, such as the day and time that updates should occur, add the following entries under HKEY_LOCAL_MACHINE\Software\Policies\ Microsoft\Windows\WindowsUpdate\AU:

➤ UseWUServer—This specifies that the client must use an SUS server to obtain updates. Set the value to 1 for clients for Automatic Updates to use an SUS server.

➤ AUOptions—Use this option to configure whether the local administrator should be notified of downloads and installations, as well as whether updates should be installed on a defined schedule. The possible values are 2 (notify of download and installation), 3 (automatically download and notify of installation), or 4 (automatic download and schedule installation).

➤ ScheduledInstallDay—This defines the day that updates should be installed. The values range from 0 to 7, where 0 indicates every day and 1–7 indicate specific days of the week (1 = Sunday and 7 = Saturday).

➤ ScheduledInstallTime—This defines the time of day that updates should be installed. The value is specified in 24-hour format.

➤ ResCheduleWaitTime—This defines when updates should occur when the predefined scheduled time has passed. The value is specified in minutes (1–60).

➤ NoAutoRebootWithLoggedOnUsers—This defines whether Automatic Updates can reboot a computer when a user is logged on. Set this value to 1 to enable the logged-on user to choose whether to reboot the computer.

➤ NoAutoUpdate—This enables or disables automatic updates.

Monitoring Network Protocol Security

Organizations want to ensure that communications remain secure. Therefore, it's important for network administrators to monitor network communications to ensure that communications are indeed trustworthy. A number of tools included with Windows Server 2003 can be used to monitor network protocol security. The following sections introduce you to some of these tools and how they can be used.

Using the IP Security MMC Snap-In

Internet Protocol Security (IPSec) is a protocol used to secure communications between two hosts. (The IPSec protocol is covered in more detail in Chapter 5, "Routing and Remote Access.") As part of managing and maintaining network security, administrators can use the IP Security Monitor tool to validate that communications between hosts are indeed secure. It provides information such as which IPSec policy is active and whether a secure communication channel is being established between computers.

The IP Security Monitor tool included with Windows Server 2003 contains many new features not found in the Windows 2000 version. The IP Security Monitor tool in Windows 2000 was simply an executable program called ipsecmon.exe. Now in Windows Server 2003, it is implemented as a Microsoft Management Console (MMC) snap-in. Some of the additional enhancements include the following:

➤ Administrators now have the capability to monitor IPSec on the local computer or on a remote system.

➤ It provides information such as the name and description of active IPSec policies.

➤ Administrators can view main mode and quick mode statistics. Main mode and quick mode are the two phases of IKE negotiations.

➤ The refresh rates can now be customized.

➤ Administrators can search for filters based on a source or destination IP address.

Be prepared to encounter exam questions pertaining to IP Security Monitor because it contains many new enhancements over the version included with Windows 2000. Remember, the **ipsecmon.exe** command is used to launch the tool in Windows 2000. In Windows Server 2003, it is implemented as an MMC snap-in.

To open the IP Security Monitor snap-in, perform the following steps:

1. Click Start and click Run.

2. Type **MMC** and click OK.

3. Within the Microsoft Management Console, click File and then click Add/Remove Snap-In.

4. From the Add/Remove Snap-In window, click Add.

5. From the list of available snap-ins, select IP Security Monitor and click the Add button (see Figure 4.10). Click Close.

6. Click OK.

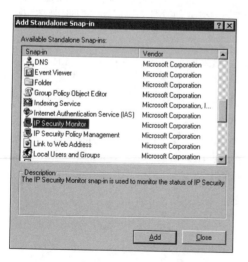

Figure 4.10   Adding the IP Security Monitor snap-in.

You can use the IP Security Monitor console, shown in Figure 4.11, to view IPSec information locally or on a remote computer. To add another computer to the console, right-click the IP Security Monitor container within the console and click Add Computer. Type the name of the computer that you want to connect to, or click the Browse button to search for it.

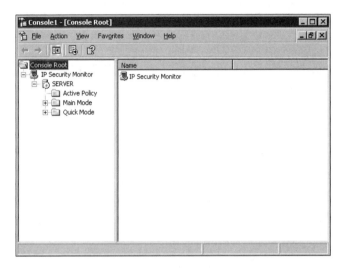

Figure 4.11 The IP Security Monitor snap-in.

 IP Security Monitor can be used only to monitor computers running Windows XP and Windows Server 2003. The version of IP Security Monitor included with Windows Server 2003 cannot be used to monitor a computer running Windows 2000.

Expanding the IP Security Monitor container displays the name of the local computer or any remote computer that you are connected to. By expanding the computer, you will see three containers: Active Policy, Main Mode, and Quick Mode.

As noted previously, IP Security Monitor can be used to view the active IPSec policies on a computer. Clicking the Active Policy container within the console displays the following information:

➤ *Policy Name*—Lists the name of the active IPSec policy.

➤ *Policy Description*—Lists an optional description of the policy outlining the purpose of the policy.

➤ *Policy Last Modified*—Indicates when the policy was last modified. This option is applicable only to policies applied to a local computer.

➤ *Policy Store*—Specifies the storage location for the active IPSec policy.

➤ *Policy Path*—Specifies the Lightweight Directory Access Protocol (LDAP) path to the IPSec policy.

➤ *Organizational Unit*—Specifies the Organizational Unit to which the group policy is applied.

➤ *Group Policy Object Name*—Specifies the name of the group policy object to which the IPSec policy is applied.

You'll notice two other containers listed under your server within the IP Security Monitor console: Main Mode and Quick Mode. Clicking on either of these containers displays a number of other containers (see Figure 4.12). In any case, you can use these different options to monitor communications between hosts. A multitude of statistics can be used to monitor IPSec.

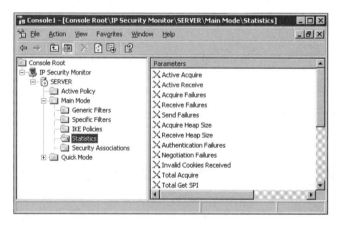

Figure 4.12   Viewing main mode statistics.

Using the Support Tools

Windows Server 2003 also includes a number of other tools that can be used to monitor network protocol security. These tools are not installed by default. To install the support tools, perform the following steps:

1. Insert the Windows Server 2003 CD.

2. From the Welcome screen, click Browse This CD.

3. Locate the Support\Tools directory on the CD.

4. Double-click suptools.msi and follow the instructions to complete the installation.

Some of the tools that you might find useful for monitoring network protocol security include the following:

➤ *Netdiag*—Netdiag can be used to obtain basic network information. One thing to note is that the version of Netdiag included with Windows Server 2003 does not display any IPSec-specific statistics.

➤ *Netsh*—This command-line utility can be used to view or modify the network configuration of a computer.

Troubleshooting Network Protocol Security

Monitoring network protocol security is an important aspect of maintaining overall security. By regularly monitoring network communications, you can more easily identify problems that might be occurring. This is another important aspect of an administrator's job: troubleshooting problems and resolving them as quickly and as efficiently as possible. When it comes to troubleshooting network protocol security, a number of different tools are available for determining the cause of the problem.

Using the IP Security Monitor MMC Snap-In

As previously mentioned, IP Security Monitor can be used to monitor and fine tune IPSec performance. However, it is also a very useful tool for troubleshooting. The IP Security snap-in can be used to determine which IPSec policy is being assigned. For example, if IPSec communication is not functioning as it should, you can use IP Security Monitor to verify which IPSec policy is currently in effect on the computer.

IP Security Monitor can also be used to view IPSec statistics, which can provide useful information for troubleshooting. For example, if you are experiencing a large number of failures when attempting IP-secured communications, you can use IP Security Monitor to view related statistics.

Event Viewer

One of the most useful tools for troubleshooting is the Event Viewer. Using this tool, you can view events that are recorded in the event logs. By default, a computer running Windows Server 2003 typically has three logs listed within the Event Viewer: the application, system, and security logs. You might have additional logs listed, depending on the services installed. For example, a log file is created for the DNS service when it is installed. If the computer running Windows Server 2003 is configured as a domain controller, it will also contain the File Replication Service log and the Directory Service log. Each of the different logs is summarized in the following:

> *Application*—This log contains events pertaining to applications and programs running on the computer.

> *Security*—This log contains events pertaining to security as defined in the Audit policy. For example, this includes successful logons, resource access, and use of user rights. By default, security logging is now enabled in Windows Server 2003.

> *System*—This log contains events generated by Windows system components.

> *Directory Service*—This log contains events generated by Active Directory. This log is available only if the computer is configured as a domain controller.

> *File Replication Service*—This log contains events generated by the Windows File Replication Service. For example, any errors generated while the sysvol on domain controllers is being updated are written to this log. Again, this log file is present only if the computer is configured as a domain controller.

> *DNS Server*—This log contains events generated by the DNS service. This log is present only if the computer is configured as a DNS server.

You can open the Event Viewer by clicking Start, pointing to Administrative Tools, and selecting the Event Viewer for the submenu (see Figure 4.13).

With Event Viewer open, you can view the contents of a log file by selecting it. The entries contained with the log file are displayed on the Details pane (see Figure 4.14).

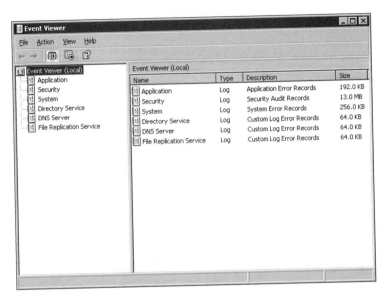

Figure 4.13 Opening the Event Viewer to view system events.

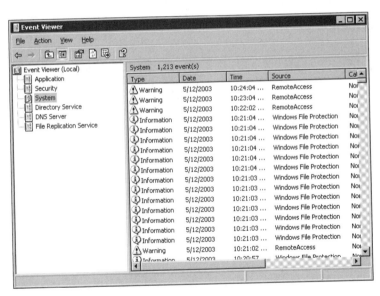

Figure 4.14 Viewing the contents of a log file.

There is detailed information about every event that is written to one of the log files. By double-clicking a specific event, you can view the event header information (see Figure 4.15). Table 4.2 summarizes the available information.

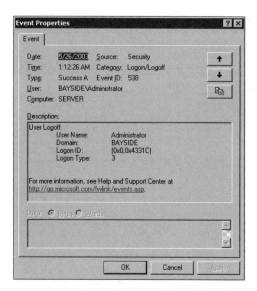

Figure 4.15 Viewing the event detail information.

Table 4.2	Fields Contained in the Event Detail Pane
Information	**Description**
Date	The date when the event occurred.
Time	The specific time of day when the event occurred.
User	The name of the user under which the event occurred.
Computer	The name of the computer the event occurred on. Normally, this is the local computer unless you are viewing the contents of a log file on a remote computer.
Source	The software that logged the event. This can be a program or a system component.
Event	A number identifying the event that has occurred. This number can help support personnel to troubleshoot the event.
Type	The type of event. The system and application logs define an event as a warning, error, or information.
Classification	The classification of the event by the event source.

As already noted in Table 4.2, different types of events can occur. The type of event depends on which log file you are examining. Event viewer displays five different types of events, as summarized in Table 4.3.

Table 4.3	Event Types
Event Type	**Description**
Information	An event successfully occurred, such as the loading of a device driver.
Warning	An event has occurred that might lead to future problems. For example, a hard drive might be running low on disk space.
Alert	A significant problem has occurred, such as the failure of a service to start.
Success audit	A successful action has been performed that is defined in the audit policy.
Failure audit	An unsuccessful action has been performed that is defined in the audit policy.

You can use the Event Viewer to perform the following actions:

➤ *Troubleshoot IKE (Internet Key Exchange) Negotiations*—If you've enabled successes and failures for Audit Logon Events, IKE negotiation successes and failures are logged in the Security log. During the IKE negotiations two computers generate a shared, secret key used to secure communications between them.

➤ *Troubleshoot IPSec Policies*—If Audit Policy Changes has been enabled, you can monitor any changes that are made to the IPSec policies. Changes made to the IPSec policy result in an event being written to the Security log.

➤ *Monitor Dropped Packets*—If packet event logging is enabled through the Registry, you can monitor dropped inbound and outbound packets using the System log.

Network Monitor

As an organization increases in size, new services and applications are installed; as network shares are created, traffic on a network can increase greatly. Take, for example, the Dynamic Host Configuration Protocol (DHCP). Adding DHCP to a network most definitely has an impact on network traffic during the IP lease and the renewal process.

 Remember that one of the ways in which you can optimize network traffic is to configure the bindings as well as disable unnecessary protocols and services.

Using a tool called Network Monitor, you can monitor and log network activity and then use the information to manage and optimize traffic. Another use for this tool is for troubleshooting network communications. For example, you can use Network Monitor to view and troubleshoot IPSec communication.

Network Monitor consists of the following components:

➤ *Network Monitor Driver*—The Network Monitor Driver is responsible for capturing the frames coming to and from a network adapter.

➤ *Network Monitor Tools*—These tools are used to view and analyze the data captured by the Network Monitor Driver.

Installing Network Monitor

Network Monitor Tools are not installed with Windows Server 2003 by default, but they can be installed using the following process. Installing Network Monitor Tools automatically installs the Network Monitor Driver.

1. Select Start, Control Panel, Add or Remove Programs.

2. Click Add/Remove Windows Components.

3. Within the Windows Component Wizard, select Management and Monitoring Tools, and click the Details button.

4. Select the Network Monitor Tools check box (see Figure 4.16). Click OK.

5. Click Next. Click Finish.

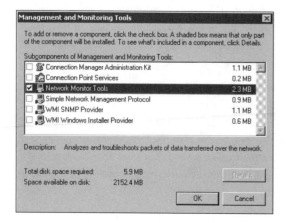

Figure 4.16 Installing Network Monitor.

In some instances, you want to install only the Network Monitor Driver. For example, a computer running Network Monitor Driver can capture the information and forward it to a Systems Management Server (SMS) machine. It is also useful to capture network traffic on a subnet that is remote to where Network Monitor Tools are being run. To install the Network Monitor Driver component, perform the following steps:

1. Within the Network Connections applet, right-click the local area connection and choose Properties.

2. From the Properties window for the local area connection, click Install.

3. Click Protocol and click Add.

4. Within the Network Protocol window, click the Network Monitor Driver.

5. Click OK.

Using Network Monitor

Network Monitor can display a large amount of information about the frames captured to and from a network adapter card. When Network Monitor is first opened, four panes are displayed within the console. The Graph pane displays the network activity in a bar chart. The Sessions Stats pane displays information about individual sessions. The Station Stats pane displays statistics about the sessions the server is participating in. The Total Stats pane displays summary statistics since the capture was started.

To view statistics about network traffic, you must first start a capture. To do so, click the Start option from the Capture menu. To view the captured data, click the Start and View option from the capture menu. Network Monitor displays all the frames captured during the capture period with a Summary window. To view specific information about a frame, click the frame within the Summary window.

Now when you run Network Monitor, all frames going to and from the computer are captured. If you're looking for specific types of traffic, you can create a capture filter to define what types of frames should be captured. However, keep in mind that this increases the load on a server because it must examine each frame to determine whether it matches the criteria of the filter. To configure capture filters within Network Monitor, choose the Filter option from the Capture menu.

Exam Prep Questions

Question 1

> Which of the following tools can be used to view IPSec statistics?
>
> ○ A. Network Monitor
>
> ○ B. IP Security Monitor
>
> ○ C. System Monitor
>
> ○ D. IP Security Policy Management

Answer B is correct. IP Security Monitor can be used to gather and monitor IPSec statistics. Answer A is incorrect because Network Monitor is used to capture and analyze IP packets. Answer C is incorrect because System Monitor is used to monitor server performance. Answer D is incorrect because IP Security Policy Management is used only to create and manage IP Security policies.

Question 2

> You are trying to install Software Update Services on a computer running Windows Server 2003. The installation of the software continually fails. You verify that the computer meets the hardware requirements. The server is also running IIS 5.0 and Internet Explorer 6.0, and all partitions except the system partition are formatted with FAT. What could be causing the problem?
>
> ○ A. Service pack 1 is not installed.
>
> ○ B. The partition storing the updates is not formatted with FAT.
>
> ○ C. IIS must be uninstalled.
>
> ○ D. The system partition must be formatted with NTFS.

Answer D is correct. Software Update Services requires that the system partition be formatted with NTFS along with the partition on which the software will be installed. Answer A is incorrect because no service pack is required. Answer B is incorrect because the partition on which SUS is installed must be NTFS as well. Answer C is incorrect because IIS 5.0 is required.

Question 3

John is the network administrator for a small organization. He wants to configure Automatic Updates settings through a group policy. He creates a new group policy object for the appropriate Organizational Unit. When he opens the policy, he cannot find any Automatic Updates settings to configure. What is causing the problem?

- ○ A. John is not permitted to edit group policy objects.
- ○ B. Software Update Services has not been installed.
- ○ C. The Automatic Updates ADM file has not been loaded.
- ○ D. Automatic Updates settings must be configured on each local computer.

Answer C is correct. To deploy the Automatic Updates settings using a group policy, the ADM file must first be loaded. If not, the Automatic Updates settings will not be available within a group policy object. Answer A is incorrect because the user is already an administrator. Answer B is incorrect because installing the SUS software does not automatically add the Automatic Updates settings into a group policy object. Answer D is incorrect because settings can be configured locally or through a group policy.

Question 4

Bob is planning the deployment of Software Update Services. He has a number of workstations on the network that are running various client operating systems. Which clients on the network will support the updated version of Automatic Updates? (Choose all that apply.)

- ❑ A. Windows 98
- ❑ B. Windows Me
- ❑ C. Windows 2000
- ❑ D. Windows XP

Answers C and D are correct. The updated version of the Automatic Updates software can be installed on Windows 2000 platforms and later. Therefore, answers A and B are incorrect.

Question 5

Mary is concerned that some of the servers on the network no longer meet the security requirements outlined by her organization. Different network administrators often troubleshoot problems and make configuration changes while doing so. She wants to verify the current security settings and compare them against the initial template used to configure new servers. What tool can she use?

○ A. IP Security Monitor

○ B. Security Configuration and Analysis

○ C. Network Monitor

○ D. Security Templates

Answer B is correct. The Security Configuration and Analysis tool can be used to analyze the current security settings of a computer and compare them against the settings within an existing template. Answer A is incorrect because IP Security Monitor is used to monitor and troubleshoot IPSec communications. Answer C is incorrect because Network Monitor is used to capture and analyze network traffic. Answer D is incorrect because the Security Templates snap-in is used to configure existing templates and create new ones.

Question 6

Mary is implementing a secure baseline for all new servers configured on the network. She wants each server to be configured with a standard set of security settings. What is the simplest way for Mary to configure the security settings on all new servers to be identical?

○ A. Mary must manually configure the settings on each server.

○ B. Mary can create a security template using the Security Templates snap-in with all the required security settings and deploy it through a GPO.

○ C. Mary can use the Security Configuration and Analysis tool to create a new template with all the required security settings.

○ D. Mary can use Software Update Services to configure each new server with the required security settings.

Answer B is correct. Mary can use the Security Templates snap-in to create a new template with the required security settings. The template can then be imported when new servers are configured. Answer A is incorrect. Although this is a viable solution, it is not the most efficient one. It requires configuring the same settings on each server. Answer C is incorrect because this tool cannot be used to create new templates. Answer D is incorrect because SUS is used to deploy software updates to clients.

Question 7

You are editing the Registry to configure Automatic Updates on a Windows XP workstation. You want to specify which server the client will retrieve the updates from. Which of the following Registry options should you configure to specify the SUS server that the updates will be downloaded from?

- ○ A. **UseWUServer**
- ○ B. **AUOptions**
- ○ C. **WUServer**
- ○ D. **SUSServer**

Answer C is correct. To specify which server a client will download the updates from, you must configure the WUServer value. Answer A is incorrect because it only enables Automatic Updates to use an SUS server. Answer B is incorrect because this option is used to specify how updates are downloaded and installed. Answer D is incorrect because there is no such option.

Question 8

Which of the following command-line utilities can be used to view IPSec statistics?

- ○ A. netdiag
- ○ B. ipsecmon
- ○ C. ping
- ○ D. netsh

Answer D is correct. The netsh command-line utility can be used to view IPSec statistics. Answer A is incorrect because this command-line utility is no longer used to view IPSec-specific statistics. Answer B is incorrect because this command is used to launch the IP Security Monitor in Windows 2000. Answer C is incorrect because ping is used to test TCP/IP connectivity.

Question 9

The IPSec policy configured for domain controllers is not behaving normally. You suspect that a configuration change was made by another administrator. Which tool can you use to determine whether a policy change was indeed made?

○ A. IP Security Monitor

○ B. Security Configuration and Analysis

○ C. netsh

○ D. Network Monitor

Answer C is correct. As long as auditing of policy changes has been enabled, you can monitor when changes are made to an IPSec policy using the Event Viewer. Therefore answers A, B, and D are incorrect because these tools cannot be used to monitor whether an IPSec policy change was made.

Question 10

IP Security Monitor will be used to monitor IPSec communications on several servers. Your organization is still in the process of migrating to Windows Server 2003, so some of the servers are still running Windows 2000. You use the IP Security Monitor snap-in from your computer to monitor the servers across the network. However, you discover that you are able to monitor only other computers running Windows Server 2003. What is causing the problem?

○ A. You do not have administrative permissions on the servers running Windows 2000.

○ B. IP Security Monitor cannot be used to monitor computers running Windows 2000.

○ C. The Windows 2000 servers are not members of the local domain.

○ D. The Network Monitor driver is not installed on the Windows 2000 servers.

Answer B is correct. The IP Security Monitor included with Windows Server 2003 cannot be used to monitor computers running Windows 2000. Therefore answers A, C, and D are incorrect.

Need to Know More?

 Search the online version of TechNet and the Windows Server 2003 Server Resource Kit using keywords such as "IP Security Monitor," "Security," and "Security Configuration and Analysis."

 Search the Windows Update site at the following URL for more information about Software Update Services: www.microsoft.com/windows2000/windowsupdate/sus/default.asp.

Routing and Remote Access

Terms you'll need to understand:

✓ Authentication
✓ Remote Access Service (RAS)
✓ Internet Authentication Server
✓ Routing Information Protocol (RIP)
✓ Open Shortest Path First (OSPF)
✓ IP routing
✓ IPSec

Techniques you'll need to master:

✓ Configuring a remote access server
✓ Configuring the different authentication and encryption protocols
✓ Understanding the components of a remote access policy
✓ Understanding how remote access policies are evaluated
✓ Configuring routing and remote access for Dynamic Host Configuration Protocol (DHCP) integration
✓ Configuring a virtual private network (VPN)
✓ Understanding the different routing protocols
✓ Implementing and configuring demand-dial routing
✓ Understanding the difference between dynamic and static routing
✓ Understanding and implementing IPSec
✓ Troubleshooting routing and remote access

As technology advances and enables users to be more mobile, the need for remote access is quickly increasing. Providing users with access to network resources from remote locations, such as home offices and client and business sites, is becoming a necessity. Organizations need the flexibility of providing mobile users access to network resources without a compromise in security or a drastic increase in administrative overhead.

Also, as networks continue to become interconnected, businesses are always looking for cost-effective and practical ways to implement routing. The option is always available to purchase high-end dedicated, complex routing solutions. However, with Windows Server 2003, a simple, efficient, and effective routing solution is built into the operating system.

This chapter covers important topics related to Windows Server 2003 routing and remote access. You learn how to configure a remote access server and provide access to the network without compromising security, and you learn about some of the management and monitoring tasks that go along with remote access. You also learn how to configure a virtual private network (VPN), and how to enable and configure the routing feature that is included with routing and remote access.

It's crucial that you have a thorough understanding of all the topics presented in the chapter. Because remote access is one of the most popular exam areas, you'll likely run into several remote access questions.

Configuring Remote Access

Windows Server 2003 includes the Routing and Remote Access Service (RRAS), which enables remote clients to connect to a remote access server and use resources as though they were directly attached to the network. RRAS can be used to configure VPNs, thus expanding your LAN over the Internet.

Windows 2000 introduced routing and remote access, which replaced the remote access service of Windows NT 4.0. RRAS in Windows Server 2003 now includes the following new features:

➤ RRAS servers can be configured to use a preshared key instead of a certificate for VPN connections using the Layer 2 Tunneling Protocol (L2TP) and IP Security (IPSec).

➤ Network Address Translation (NAT) now supports both dynamic and static packet filtering. Dynamic filtering is implemented through the use of Basic Firewall.

➤ In Windows 2000, NAT did not support L2TP/IPSec connections. NAT in Windows Server 2003 can now translate L2TP/IPSec VPN connections.

Windows Server 2003 remote access provides two connectivity methods:

➤ *Dial-up*—Using dial-up remote access such as an ISDN or a phone line, clients can connect to a remote access server.

➤ *VPN*—Clients connect to a remote access server configured as a VPN server using an IP-based internetwork (most often the public Internet).

Enabling Routing and Remote Access

RRAS is installed by default with Windows Server 2003. However, before you can begin using RRAS, it must first be enabled. To enable RRAS, follow these steps:

1. Click Start, point to Administrative Tools, and click Routing and Remote Access.

2. Right-click the server and select Configure and Enable Routing and Remote Access. Click Next.

3. The Routing and Remote Access Server Setup Wizard opens. From the list of common configurations, select Remote Access (dial-up or VPN). The remaining options are summarized in Table 5.1. Click Next.

4. Select the connection methods clients can use to connect to the remote access server (VPN and/or dial-up). Click Next.

5. Choose the network interface for clients to use. Click Next.

6. On the IP Address Assignment screen, select how remote access clients will receive an IP address (see Figure 5.1). IP addresses can be assigned automatically using a Dynamic Host Configuration Protocol (DHCP) server on the internal network, or you can configure a range of IP addresses on the remote access server to assign to remote access clients. If you choose the second option, the resulting wizard screen enables you to configure the range of IP addresses that are available to remote clients. Click Next.

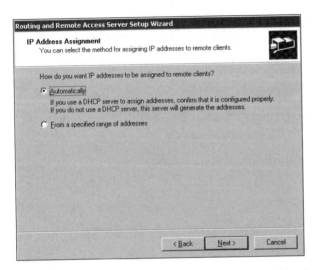

Figure 5.1 You must configure IP address assignments for remote clients.

7. Specify whether to use a Remote Authentication Dial-In User Service (RADIUS) server. If you choose to use a RADIUS server, the resulting wizard screen enables you to specify the name of the primary and alternative RADIUS servers and the shared secret. Click Next.

8. Click Finish.

Table 5.1   Common Remote Access Configurations

Configuration	Description
Remote Access (dial-up or VPN)	Enables computers to connect to the server using a dial-up or VPN connection
Network Address Translation (NAT)	Allows internal computers to access the Internet using a single public IP address
Virtual private network (VPN) access and NAT	Allows computers to access the remote access server through the Internet, and allows internal clients to access the Internet using a single public IP address
Secure communications between two private networks	Connects the network to a remote network
Custom configuration	Allows you to choose any combination of features

When you click the Finish button to exit the wizard, a warning message appears if you chose to use a DHCP server to assign IP addresses to remote clients (see Figure 5.2). The message warns you that to have DHCP messages relayed from remote clients to a DHCP server on the internal network, the remote access server must be configured as a DHCP Relay Agent. (This issue is covered in more detail in the section entitled "Configuring Routing and Remote Access for DHCP.")

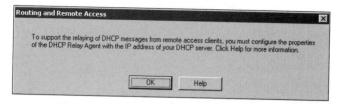

Figure 5.2   To complete the remote access process, you must configure a DHCP Relay Agent.

Configuring Inbound Connections

The two main communication protocols used by dial-up remote access clients are the *Point-to-Point Protocol (PPP)* and the *Serial Line Internet Protocol (SLIP)*. PPP has become an industry-standard communications protocol because of its popularity; it provides support for multiple network protocols, including TCP/IP, IPX/SPX, and NetBEUI.

SLIP is a legacy communication protocol used primarily to connect to Unix systems. One of the major disadvantages of SLIP is the lack of security (for example, sending passwords in clear text). Windows Server 2003 remote access supports the use of SLIP for outbound connections only. SLIP also does not support the DHCP functionality on a RAS server to assign dial-in clients an IP address.

NOTE | The two protocols used for accessing a VPN server are the Point-to-Point Tunneling Protocol (PPTP) and the Layer 2 Tunneling Protocol (L2TP). PPTP is used over a PPP connection to create a secure tunnel.

You can configure PPP using the PPP tab in the Properties window of the remote access server (see Figure 5.3). You can enable the Multilink Connections option to allow remote access clients to aggregate multiple phone lines into a single logical connection, which increases bandwidth. For example, you can combine two B channels from an ISDN BRI connection. Although multilink enables multiple connections to act as a single logical connection, on its own it does not provide a way of dynamically adding and dropping links based on bandwidth requirements. The Bandwidth Allocation Protocol (BAP) provides this feature. BAP enables multilink connections to be added and dropped as bandwidth requirements change. For example, if the bandwidth utilization for a link goes beyond a configured level, the client who is requesting an additional link can send a BAP request message. The Bandwidth Allocation Control Protocol (BACP) works in conjunction with the Link Control Protocol (LCP) to elect a favored "peer" so that a favored peer can be identified if multiple BAP requests are received simultaneously. You can also enable or disable BAP, BACP, LCP, and software compression for PPP connections from the Properties window shown in Figure 5.3.

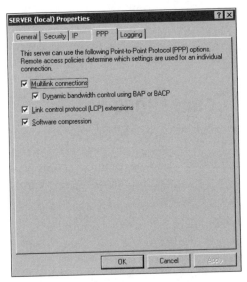

Figure 5.3 You configure PPP via the PPP tab in the Properties window of the remote access server.

To apply multilink at the remote access policy level, you must first enable it at the server level. This means that if multilink is not enabled through the Properties window for the remote access server, you will not be able to apply it in a remote access policy.

Configuring Ports

Configuring inbound connections allows a remote access server to accept incoming connections from remote access clients. After RRAS has been enabled, a number of ports are created. Additional ports can be created, if necessary. You can configure the ports by right-clicking the Ports icon under the RAS server and selecting Properties. Select the ports that you want to configure and click the Configure button. Keep in mind that the configuration changes made apply to all ports. The configurable options are the same for PPTP and L2TP ports (see Figure 5.4). From this Properties window, you can also increase the number of ports by changing the Maximum Ports setting.

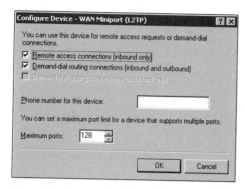

Figure 5.4 You configure ports via the Ports Properties icon on the RAS server.

In the Configure Device dialog box shown in Figure 5.4, you can configure the ports for inbound use only, or for inbound and outbound use if the server is used for demand-dial routing. This is also where you can configure additional ports by setting the Maximum Ports value.

NOTE
Demand-dial routing enables on-demand connections using physical or virtual links. The benefits of a demand-dial connection, as opposed to a dedicated link, include reduced costs and increased security. For example, you can use demand-dial routing to enable two offices in different geographical locations to connect without incurring the cost of a dedicated link. This way, the connection is established only when necessary.

Modem and serial ports are also created for any modems that are installed on the server, and for any serial or parallel connections. These ports can also be configured in the Ports Properties dialog box.

Configuring Routing and Remote Access User Authentication

With remote access, you are basically opening the door for remote access clients to access the internal network. With remote access arises the topic of security. You must be able to allow certain "trusted" clients to have remote access while denying access to everyone else. You also want to ensure that the data that is being sent between a remote access client and a remote access server is secure. To meet these requirements, Windows Server 2003 supports a number of authentication and encryption protocols.

Configuring Remote Access Authentication Protocols

Windows Server 2003 supports a number of authentication protocols that can be used to authenticate dial-up clients. The supported protocols are as follows:

➤ *Password Authentication Protocol (PAP)*—PAP is the least secure of all of the authentication protocols because it sends the username and password in clear text.

➤ *Shiva Password Authentication Protocol (SPAP)*—SPAP can be used to authenticate against Shiva remote access servers and to authenticate against Windows 2003 Servers. This protocol is typically more secure than PAP but not as secure as CHAP or MS-CHAP.

➤ *Challenge Handshake Authentication Protocol (CHAP)*—CHAP does not send the username and password across the network. Instead, it uses a challenge response with a one-way hash algorithm. It is an industry-standard protocol that can be used to authenticate non–Windows-based clients.

➤ *Microsoft Challenge Handshake Authentication Protocol (MS-CHAP)*—MS-CHAP is a Microsoft version of CHAP that uses mutual authentication and encryption for Windows-based clients. MS-CHAP version 2 provides strong encryption and separate encryption keys for sending and receiving data.

➤ *Extensible Authentication Protocol (EAP)*—EAP is an extension of PPP that provides support for other authentication mechanisms, such as smart cards. This authentication protocol requires the presence of a public key (PK) infrastructure.

 Knowing the features and the differences among the preceding authentication protocols is important for achieving success on the exam.

Using the Properties dialog box for the remote access server that is shown in Figure 5.5, you can configure which authentication protocol the remote access server can use to authenticate remote clients. Clicking the Authentication Methods button from the Security tab opens the Authentication Methods dialog box, from which you can select the authentication protocols that are available on the server.

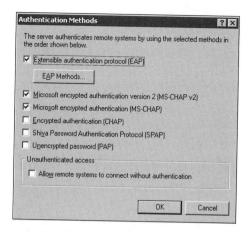

Figure 5.5 You configure authentication methods by clicking the Authentication Methods button on the Security tab.

When you have enabled the authentication protocols at the server level, you can use the Authentication tab in the policy's Properties dialog box (see Figure 5.6) to specify which of the authentication protocols are available for each remote access policy. To do so, click the Remote Access Policies container, right-click the appropriate policy within the Details pane, and click Properties. You can access the Authentication tab by clicking the Edit Profile button.

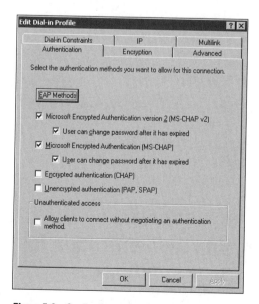

Figure 5.6 Configuring authentication methods in a remote access policy via the Authentication tab.

Configuring Encryption Protocols

If you're sending sensitive data across the network, you might want to add another level of security by implementing some form of data encryption. The two types of encryption available are as follows:

➤ *Microsoft Point-to-Point Encryption (MPPE)*—MPPE can use 40-bit, 56-bit, and 128-bit encryption keys. MPPE encryption can be used for PPP connections, including PPTP VPN connections. MPPE is used in conjunction with EAP-TLS and MS-CHAP authentication protocols.

➤ *IP Security (IPSec)*—IPSec is used with L2TP connections. It supports the Data Encryption Standard (DES) and triple DES (3DES).

 | Some older Microsoft operating systems do not support 56-bit encryption. To support these clients, you must use 40-bit encryption instead. Otherwise, you should use 56-bit encryption. Also keep in mind that 128-bit encryption is supported only in North America.

Encryption for a dial-up connection is configured at the policy level. Right-click the remote access policy within the Details pane for the Remote Access Policies container. Open the Properties dialog box for the remote access policy, click the Edit Profile button, and select the Encryption tab (see Figure 5.7). Select one or more of the following encryption levels:

➤ *No Encryption*—Select this option to allow remote access clients to connect without requiring a form of encryption.

➤ *Basic*—This specifies whether remote access clients can connect using MPPE 40-bit or IPSec 56-bit DES encryption.

➤ *Strong*—This specifies whether remote access clients can connect using MPPE 56-bit or IPSec 56-bit DES encryption.

➤ *Strongest*—This specifies whether remote access clients can connect using MPPE 128-bit or IPSec 3DES.

Configuring Internet Authentication Services (IAS) to Provide Authentication for Routing and Remote Access Clients

As your networks increase in size, you might need to implement multiple remote access servers. To ease the administrative overhead of managing multiple RAS servers, you can implement a RADIUS server to centralize the authentication of remote access clients and the storage of accounting information.

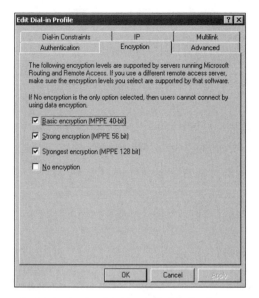

Figure 5.7 Configuring the encryption level for a profile.

Windows Server 2003 can be configured for RADIUS by installing the Internet Authentication Service (IAS) through the Add/Remove programs applet in the Control Panel. With IAS, a server can be configured as a RADIUS server and a RADIUS proxy. When configured as a RADIUS server, RAS servers can forward authentication requests from RAS clients to the IAS server. IAS provides the benefit of centralizing user authentication and centralizing the storage of auditing and accounting information collected from the RAS servers. When RADIUS is implemented, the remote access server is configured as a RADIUS client. You can configure a RADIUS client when enabling routing and remote access. Any authentication requests to the remote access server are sent to the server running IAS. The server running IAS provides authentication, auditing, and accounting services for RADIUS clients.

When configured as a RADIUS proxy, an IAS server can forward authentication and accounting information to other RADIUS servers. The IAS server functions as a message router and forwards messages to another specified RADIUS server or client. Connection request–processing rules are configured to tell the IAS server where to forward the authentication request messages. Keep in mind that an IAS server can function as a RADIUS server and a RADIUS proxy. Depending on the connection request–processing rules configured, some connection requests can be authenticated and others can be forwarded.

Installing IAS

IAS can be installed using the Add or Remove Programs applet within the Control Panel by performing the following steps:

1. Click Start, point to the Control Panel, and click Add or Remove Programs.

2. Click Add/Remove Windows Components.

3. From the list of Windows components, select Networking Services and click the Details button.

4. From the list of subcomponents, select Internet Authentication Service. Click OK. Click Next.

5. Click Finish.

When IAS has been installed, you can use the Internet Authentication Service MMC snap-in, which is located within the Administrative Tools menu, to configure IAS.

Configuring Routing and Remote Access Policies to Permit or Deny Access

A *remote access policy* enables you to control which users are permitted remote access to the network and specify the characteristics of the connection. In terms of remote access, Windows 2000 introduced some major changes from Windows NT 4.0. One of these changes is the use of remote access policies. Before Windows 2000, remote access was controlled through the Properties dialog box of a user account. Windows 2000 and now Windows Server 2003 use both user account properties and remote access policies to control remote access.

With remote access policies, administrators can permit or deny connection attempts based on a number of criteria (such as the time of day or group membership), giving administrators much more flexibility and granular control. When a connection has been permitted, administrators can further control the session by defining the maximum session time and encryption settings.

A remote access policy consists of the following elements, which work together to provide secure access to remote access servers:

➤ Conditions

➤ Permissions

➤ Profile

When remote access is enabled, two default remote access policies are created automatically: connections to Microsoft Routing and Remote Access Server and connections to other access servers.

You can create additional policies by right-clicking the Remote Access Policies icon within the Routing and Remote Access management console and selecting the New Remote Access Policy option. The wizard prompts with the option of creating a typical policy for a common scenario using the wizard or to create a custom policy. The elements of a policy are discussed in the following section.

Managing Remote Access Conditions

Conditions define the parameters that must match those configured on the remote access client before the server will grant remote access. These can include parameters such as the time of day and Windows group membership. Before the permissions of a remote access policy are evaluated, the connection attempt must match the conditions within a remote access policy. For example, the conditions of the policy might specify that you must be a member of the Sales group. If the user account is a member of the Sales group, the conditions have been met and the policy evaluation continues by checking the permissions of the user account. If multiple policies are configured, the first policy that matches the conditions of the connection attempt is then further evaluated for permissions and profile settings. Table 5.2 summarizes some of the commonly used conditions that can be configured for a remote access policy.

Table 5.2 Conditions That Can Be Configured in a Remote Access Policy	
Condition	Description
Called station ID	The number dialed by the remote access client
Calling station ID	The number from which the remote access client called
Day and time restrictions	The days of the week and time of day users are allowed remote access
Windows groups	The Windows groups to which the user must belong

To configure the conditions of a remote access policy, follow these steps:

1. Open the Routing and Remote Access management console and click the Remote Access Policies container.

2. Right-click the remote access policy and click Properties.

3. From the Properties dialog box for the policy, click the Add button.

4. In the Select Attribute dialog box, select the attributes that you want to configure and click Add (see Figure 5.8).

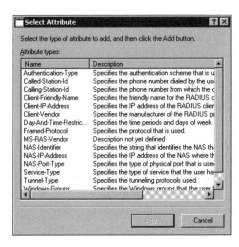

Figure 5.8   You can configure remote access conditions to further control how remote access is handled.

Controlling Remote Access Permissions

If the connection attempt matches the conditions of a remote access policy, the permissions of that policy are then evaluated. The remote access permissions determine whether a specific user is granted or denied remote access. Windows Server 2003 uses a combination of the dial-in properties of a user account and the permissions in the remote access policy to determine whether the connection attempt is allowed. Remote access permissions can be explicitly allowed or denied through user account properties. When configuring remote access permissions using the Dial-In tab in the Properties dialog box for a user account, you have the following three options (see Figure 5.9):

➤ Allow Access

➤ Deny Access

➤ Control Access Through Remote Access Policy

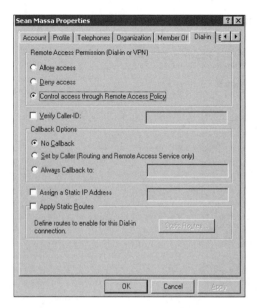

Figure 5.9   Configuring remote access permissions through the user account properties.

 If the Control Access Through Remote Access Policy option is unavailable, switch the domain from Windows 2000 native mode to Windows Server 2003 mode. This option is not available when operating in Windows 2000 native mode.

If you explicitly allow remote access by selecting the Allow Access option, the connection attempt can still be denied if the properties configured for the user account do not match the remote access policy or if the profile settings are not met.

If you choose to have the policy control remote access permissions, you can grant or deny permission through the policy's Properties window (see Figure 5.10). If you are using the default policy, remote access permission is denied by default. You must change this setting to allow access.

From the Dial-In tab, several other settings can be configured, including caller ID, callback options, and static IP routes. Again, if you configure the settings for the user account, they must match the settings configured on the client or the connection attempt will be denied.

 Using the callback feature, a RAS server can be configured to call a remote access client back at a preconfigured number or at a number set by the caller. This provides an added level of security because users are permitted to dial in to the remote access server only from the number specified.

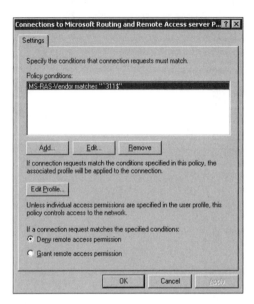

Figure 5.10   Controlling access through the remote access policy.

Configuring a Remote Access Profile

The final element of the remote access policy is the remote access profile. When the remote access client has been granted permission, the profile determines the settings of the connection. Again, the settings in the profile must match those of the connection attempt or it will be denied.

To configure the profile settings, click the Edit Profile button in the policy's Properties window. This opens the Edit Dial-In Profile dialog box, shown in Figure 5.11. Several tabs are available, as summarized in Table 5.3.

Table 5.3 Remote Access Profile Settings	
Property Tab	**Description**
Dial-In Constraints	Configure the Disconnect If Idle time, maximum session time, day and time restrictions, and media and number restrictions.
IP	Define how IP addresses are assigned to clients, and configure packet filtering for inbound and outbound connections.
Multilink	Enable and configure multilink and the Bandwidth Allocation Protocol.
Authentication	Configure the authentication methods that are available for the connections in the remote access policy.
Encryption	Configure the different levels of encryption for the policy.
Advanced	Specify additional connection parameters.

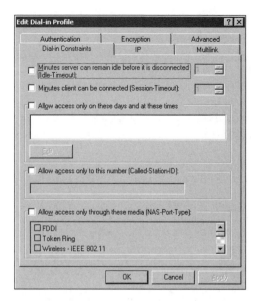

Figure 5.11   You can configure a remote access profile via a remote access policy.

Evaluating Remote Access Policies

Given the many options and the complexity of remote access policy elements, it is important to have a good understanding of how policies are
applied when a remote access client attempts a connection. Assuming that
your domain functional level is Windows Server 2003, the following points
outline the connection process:

➤ When a user attempts to establish a remote access connection, the RAS
server determines whether a policy exits. The first policy in the ordered
list of remote access policies is checked. If there is no policy configured
(and the default policy has been deleted), the connection attempt is
rejected. If a policy does exist, the evaluation process continues.

➤ The conditions of the first policy in the list are evaluated. If the connection attempt matches all the conditions, the evaluation process continues. If all conditions do not match the connection attempt, the next
policy in the list is evaluated. If no more policies exist, the connection
attempt is rejected.

➤ If the connection attempt matches the conditions in one of the policies,
the permissions for the user are evaluated. If the user's account property
is set to Deny Access, or if the permission within the policy is set to
Deny Access, the connection attempt is rejected. If the policy or the
account property is set to Allow Access, the process continues.

➤ The settings of the remote access profile and the properties of the user account are evaluated against the connection attempt. If the connection attempt matches both the profile and account settings, the user is granted remote access. If not, the connection attempt is rejected.

 Remote access policies are a popular topic on the exam. Be sure you are familiar with how remote access policies and the policy elements are evaluated. Also keep in mind that remote access policies are not stored within Active Directory; they are stored on each server.

 If you are running in Windows 2000 native functional level, keep in mind that, unless they are set to Deny Access, the permission settings configured using the Dial-In tab for a user account override those in the policy. For example, if the account property is set to Allow Access but the profile denies it, the user is granted access and the process of evaluation continues. On the other hand, if the account property is set to Deny Access and the profile permits access, the connection attempt is rejected. By default, the Administrator and Guest accounts on a standalone remote access server or in a Windows Server 2003 functional-level domain are set to control access through the remote access policy; for a Windows 2000 native functional-level domain, they are set to Deny Access.

Configuring Routing and Remote Access for DHCP

As you saw when enabling RRAS, you can configure the remote access server with a range of IP addresses to assign to remote access clients. (If you do, make sure the range does not conflict with the range of IP addresses configured on the DHCP server, to avoid duplicate addresses.) You can also configure the RAS server to obtain IP addresses from the DHCP server to lease to clients.

When you choose to use a DHCP server, the remote access server obtains, by default, 10 IP addresses to lease to clients. If all 10 IP addresses are in use, the remote access server obtains 10 more from the DHCP server. (10 is the default number but can be changed through the Registry.) The benefit of using DHCP with RAS is that IP address assignment remains centralized.

For DHCP to be used with RAS, the DHCP Relay Agent must be configured on the RAS server. When you configure the DHCP Relay Agent, clients still receive IP addresses from the RAS server, but they can use DHCPInform messages to obtain optional parameters, such as the IP addresses of WINS and DNS servers, directly from the DHCP server. The relay agent component allows the RAS server to relay the DHCPInform messages between the remote access clients and the DHCP server.

To configure DHCP to work with remote access, follow these steps:

1. Within the Routing and Remote Access management console, right-click General under the IP Routing icon and select New Routing Protocol.

2. In the Select Routing Protocol window, select the DHCP Relay Agent and click OK.

3. Right-click the DHCP Relay Agent icon, listed under IP Routing, and select New Interface. Select the network connection over which DHCP messages will be routed and click OK.

4. Right-click the DHCP Relay Agent and select Properties. Type the IP addresses of the DHCP server or servers to which the RAS server should forward the DHCPInform requests (see Figure 5.12).

Figure 5.12   You must configure the RAS server with the IP address of the DHCP server.

5. Right-click the interface to bring up the Properties window. From the Properties window, you can disable or enable the relaying of DHCP packets, and configure the hop count and the boot threshold.

Configuring a Virtual Private Network (VPN)

A VPN enables you to connect to a remote server using the Internet. When a remote access client has established a connection to the Internet, a connection is created with the VPN server using a tunneling protocol (PPTP or L2TP). The tunnel provides secure communication between the user and the private network. One of the biggest advantages to implementing a VPN is the cost reduction. Remote clients can dial into a local ISP and then connect to the remote server rather than incurring possible long-distance charges.

Two types of tunneling protocols can be used to connect to a VPN server: the Point-to-Point Tunneling Protocol (PPTP) and the Layer 2 Tunneling Protocol (L2TP). Both protocols are automatically installed by default. PPTP is used over PPP connections on an IP-based network and supports the encryption and encapsulation of IP, IPX, and NetBEUI packets. L2TP can encapsulate IP traffic over a variety of networks, including Frame Relay, ATM, and X.25.

Both PPTP and L2TP encrypt data that is being transferred. PPTP has built-in encryption technologies and uses MPPE 40-bit to 128-bit encryption. L2TP uses IPSec for data encryption. IPSec uses the Data Encryption Standard (DES) to encrypt data with supported key lengths between 56-bit (DES) and 168-bit (3DES).

In terms of authentication, a user attempting to establish a VPN connection can be authenticated using EAP, MS-CHAP, CHAP, SPAP, or PAP. Computer-level and user-level authentication are provided if you are using L2TP over IPSec. The mutual authentication of computers occurs through the exchange of computer certificates; in other words, certificates must be installed on both the VPN client and the VPN server. EAP, CHAP, MS-CHAP, SPAP, and PAP can perform the user-level authentication.

Table 5.4 summarizes the differences between the two tunneling protocols.

Table 5.4 Differences Between PPTP and L2TP	
PPTP	L2TP
Used only for IP-based networks	Supports any point-to-point connection, including IP, ATM, and frame relay
Uses PPP encryption	Encryption is handled by IPSec

(continued)

Table 5.4 Differences Between PPTP and L2TP *(continued)*	
PPTP	**L2TP**
Allows IP, IPX, and NetBEUI traffic to be encrypted	Allows IP traffic to be encrypted
Tunnel authentication	No tunnel authentication

To enable a Windows Server 2003 as a VPN server, use the same process outlined when enabling a remote access server, but select the option to configure a VPN server. (Two network interfaces are required to configure VPNs.) When a VPN server is enabled, five PPTP and five L2TP ports are automatically created. Additional ports can be created and configured using the Ports container within the Routing and Remote Access console.

Managing TCP/IP Routing

With Routing and Remote Access (RRAS), a computer running Windows Server 2003 can function as a network router, which routes IP packets between networks. This router service allows LANs and WANs to be interconnected easily. The routing technology is built into the operating system, providing small and large businesses with a cost-effective and secure way of interconnecting their networks.

IP Routing

Routing is the process of sending a packet from the source address to the destination address. Because all IP packets have a source and destination IP address, it is possible to deliver them to the proper location. Of course, how the routing of IP packets actually occurs is much more complex.

Because each IP packet has addressing information within the header, routers can use this information to determine where a packet should be sent so that it can reach the destination host. Routers maintain information about the physical network, such as the path to a destination network and the metric associated with the route. The metric is the cost associated with using a route. Typically, this is the number of hops to the destination network. If there are multiple routes to a destination network, the route with the lowest metric is favored. For routers to know the location to which packets must be forwarded, they must also know about their neighboring routers. This information is stored within the routing table. When a router receives a packet, it checks the routing table to determine where the packet must be sent to reach the destination host. The information within a routing table can be generated statically or dynamically.

Static Routing

With *static routing*, an administrator must manually configure the routing table by adding entries that tell the router how to reach other networks. Using the `route` command, an administrator updates the routing table by specifying the network addresses, the subnet masks, and the metric associated with each route.

When deciding whether to use static routing, keep in mind that it works best for networks that do not change on a regular basis. If the network configuration is constantly changing, the administrative overhead associated with having to update the routing tables every time something changes increases greatly because the changes must be made on each router. In such cases, it might be more beneficial to implement dynamic routing.

Dynamic Routing

Dynamic routing eliminates the overhead associated with manually updating routing tables. Routers can dynamically build their own routing tables by communicating with other routers on the network.

With dynamic routing, the routing tables are built automatically through router communication. Using a routing communication protocol, routers periodically exchange messages containing location information about routes through the network. This information is used to build and update routing tables.

The major advantage of dynamic routing is that it reduces the administrative overhead associated with manually updating routing tables. For example, if a router goes down, the change is automatically propagated to all routers on the network so that they are all aware of the change in the network topology. One of the major disadvantages is the high amount of traffic it generates.

Managing Routing Protocols

For routers to share information and dynamically update their routing tables, a routing protocol must be used. As already mentioned, the two routing protocols supported by Windows Server 2003 are Routing Information Protocol (RIP) and Open Shortest Path First (OSPF). Although both routing protocols are used for dynamic routing, there are some distinct differences between the two.

Routing Information Protocol (RIP)

The RIP is designed for small to medium-size networks. One of the main benefits in choosing RIP is that it's easy to configure and deploy. One of the major drawbacks associated with this protocol is that it is limited to a maximum hop count of 15. This means that any networks more than 15 hop counts away are considered unreachable. Also, as a network increases in size, excessive traffic can be generated from RIP announcements.

> As mentioned previously, all routes to a destination network are assigned a metric, which defines the distance between the source and destination. RIP uses a hop count to identify the distance between two networks. A value of **1** is added to the hop count for each router that resides between a source and destination network.

When a router is first configured as a RIP router, the only entries in the routing table are for those networks to which it is physically connected. It then begins to send announcements of its availability to notify other routers of the networks it services. RIPv1 sends the announcements as broadcasts, whereas RIPv2 can broadcast multicast packets for the announcements.

When changes occur to the network topology, RIPv2 uses triggered updates to communicate the changes to other routers. With triggered updates, the change to the network topology can be propagated immediately.

> If you are considering using RIPv1, keep in mind that it does not support multicasting, it does not support any type of security between routers, and it does have known issues with routing loops. Because it might take several minutes for routers to reconfigure themselves after a change in network topology—for example, when an existing router becomes unavailable—routing loops can occur in which routers send data in a circle.

> RIPv2 supports multicasting for updating the routing tables. RIPv1 does not support this feature. RIPv1 routers cannot communicate with RIPv2 routers using multicasting for updates.

Open Shortest Path First (OSPF)

OSPF is designed for large internetworks (especially those spanning more than 15 router hops). The disadvantage of OSPF is that it's generally more complex to set up and requires a certain amount of planning.

OSPF is not supported for nonpersistent, demand-dial connections.

OSPF uses the Shortest Path First (SPF) algorithm to calculate routes. The shortest path (the route with the lowest cost) is always used first. Unlike RIP, which uses announcements only to update and share routing information, OSPF maintains a map of the network known as the *link-state database*. This map is synchronized between adjacent routers, or those neighboring OSPF routers. When a change is made to the network topology, the first router to receive the change sends out a change notification. Each router then updates its copy of the link state database, and the routing table is recalculated.

Poison reverse is a method by which a gateway informs its neighboring gateways that a connected gateway is no longer available. The gateway that knows about the unavailable one sets the hop count to the unconnected gateway to infinite, which means it is unreachable.

One of the main differences between OSPF and RIP is that OSPF divides the network into different areas. Each of the routers maintains information in the link-state database only about those areas to which it is connected. Another difference is that OSPF replicates the changes only to the routing table, not to the entire table.

An *area* is a group of neighboring networks. The areas are connected to a *backbone area*. Area border routers connect the different areas to the backbone area.

Installing and configuring RIP and OSPF is discussed in the section entitled "Managing Remote Access."

Manage Routing Tables

In some instances you need to add a static route to your Windows Server 2003 router. This, of course, has its advantages and disadvantages. Creating a static route is simple; however, the routes you configure are not shared between routers. Static routes specify the network address and subnet mask that tell the router how to reach a certain destination. The router uses the information to determine which gateway to forward the packet to so that the packet can reach the destination host.

Static routes can be configured in one of two ways. First, they can be configured using the `route add` command. Using the `route add` command, you can add static entries to the local routing table on a router. (You can also use the -p parameter to specify whether they should be persistent routes, meaning that they will remain in the routing table when the system reboots.)

The syntax for the `route add` command is as follows:

```
route add <destination> mask <netmask> <gateway> metric <interface>
```

The second option is to configure a static route within the RRAS management console. To configure a static route using this method, perform the following steps:

1. Within the RRAS management console, expand IP Routing.

2. Right-click Static Routes and select New Static Route. The Static Route window appears (see Figure 5.13).

3. Using the drop-down arrow, select the interface that will be used to route IP packets.

4. Type the destination IP address and subnet mask.

5. Type the IP address of the gateway for the RRAS server.

6. Click OK.

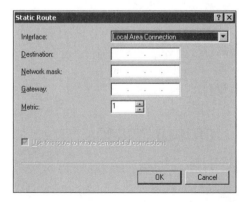

Figure 5.13   Creating a new static route via the Static Route window.

Managing Remote Access

As with most server roles, when a server has been configured, you most likely have to perform management tasks in the form of configuration changes or daily management tasks. The following section discusses some of the topics that pertain to managing a remote access server.

Managing Packet Filters

Packet filtering enables an administrator to specify the type of inbound and outbound traffic that is allowed to pass through a Windows Server 2003 router. When configuring packet filters, you can allow all traffic except traffic prohibited by filters. Or, you can deny all traffic except traffic that is allowed by filters.

Packet filters can be created and configured through the RRAS console by performing the following steps:

1. Within the Routing and Remote Access console, expand the IP Routing container listed under your remote access server.

2. Select the General container and, within the Details pane, right-click the interface for which you want to configure packet filtering; click Properties.

3. From the General tab, select either Inbound Filters or Outbound Filters.

4. From the Inbound or Outbound Filters dialog box, click New. Specify the settings for the IP filter. Click OK.

5. Specify the action for the new packet filter. Click OK.

After a packet filter is created, it can be edited at any time by selecting the filter from the list and clicking the Edit button.

Manage Routing and Remote Access Routing Interfaces

Two types of demand-dial connections can be created for routing: *on-demand connections* and *persistent connections*. With demand-dial connections, a connection with the remote router is established only when necessary. A connection is established to route information and is terminated when the link is not in use. The benefit of this connection is obviously the cost savings associated with not using a dedicated link. With persistent connections, the link does not need to be terminated. Even when it is not in use, it remains open. Connections between network routers can be one-way or two-way initiated, meaning that a connection can be initiated by only one router or by both the routers. With one-way initiated connections, one router is designated as the answering router and the other is designated as the calling router, which is responsible for initiating any connections.

To enable routing, right-click the remote access server and click Properties. On the General tab, select the Router option.

Creating a One-Way Demand-Dial Interface

Demand-dial connections can be created within the Routing and Remote Access snap-in. How you configure the connection depends on whether you are configuring a one-way or two-way initiated connection. To create a demand-dial interface on the calling router, perform the following steps:

1. Right-click Network Interfaces within the RRAS console and click New Demand-Dial Interface. This launches the Demand-Dial Interface Wizard. Click Next.

2. Type a name for the interface. Click Next. Select the connection type. Click Next. Select the device that is used for making the connection. Click Next.

3. Type in the phone number of the remote server you are dialing. Click Next.

4. From the Protocols and Security window (see Figure 5.14), select the necessary options from the list that follows.

   ➤ Route IP Packets on This Interface

   ➤ Add a User Account So a Remote User Can Dial In

   ➤ Send a Plain-Text Password If That Is the Only Way to Connect

   ➤ Use Scripting to Complete the Connection with the Remote Router

5. Configure a static route to the remote network. Click Next.

6. From the Dial Out Credentials window, specify the username and password that the dial-out router will use to connect to the remote router (see Figure 5.15). Click Next.

7. Click Finish.

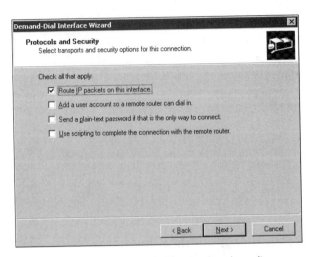

Figure 5.14 Configuring demand-dial protocols and security.

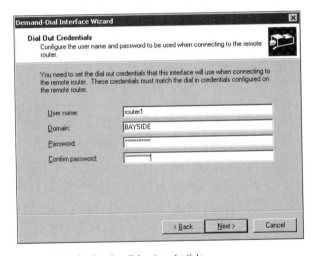

Figure 5.15 Configuring dial-out credentials.

Before you attempt to create a new demand-dial interface, make sure the router is enabled for LAN and demand-dial routing instead of just a LAN router. You can enable this option by right-clicking the RRAS server and choosing Properties. From the General tab, select the LAN and demand-dial routing.

The answering router also needs to be configured for one-way demand-dial connections. A user account must be created on the answering router with dial-in permissions and the appropriate policy permissions. The user account is used to authenticate connections from the calling routers. A static route can then be configured on the user account. Also make sure when creating a user account that the Password Never Expires option is selected and the User Must Change Password at Next Logon option is not selected.

When configuring the calling router, make sure that the dial-out credentials match the user account name configured on the answering router.

Creating a Two-Way Demand-Dial Interface

Creating a two-way demand-dial connection is similar to configuring a one-way connection, but there are a few distinct differences. A demand-dial interface is created on each RRAS server using the process outlined previously to create a one-way demand-dial connection. You must assign a name to the interface and specify the phone number to dial, the device to be used, the protocol and security settings, and the dial-out credentials. You must also configure a user account, with the appropriate remote access permissions, on each RRAS server. Keep in mind that the user account name must be identical to the name assigned to the demand-dial interface of the calling router. Finally, you must configure a static route using the demand-dial interface.

Remember when you are configuring two-way demand dialing that the user account names on the answering router must be identical to the demand-dial interface names on the calling routers.

Configuring a Demand-Dial Connection

When a demand-dial connection has been created, you can configure it further using the Properties window for the connection. From the Options tab (see Figure 5.16), configure the connection type: either demand dial or persistent. You can also set the dialing policy by specifying the number of times that the calling router should redial if there is no answer and by specifying the interval between redial attempts.

The Security tab enables you to configure the security options for the dial-out connection (see Figure 5.17). This configuration includes whether unsecured passwords are permitted, whether the connection requires data encryption, and whether a script will be run after dialing.

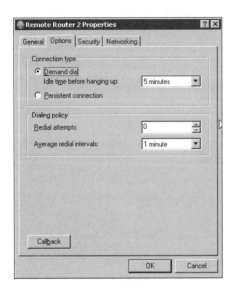

Figure 5.16 Using the Options tab to configure a connection type.

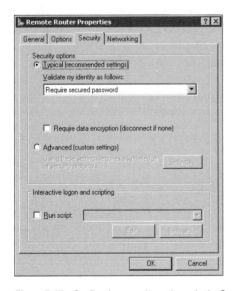

Figure 5.17 Configuring security options via the Security tab.

As shown in Figure 5.18, the Networking tab is used to configure the type of dial server you use and the different network components that the connection uses.

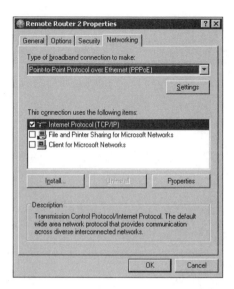

Figure 5.18   Configuring network settings for a demand-dial connection.

You can make several other configurations to a demand-dial interface. Demand-dial filtering enables you to control the type of IP traffic that can initiate a connection. You can allow or deny a connection based on the type of IP traffic. For example, you might want only Web and FTP traffic to initiate the demand-dial connection. Dial-out hours determine the times of day that a connection can be initiated. This enables an administrator to control when the demand-dial connection is used.

Managing Routing Protocols

After the demand-dial or LAN interfaces have been created, configuring the appropriate routing protocol interfaces is the last step to configure the RRAS server as a network router. You must first add the routing protocol; you right-click the General node and choose New Routing Protocol. The window that appears lists the protocols from which you can choose (see Figure 5.19). Select RIPv2 or OSPF and click OK.

After the routing protocol has been added, you must add the interfaces. To do so, right-click the appropriate routing protocol and select New Interface. After you select an interface and click OK, the Properties window for the interface appears, enabling you to configure it. The available options are discussed in the sections entitled "Configuring RIP Interface Properties" and "Configuring OSPF Interface Properties."

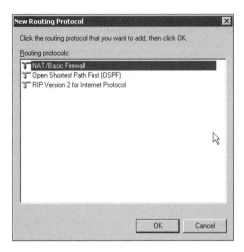

Figure 5.19   Adding a new routing protocol to the General node.

Configuring Routing Protocols

After RIP or OSPF has been installed, you can configure a general set of properties for each of the protocol types. Because RIP requires little configuration, the Properties window for the protocol has only two tabs, as shown in Figure 5.20.

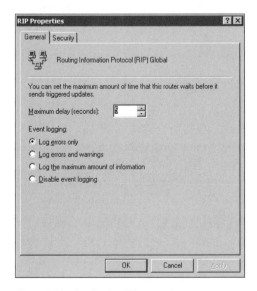

Figure 5.20   Configuring RIP properties.

From the General tab, you can configure the Maximum Delay value, which determines how long a router waits to send an update notification message to other routers on the network. The remaining options enable you to set up event logging for the protocol. The Security tab enables you to configure from which routers the local router can accept announcements.

Because OSPF is slightly more complex than RIP, it requires more detailed configuration and, as a result, has more options in its Properties window (see Figure 5.21).

Figure 5.21 Configuring OSPF properties.

From the General tab, the router can be assigned an IP address that it can use to identify itself. You can also enable autonomous system boundary router, which means that the router will advertise external routes that it learns from other sources. Using the remaining options, you can enable OSPF event logging.

The Areas tab lists all the areas for the router. With OSPF, areas can be used to subdivide a network. This can be done to reduce the size of the database routers within an area by maintaining database information only for the area in which they belong. Using this tab, areas can be added, deleted, and edited. The Virtual Interface tab lists all the configured virtual interfaces. A virtual interface is a virtual connection between an area border router and a backbone area border router. This logical connection allows the two routers to share information.

If the Enable Autonomous System Boundary Router option is selected, you can use the External Routing tab to control which sources from which routes are accepted or ignored. The Ignore Filters button defines the specific routes that should be accepted or ignored.

Configuring RIP Interface Properties

Every RIP interface has it own Properties window from which you can configure a number of options. Within the RRAS console, expand IP Routing, RIP; then right-click one of the available interfaces and click Properties.

The General tab enables you to configure the operation mode. You can select either Autostatic Update Mode or Periodic Update Mode. With *autostatic update*, RIP announcements are sent when other routers request updates. Any routes learned while in autostatic update mode are marked as static and remain in the routing table until the administrator manually deletes them. In *periodic update mode*, announcements are sent out periodically. (The Periodic Announcement Interval determines how often.) These routes are automatically deleted when the router is stopped and restarted. The outgoing and incoming packet protocol enables you to configure the type of packets, such as RIPv1 or RIPv2, the router sends and accepts.

The Activate Authentication and Password options enable you to maintain an added level of security. If authentication is enabled, all outgoing and incoming packets must contain the password specified in the password field. When using authentication, make sure that all neighboring routers are configured with an identical password.

From the Security tab, an administrator can configure RIP route filters. The router can be configured to send and accept all routes, send and accept only routes from the ranges specified, or accept and send all routes except for those specified.

The Neighbors tab is used to configure how the router will interact with other RIP routers. The Advanced tab has several configurable options, which are summarized in Table 5.5.

Table 5.5 Advanced RIP Options	
Option	**Description**
Periodic Announcement Interval	Controls the interval at which periodic update announcements are made.
Time Before Route Expires	Determines how long a route remains in the routing table before it expires.
Time Before Route Is Removed	Determines how long an expired route remains in the routing table before being removed.

(continued)

Table 5.5 Advanced RIP Options *(continued)*	
Option	**Description**
Enable Split Horizon Processing	Ensures that routing loops do not occur because the routes learned from a router are not rebroadcast to that network.
Enable Triggered Updates	Controls whether changes in the routing table are sent out immediately.
Send Clean-Up Updates when Stopped	Controls whether the router sends an announcement when it is stopped, to notify other routers that the routes for which it was responsible are no longer available.
Process Host Routes in Received Announcements	Controls whether host routes received in RIP announcements are accepted or denied.
Include Host Routes in Send Announcements	Controls whether host routes are included in RIP announcements.
Process Default Routes in Received Announcements	Controls whether default routes received in RIP announcements are accepted or denied.
Process Default Routes in Send Announcements	Controls whether default routes are included in RIP announcements.
Disable Subnet Summarization	This option is available only for RIPv2. It controls whether subnets are advertised to routers on different subnets.

NOTE

Demand-dial interfaces are configured by default for autostatic update mode, whereas LAN interfaces are configured for periodic update mode.

Configuring OSPF Interface Properties

If OSPF has been installed, each of the OSPF interfaces can be configured using its Properties window, just as RIP interfaces can be configured. An OSPF interface can be added the same way as a RIP interface. Simply right-click OSPF under the General node and click New Interface. Select the interface that the protocol will run on and click OK. Figure 5.22 shows the OSPF Properties window that appears.

From the General tab, you can enable OSPF and configure the area ID, router priority, cost, and password. The Network Type options enable you to configure whether the OSPF is a broadcast interface, a point-to-point interface, or a nonbroadcast multiple access interface.

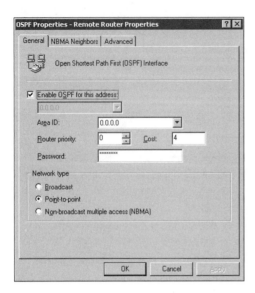

Figure 5.22   Configuring an OSPF interface via the Properties window.

The NBMA Neighbors tab enables you to specify the IP address of neighboring routers and associate a priority with the neighbor. Table 5.6 summarizes the options available from the Advanced tab.

If you are on a nonbroadcast multiple access (NBMA) network—a Frame Relay network that does not support broadcasts—the NBMA option on the General tab must be selected. You must also configure the IP addresses of OSPF neighbors using the NBMA Neighbors tab.

Table 5.6 Advanced OSPF Options	
Option	**Description**
Transit Delay	An estimation of the number of seconds for a link-state update to be transmitted over the network
Retransmit Interval	The number of seconds between link-state advertisement retransmissions
Hello Interval	How often hello packets are sent out to discover other routers
Dead Interval	The number of seconds until a neighboring router determines this router to be down
Poll Interval	The number of seconds between poll intervals sent to a dead neighbor
Maximum Transmission Unit (MTU) Size (Bytes)	The maximum byte size of an OSPF IP packet

Managing Devices and Ports

Devices and ports can be managed through the RRAS console. To do so, right-click the Ports container under your remote access server and click Properties. Select the device you want to configure and click the Configure button. From the Configure Devices window, you can enable remote access inbound connections, demand-dial inbound and outbound connections, and demand-dial outbound connections only. You can also configure a phone number for the device and configure additional ports.

Managing Routing and Remote Access Clients

Managing a remote access server also entails managing the clients that are connecting to it. You can use a number of tools with the Routing and Remote Access management console to manage remote access clients.

The management console provides administrators with a quick and easy way of viewing which clients are currently connected to a remote access server. To do so, click the Remote Access Clients container listed under your remote access server. The left pane displays the users currently connected. You can view status information for specific users by right-clicking their username and clicking the Status option. You can also disconnect a specific user by right-clicking the username and selecting the Disconnect option.

You also have the option of sending a message to a single user or all users connected to a remote access server. For example, if the server is going offline for maintenance, you can send a message to all connected users informing them of this. To send a message to a specific user, right-click the username and select Send Message. To send a message to all users currently connected to the server, right-click the Remote Access Clients container and select Send to All.

Implementing Secure Access Between Private Networks

As networks throughout the world become more interconnected, network administrators are challenged with ensuring that data transferred across a network is secure. This is where the IP Security (IPSec) protocol comes into play and allows for authentication of hosts, data integrity, and data encryption.

IPSec is used to protect data that is sent between hosts on a network, which can be remote access, VPN, LAN, or WAN. IPSec ensures that data cannot be viewed or modified by unauthorized users while being sent to its destination. Before data is sent between two hosts, the source computer encrypts the information. It is decrypted at the destination computer. IPSec provides the following benefits:

➤ Secure end-to-end communication between hosts

➤ Secure connections for remote access clients using the Layer 2 Tunneling Protocol (L2TP)

➤ Secure router-to-router connections

As you will see when you begin to configure IPSec, different levels of security can be implemented to meet varying needs. IPSec is implemented through IPSec policies. The policies are created and assigned to individual computers or groups of computers (or groups of users). The policies determine the level of security that will be used.

IPSec consists of three components that work together to provide secure communications between hosts:

➤ *IPSec Policy Agent*—This component is responsible for retrieving policy information from the local computer or Active Directory.

➤ *ISAKMP/Oakley Key Management Service*—This component is responsible for establishing a secure channel between hosts and creating the shared key that is used to encrypt the data. It also establishes a security association between hosts before data is transferred. The security association determines the mechanisms that are used to secure data.

➤ *IPSec Driver*—On the sending computer, this component monitors IP packets. Packets matching a configured filter are secured using the security association and shared key. The IPSec driver on the receiving computer decrypts the data.

The following steps outline how the different components work together to provide secure communications:

1. When Computer1 starts, the IPSec policy agent retrieves policy information from the local computer or Active Directory.

2. When Computer1 attempts to send data to Computer2, the IPSec driver examines the IP packets to determine whether they match the configured filters. If a match is determined, the IPSec driver notifies the ISAKMP/Oakley.

3. The ISAKMP/Oakley service on the two computers is used to establish a security association and a shared key.

4. The IPSec driver on Computer1 uses the key and security association to encrypt the data.

5. The IPSec driver on Computer2 decrypts the information and passes it to the requesting application.

In summary, before any data is transferred between two hosts, the security level must be negotiated. This negotiation includes agreeing on an authentication method, a hashing method, and an encryption method.

Configuring IPSec

You can enable IPSec using the Local Security Policy snap-in. The following list describes the three default policies. You can enable any policy for the local computer by right-clicking the policy and choosing the Assign option.

➤ *Client (Respond Only)*—This is used for computers that should not secure communications most of the time, but if requested to set up a secure communication, they can respond.

➤ *Server Secure (Require Security)*—When this option is selected, the server requires all communications to be secure. If a client is not IPSec-aware, the session will not be allowed.

➤ *Server (Request Security)*—This is used for computers that should secure communications most of the time. In this policy, the computer accepts unsecured traffic but always attempts to secure additional communications by requesting security from the original sender.

If you are running Active Directory, you can create an IPSec policy that is stored within Active Directory. To view the policies, open the Group Policy snap-in, shown in Figure 5.23.

The three policies that exist by default are Client, Server Secure, and Server. (The process of creating new IPSec policies is outlined in the following section.) To assign an IPSec policy to Group Policy, right-click the policy and click the Assign option.

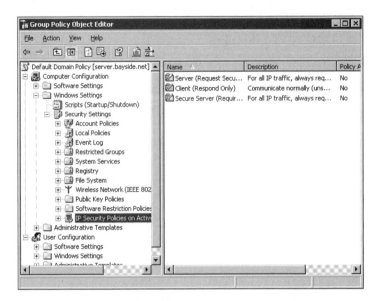

Figure 5.23 IPSec policies within the Group Policy snap-in.

Configuring IPSec for Transport Mode

IPSec can be used in one of two modes: transport mode or *tunnel mode*. Tunnel mode is used for server-to-server or server-to-gateway configurations. The tunnel is the path a packet takes from the source computer to the destination computer. This way, any IP packets sent between the two hosts or between the two subnets, depending on the configuration, are secured.

Two formats can be used with tunneling mode: ESP tunnel mode and AH tunnel mode. With Authentication Header (AH) tunnel mode, the data itself is not encrypted. It provides authentication and integrity, and it protects the data from modification, but it is still readable. With Encapsulating Security Payload (ESP) tunnel mode, authentication, integrity, and data encryption are provided.

 Tunnel mode is not used for remote access VPNs. IPSec/L2TP or PPTP is used for VPN connections. Tunnel mode is used for systems that cannot use IPSec/L2TP or PPTP VPNs.

To create a new IPSec policy, perform the following steps:

1. Click Start and click the Run command. Type **mmc** and click OK.

2. Click File and select Add/Remove snap-in. Click Add.

3. From the List of available snap-ins, select IP Security Policy Management. Click Add. Click Finish. Click Close.

4. Click OK.

5. To create a new policy, right-click IP Security Policies on Local Computer and select Create IP Security Policy. Click Next.

6. Type a name for the new policy. Click Next.

7. From the Requests for Secure Communications window, leave the default option of Activate the Default Response Rule selected to have the computer respond to those that request security. Click Next.

8. Select the authentication method. You can choose Kerberos, certificates, or a preshared key. You can edit the policy afterward to add multiple authentication methods. Click Next.

9. Click Finish.

To configure an IPSec tunnel, perform the following steps:

1. From the Properties window of the IPSec policy that you want to manage, select the rule you want to edit and click the Edit button.

2. Select the Tunnel Setting tab.

3. Select the tunnel endpoint that is specified by this IP address option and type the IP address of the tunnel endpoint.

4. After the tunnel endpoint has been specified, you can configure the tunneling mode using the Filter Actions tab. For ESP tunnel mode, select High. For AH tunnel mode, select Medium.

Customizing IPSec Policies and Rules

Each of the policies can be edited using the policy's Properties window. IPSec policies consist of several components, including the following:

➤ *Rules*—IPSec rules determine how and when communication is secured.

➤ *Filter lists*—Filter lists determine what type of IP packets trigger security negotiations.

➤ *IPSec security methods*—The security methods determine the security requirements of the rule.

➤ *IPSec authentication methods*—Authentication methods determine the ways in which hosts can identify themselves.

➤ *IPSec connection types*—This determines the types of connections, such as remote access or local area connections, to which the rule applies.

From the General tab of an IPSec policy's Properties window, you can change the name and description for the policy and configure the interval at which the computer will check for policy updates. Using the Advanced button, you can configure the Key Exchange Settings.

 When configuring the Key Exchange Settings, you can select the Master Key Perfect Forward Secrecy option. This ensures that no previously used keying material is used to generate new master keys. You can also specify the interval at which authentication and key generation must take place.

The Rules tab lists all of the rules that are configured for the policy. Other rules can be added by clicking the Add button; you can edit the existing rules using the Edit button. Clicking the Edit button brings up the Edit Rule Properties window (see Figure 5.24).

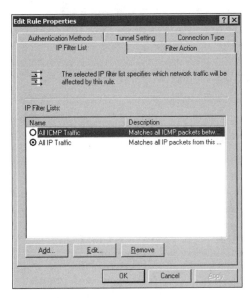

Figure 5.24 Editing IPSec rules.

The IP Filter List tab defines the type of traffic to which the rule will apply. The Filter Action tab defines whether the rule negotiates for secure traffic and how the traffic will be secured. Configuring the filter actions enables you to define the different security methods that can be negotiated. The security algorithms supported by IPSec include MD5 and SHA1. The encryption algorithms supported include DES and 3DES.

The Authentication Methods tab enables you to configure the method used to establish trust between the two computers (see Figure 5.25). If multiple authentication methods are configured for a rule, you can change the order in which they are used. The authentication methods available include these:

➤ *Kerberos*—Kerberos 5 is the default authentication method in a Windows Server 2003 domain. Users running the Kerberos protocol within a trusted domain can authenticate using this method.

➤ *Certificates*—If a trusted certificate authority is available, certificates can be used for authentication.

➤ *Preshared key*—For non–Windows Server 2003 computers or those not running Kerberos, a preshared key can be used for authentication.

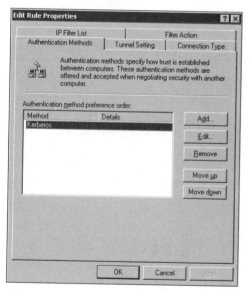

Figure 5.25 Configuring IPSec authentication methods.

The Connection Type tab enables you to define the types of connections to which the rule applies. This enables you to define different rules for different types of connections. Rules can be applied to local area connections, remote access connections, or all network connections.

The Tunnel Setting tab enables you to specify a tunnel endpoint where communication will take place between two specific computers.

You can edit the existing policies, or you can create and assign a new policy through the Group Policy snap-in. To create a new policy, right-click IP Security Policies on Active Directory within a Group Policy Object and select Create IP Security Policy. A wizard walks you through the process of creating the initial policy, which you can configure further using the Properties window for the new policy.

In Windows 2000, the **secedit /refreshpolicy machine_policy** command was used to refresh policy settings. Windows Server 2003 now uses the **gpupdate** command to refresh policy settings. When the command is used on its own, both the computer and user settings are applied. Using the command with the **/target** switch, you can specify that only the computer or user settings are applied. The **/force** switch causes all policy settings to be reapplied, regardless of whether they have changed.

Matching policies must exist on both computers before communication can take place.

Troubleshooting User Access to Remote Access Services

Troubleshooting is a major part of an administrator's job. Issues can arise related to connection problems or accessing resources beyond the remote access server. If your remote access server is configured as a router, you might encounter problems related to demand-dialing. The following section outlines some of the more common problems that you might encounter with a remote access server.

Diagnosing and Resolving Remote Access Connection Issues

One of the most common problems you might find yourself troubleshooting is related to establishing a remote access connection with a server. If a problem like this occurs, use the following points as a starting place for troubleshooting the connection problems:

➤ Verify that the modem is working and correctly configured.

➤ Verify that the remote access service is enabled and started on the server.

➤ Verify the availability of ports. If necessary, disconnect any idle sessions, or increase the number of available ports.

➤ Verify that the remote access policy is not prohibiting the connection.

Diagnosing and Resolving User Access to Resources Beyond the Remote Access Server

Remote access clients go through a remote access server to access network resources. The advantage of this is that clients can remotely access resources as though they were physically connected to the LAN. If clients are experiencing problems accessing resources beyond the RAS server, verify that IP routing has been enabled on the remote access server (using the IP tab from the server's Properties window), and also verify that any IP packet filters are not blocking the flow of traffic.

Troubleshooting Demand-Dial Routing

If on-demand connections are not being established automatically, check any of the following conditions to troubleshoot the problem:

➤ Verify that IP routing is enabled. This can be done using the IP tab from the remote access server's Properties window.

➤ Verify that you have correctly configured the static routes to the remote networks.

➤ Verify that the dial-out hours have been properly configured for the interface.

➤ Verify that any filters are not preventing the connection.

Exam Prep Questions

Question 1

Some of the users within your organization have home offices, which they work from during the weekdays. They require access to network resources, and all users can dial directly into the remote access server. For security purposes, you want to limit the dial-in hours from 8 a.m. to 6 p.m. How should you proceed?

- ○ A. Configure the properties of each user account.
- ○ B. Configure the properties of the remote access server.
- ○ C. Configure the conditions of the remote access policy.
- ○ D. Configure the port properties.

Answer C is correct. You can set day and time restrictions for remote users by configuring the conditions of the remote access policy. Answer A is incorrect because day and time restrictions are no longer configured through the properties of a user account as they were in Windows NT 4.0. You cannot configure day and time restrictions by configuring the properties of the remote access server or the ports; therefore, answers B and D are incorrect.

Question 2

You configured Windows Server 2003 as a remote access server. While enabling the service, you chose to use DHCP for IP address assignment. You are still using WINS on the internal network because you are still in the process of upgrading. Clients report that they can successfully connect but cannot access network resources using a UNC path. What must be done to resolve the problem?

- ○ A. You must configure a range of IP addresses on the RAS server, as well as assign any optional IP parameters to clients.
- ○ B. You must manually configure the IP settings on the remote access clients.
- ○ C. You must install the DHCP Relay Agent on the DHCP server.
- ○ D. You must install the DHCP Relay Agent on the RAS server.

Answer D is correct. The clients need to be configured with the IP address of the WINS server. To do this, the DHCP Relay Agent must be installed on the RAS server so that it can forward DHCPInform messages between the clients and the DHCP server. Answer A is incorrect because optional parameters cannot be configured on the RAS server. Clients can be configured with the IP address of the WINS server; however, it's easier from a management perspective to centralize IP address assignment and use a relay agent instead. Therefore, answer B is incorrect. Answer C is incorrect because the DHCP Relay Agent isn't installed on a DHCP server.

Question 3

You have multiple RAS servers on your network. You want to centralize the authentication of remote access clients and accounting information. Which of the following services should you install?

○ A. IAS

○ B. IIS

○ C. RADIUS

○ D. RRAS

Answer A is correct. To centralize the authentication of remote access clients and accounting information, the Internet Authentication Service (IAS) should be installed. Answer B is incorrect because IIS is for Web hosting. Answer C is incorrect because RADIUS is the protocol used by IAS to provide authentication and accounting services. Answer D is incorrect because Routing and Remote Access Service is used to provide a variety of services, including remote access, VPN, and routing.

Question 4

For security purposes, smart cards are being implemented for all remote access users. Which of the following protocols is required to support smart card authentication?

○ A. PAP

○ B. EAP

○ C. MS-CHAP

○ D. SPAP

Answer B is correct. The Extensible Authentication Protocol is required to support smart card authentication. Answers A, C, and D are incorrect because they do not support smart card authentication.

Question 5

You are creating a two-way demand-dial connection between two Windows Server 2003 RRAS servers. When creating the user account on the answering router, what must you remember?

- ○ A. Any user account name can be used.
- ○ B. The user account name should match the demand-dial interface name of the answering router.
- ○ C. The user account name should match the demand-dial interface name of the calling router.
- ○ D. The user account name must match the computer name of the answering router.

Answer C is correct. When creating demand-dial connections, the user account name created on the answering router must match the demand-dial interface name on the calling router. Therefore, answers A, B, and D are incorrect.

Question 6

Your internetwork consists of seven subnets. All subnets are connected using Windows Server 2000 RRAS servers. Nonpersistent demand-dial connections have been configured. You do not want to be burdened with updating the routing tables, and you want any changes to the network topology to be propagated immediately. Which of the following routing options should you implement?

- ○ A. Static routes
- ○ B. ICMP
- ○ C. OSPF
- ○ D. RIPv2

Answer D is correct. To have changes propagated throughout the network when changes occur and to reduce the administrative overhead associated with updating the routing tables, a routing protocol is required. Because OSPF cannot be used with nonpersistent connections, RIPv2 must be used (or RIPv1). Therefore, answers A and C are incorrect. Answer B is incorrect because ICMP is not a routing protocol.

Question 7

Which of the following commands would add a static route to a routing table?

- O A. **route -p 192.168.126.0 mask 255.255.255.0 192.168.125.1 metric 2**
- O B. **route add 192.168.126.0 mask 255.255.255.0 192.168.125.1 metric 2**
- O C. **route add 192.168.126.0 255.255.255.0 192.168.125.1 metric 2**
- O D. **route add 192.168.126.0 mask 255.255.255.0 gateway 192.168.125.1 metric 2**

Answer B is correct. The correct syntax when adding new static routes using the route command is route add <network> mask <subnetmask> <gateway> metric. Answers A, C, and D are incorrect because they do not use the proper syntax.

Question 8

You are configuring IP security for your network. You want all data to be encrypted, but you still want clients that do not support IPSec to be capable of authenticating with the server. Which of the following policies should you use?

- O A. Secure Server (Require Security)
- O B. Client (Respond Only)
- O C. Client (Require Security)
- O D. Server (Request Security)

Answer D is correct. By assigning the Server (Request Security) policy, the server will always attempt secure communications. Unsecured communications will still be allowed if the client is not IPSec-aware. Answer A is incorrect because communications will not be allowed if the client is not IPSec-aware. Answer B is incorrect because assigning Client (Respond Only) means that the server will respond only to requests for secure communications but will not attempt to secure all communications. Answer C is incorrect because there is no such default IP security policy.

Question 9

You are configuring IPSec between two servers in a workgroup. You assign Client (Respond Only) to each of the servers, but you notice that IP packets being sent between the two servers are not being secured. What is causing the problem?

○ A. Both are configured with the Client (Respond Only) policy.

○ B. IPSec can be used only with Active Directory.

○ C. One of the servers must be configured as an IPSec client.

○ D. The servers cannot be members of the same workgroup.

Answer A is correct. If both servers are configured with the Client (Respond Only) policy, they will respond only to requests for secure communications. One of the servers must be configured with Server (Request Security). Answer B is incorrect because IPSec can be configured through Active Directory or on the local computer. Answer C is incorrect because computers are not configured as IPSec clients. Answer D is incorrect because the workgroup membership has no impact on how servers respond to security.

Question 10

You have just updated the policy settings and want to apply changes immediately. Which of the following commands can be used?

○ A. **secedit**

○ B. **gpupdate**

○ C. **dcgpofix**

○ D. **gpresult**

Answer B is correct. To refresh policy settings, you can use the gpupdate command. Answer A is incorrect because this was the command used in Windows 2000. Answer C is incorrect because this command restores default Group Policy Objects to their original state. Answer D is incorrect because the command displays Group Policy settings for a computer.

Need to Know More?

 Search the online version of TechNet and the *Windows Server 2003 Server Resource Kit* using keywords such as "remote access," "routing," and "VPN."

 Williams, Robert and Mark Walla. *The Ultimate Windows Server 2003 Administrator's Guide*. Addison Wesley Professional, 2003.

 Minasi, Mark, Robert R. King, and Peter Hipson. *Mark Minasi's Windows XP and Windows Server 2003 Resource Kit*. Sybex, 2003.

Maintaining a Network Infrastructure

Terms you'll need to understand:

✓ Network Monitor
✓ Display filter
✓ Capture filter
✓ System Monitor
✓ Performance object
✓ Performance counter
✓ Device Manager
✓ Network Diagnostics

Techniques you'll need to master:

✓ Monitoring network traffic using Network Monitor
✓ Monitoring system performance using System Monitor
✓ Troubleshooting Internet connectivity problems
✓ Troubleshooting service dependencies
✓ Configuring service recovery options

Numerous tasks are involved in maintaining a network, from maintaining the physical network and servers to ensure performance, to troubleshooting various problems as they arise.

This chapter looks at topics pertaining to network maintenance, including monitoring network traffic, troubleshooting Internet connectivity, and managing network services. You also are introduced to the tools included with Windows Server 2003 that can be used to perform these various tasks.

Monitoring Network Traffic

As network-related services become more prevalent (because new services and applications are installed and network shares are created), traffic on a network can increase greatly. For example, a recent growth in Web-based training in many large companies to keep travel costs down would have a huge impact on network bandwidth utilization.

Network administrators must ensure that the network performs efficiently and reliably. By monitoring network performance, you can gather information that can be used for capacity planning, establishing a baseline that can help pinpoint changes in performance over time, and putting together performance-level reports. Two tools included with Windows Server 2003 can be used to monitor network traffic: Network Monitor and System Monitor.

Network Monitor

Network Monitor, which is included with Windows Server 2003, enables you to monitor and log network activity and then use the information to manage and optimize traffic. You can use the information you gather to identify unnecessary protocols and misconfigured workstations, and to detect problems with network applications and services. Some of the features of Network Monitor include the following:

> *Display filters*—Enable you to locate specific information within a capture

> *Capture filters*—Enable you to specify the type of information that is captured

> *Triggers*—Enable certain actions to be performed based on a packet's content

Network Monitor consists of the following two components:

➤ *Network Monitor Driver*—The Network Monitor Driver is responsible for capturing the frames coming to and from a network adapter.

➤ *Network Monitor tools*—The Network Monitor tools are used to view and analyze the data captured by the Network Monitor Driver.

Installing Network Monitor

Network Monitor is not installed with Windows Server 2003 by default, but it can be installed using the following process. Installing Network Monitor automatically installs the Network Monitor Driver.

1. Click Start, point to the Control Panel, and click Add or Remove Programs.

2. Click Add/Remove Windows Components.

3. Within the Windows Component Wizard, select Management and Monitoring Tools, and click the Details button.

4. Select the Network Monitor Tools check box. Click OK.

5. Click Next. Click Finish.

 Network Monitor should be used only by authorized users. The version of Network Monitor that is included with SMS can detect other instances on the network and display information such as the computer name, where the instance is installed, and the user who is currently logged onto the computer.

In some instances you want to install only the Network Monitor Driver— for example, if you want to capture traffic for multiple servers and view the captured data from your workstation. Installing the driver enables you to capture traffic on a network interface. You then need to use software such as Systems Management Server (SMS) to view the captured data. This is useful for capturing data from a number of different servers and viewing it from a central location. For example, a computer running Network Monitor Driver can capture the information and forward it to SMS. To install only the Network Monitor Driver component, perform the following steps:

1. Within the Network Connections applet, right-click Local Area Connection and choose Properties from the pop-up menu.

2. From the properties window for the local area connection, click the Install button.

3. In the list, click Protocol and then click the Add button.

4. Within the Network Protocol window, click the Network Monitor Driver.

5. Click OK.

Using Network Monitor

After Network Monitor is installed, it is added to the Administrative Tools menu. To launch the console, click Start, point to Administrative Tools, and click Network Monitor (see Figure 6.1).

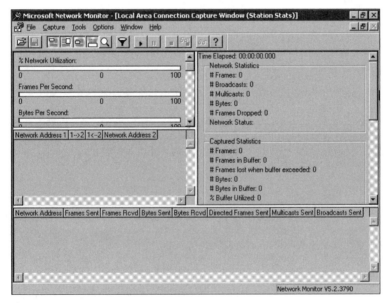

Figure 6.1 The Network Monitor console.

Network Monitor can display a large amount of information about the frames captured to and from a network adapter card. When you first open Network Monitor, four panes are displayed within the console. The Graph pane displays the network activity in the form of a bar chart. The Session Stats pane displays information about individual sessions, including statistics about the sessions in which the server is participating. The Total Stats pane displays the summary statistics since the capture was started.

To view statistics about network traffic, you must first start a capture to gather network traffic. To do so, click the Start option from the Capture menu. To view the captured data, click the Stop and View option from the Capture menu. Network Monitor displays all of the frames captured during the capture period with a Summary window. To view specific information about a frame, click the frame within the Summary window (see Figure 6.2).

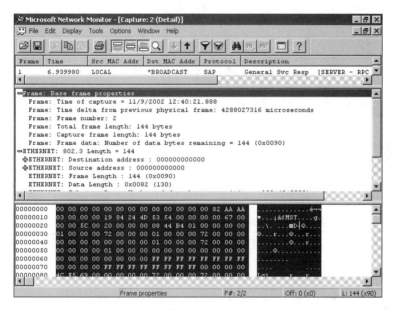

Figure 6.2   Viewing captured data within Network Monitor.

Using Capture Filters

Now when you run Network Monitor, all frames going to and from a computer are captured. During a capture, a large number of frames might be captured. If you're looking for specific types of traffic, you can create a capture filter to define which types of frames should be captured. To configure capture filters within Network Monitor, choose the Filter option from the Capture menu (see Figure 6.3).

From the Capture Filter window, you can create filters based on the following criteria:

➤ *Protocol*—Enables you to specify the protocols or the specific protocol properties that you want to capture

➤ *Address Pairs*—Specifies the computer addresses from which frames should be captured

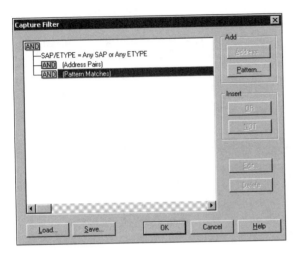

Figure 6.3 Configuring a capture filter.

> *Pattern Matches*—Enables you to configure different variables that captured frames should meet

 The Network Monitor supplied with Windows Server 2003 does not run in promiscuous mode. This means that it intercepts only packets that are intended either to or from your computer. To get the full version of Network Monitor, which includes promiscuous mode, you need SMS.

Using Display Filters

When you capture network traffic, a large number of packets can be displayed when you view the captured data, making it difficult to look for specific information.

Network Monitor enables you to configure display filters so that only specific types of traffic are displayed. To configure a display filter, select the Filter option from the Capture menu after you have run Network Monitor and captured the network traffic.

Configuring Triggers

By configuring triggers, you can perform certain actions when specific conditions are met. When Network Monitor is capturing data, it examines the contents of the packets. Any packets that meet the defined conditions trigger a specific action to be taken. To configure a trigger, click the Capture menu and click Trigger (see Figure 6.4). When the trigger criteria is met, you can configure any of the following actions to occur:

➤ The computer will beep.

➤ Network Monitor will stop capturing frames.

➤ A command-line program will be executed.

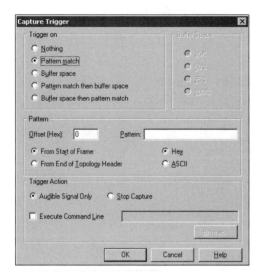

Figure 6.4 Configuring a trigger.

System Monitor

System Monitor can be used to monitor the real-time performance of the local computer or another computer on the network. System Monitor enables you to do the following:

➤ Collect real-time performance data on various aspects of system performance

➤ Control which users can view performance data locally or across the network by using the Performance Monitor Users and the Performance Log Users groups

➤ View real-time data or save data in a log file for later analysis

➤ Display captured data in various forms such as a graph or histogram

➤ Create monitoring configurations that can be used on other computers

The capability to control which users can view data using the Performance Monitor Users and Performance Log Users groups is a new feature in Windows Server 2003. Be prepared to encounter exam questions pertaining to this topic.

System Monitor enables you to monitor the performance of various server components, including hardware, services, and applications. System Monitor enables you to define the following:

➤ *The type of data you want to collect*—Performance objects enable you to select the various components you want to monitor. Each performance object has its own set of performance counters that determines what aspects of a particular counter you want to monitor. If multiple instances of an object exist (such as two network interfaces), you can select the counter instance you want to monitor.

➤ *Where you will collect the data from*—System Monitor enables you to collect data from the local computer or from another computer on the network.

➤ *How you will collect the data*—The sampling parameters enable you to define manual sampling, on-demand sampling, or automatic sampling.

Using System Monitor

System Monitor is a tool that is installed with Windows Server 2003 by default. To open the Performance console, click Start, point to Administrative Tools, and click Performance. You will find the System Monitor utility within this console (see Figure 6.5). When System Monitor is initially opened, the following three counters are displayed by default:

➤ *Memory*—Pages/Sec

➤ *Physical Disk*—Avg. Disk Queue Length

➤ *Processor*—%Processor Time

More than likely, you will also want to monitor other components and will need to add other counters—for example, if you want to monitor the performance of a service that has recently been installed. To add a counter to System Monitor, follow these steps:

1. Click Start, point to Administrative Tools, and click Performance.

2. Right-click the System Monitor Details pane and click Add Counter (see Figure 6.6), or click the Add button on the toolbar (represented by a plus sign).

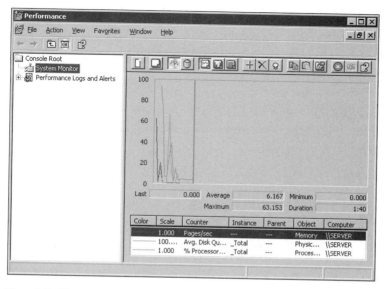

Figure 6.5   The Performance console.

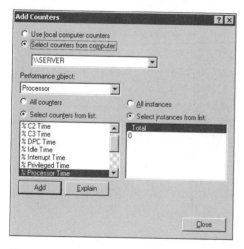

Figure 6.6   Adding counters to System Monitor.

3. To monitor the local computer, select Use Local Computer Counters. To monitor another computer on the network, click Select Counters from Computer and specify the computer name or IP address.

4. Use the Performance Object box to select the specific object you want to monitor. After you select an object, the related counters are displayed.

5. Select All Counters to monitor all counters that are related to the performance object. To select specific counters, click Select Counters from
   List. Click each counter you want to monitor and click Add. You will
   also notice an Explain button that provides information about the various counters.

6. To monitor all instances associated with a counter, select All instances.
   Otherwise, click Select Instances from List and select the instance to
   monitor.

7. Click Close.

NOTE | Before you can add a counter to a System Monitor, either you must be a member of
       the Administrators group, the Performance Logs Users group, or the Performance
       Monitor Users group, or you must be delegated the necessary permissions.

Using the System Monitor properties window (see Figure 6.7), you can further customize the settings. To do so, click the Properties button located on
the toolbar.

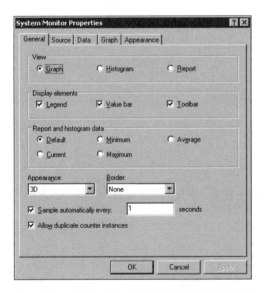

Figure 6.7 Configuring System Monitor property settings.

You can use the General tab to configure such things as the view (graph, histogram, or report), the display elements, and the counter values for a report
or histogram. By configuring the Sample Automatically Every option, you
can define the sampling interval (the default value is every 1 second).

Using the settings available on the Source tab, you can specify the data source that will be displayed (see Figure 6.8). You have three options: Display values for the current activity, store data in an existing log file, or store information in an SQL database. The remaining tabs can be used to customize the display of information within System Monitor.

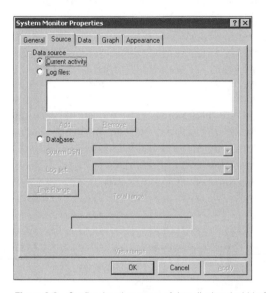

Figure 6.8   Configuring the source of data displayed within System Monitor.

Using System Monitor to Monitor Network Traffic

If TCP/IP is installed (it is installed by default), the Network Interface performance object is added to System Monitor. You can use this object to monitor data that is sent to and from a computer. When you select the performance object, you will notice that a number of counters are available. Some of the more useful counters for determining problems with a network card include these:

➤ *Packet Outbound Errors*—The number of outbound packets that could not be transmitted because of errors.

➤ *Packet Received Errors*—The number of received packets that contained errors, preventing them from being delivered to a higher-level protocol.

➤ *Packets Outbound Discarded*—The number of packets that have been discarded even though they did not contain errors. A possible cause for this scenario would be to free up buffer space.

➤ *Packets Received Discarded*—The number of received packets that were discarded even though no errors were detected.

You can also use System Monitor to monitor TCP/IP performance. Counters are available for IP, TCP, UDP, and ICMP. You can use the TCP Segments/Sec counter to monitor the number of TCP segments that the computer sent and the Segments Retransmitted/Sec counter to monitor the number of segments that the computer must resend because of errors. The IP Datagrams/Sec counter can be used to monitor the amount of TCP/IP traffic on the network. A number of other counters are available for the various protocols in the TCP/IP suite.

If your computer is functioning as a domain controller, you can use System Monitor to monitor the performance of the server service. In terms of network traffic, you should monitor the Logon Total and Logons/Sec counters, which determine the total number of logon requests the server has received since it was last restarted and the number of logon requests received per second.

Troubleshooting Internet Connectivity

You can establish Internet connectivity in a number of ways. You can use a remote access server, Internet Connections Sharing (ICS), Network Address Translation (NAT), or a direct connection using a network card, a modem, or another device. Because many organizations now rely heavily on the Internet for day-to-day operations, it is important that you have some understanding of how to troubleshoot Internet connectivity issues as they arise and the tools available to assist you.

 Refer to Chapter 5, "Routing and Remote Access," for specific information about troubleshooting remote access.

If you are troubleshooting Internet Connectivity, the following are some of the common steps you can take initially:

➤ If you are using a dialup connection, verify the number and credentials being used.

➤ Verify that the hardware being used is connected.

➤ Ensure that the hardware being used to connect to the Internet (such as a modem) is functioning.

➤ Use the IPCONFIG command to check the local host's TCP/IP configuration.

➤ If you access the Internet through a gateway, verify that the gateway is operational. This can be done by pinging the gateway's IP address.

➤ For name-resolution errors, make sure that DNS is properly configured and the DNS servers are online.

➤ If Internet access is through a proxy server, verify that the outgoing traffic is permitted.

The following section examines some of the tools and utilities included with Windows Server 2003 that can be used to assist you in troubleshooting Internet connectivity.

Hardware

Whether you have a direct connection to the Internet or have access through another computer, some form of hardware is used. If you experience hardware problems, whether with a modem, a network adapter, or another device, you can use Device Manager to attempt to troubleshoot and diagnose the problem.

You can access Device Manager by right-clicking My Computer and choosing Properties. Select the Hardware tab and click the Device Manager button. As you can see from Figure 6.9, Device Manager lists all the hardware that is currently installed on the computer.

By opening the properties window for a device, such as the network interface card, you can verify its status. If there are problems with the device, click the Troubleshoot button, which gives you some basic suggestions for troubleshooting the issue at hand. If you are troubleshooting a modem problem, you can also use the Diagnostics tab, which is found on the properties window for the modem within the Phone and Modem applet.

Troubleshooting Utilities

Aside from Device Manager, which can be used to troubleshoot hardware problems, a number of other utilities available can assist in diagnosing Internet connectivity problems. The following sections outline some of the tools that are included with Windows Server 2003.

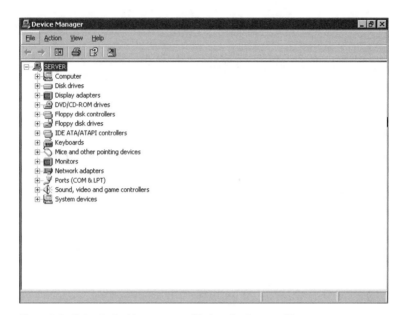

Figure 6.9   Using Device Manager to troubleshoot hardware problems.

Network Diagnostics

Network Diagnostics is a tool that gathers information about the hardware, software, and network connections on a local computer and displays the results. It can be used to verify network connectivity and determine whether network-related services are running. The result of the network diagnostics analysis can then be used to identify connectivity problems.

 You can also configure the scanning option for Network Diagnostics and specify what actions to take and what categories to include in the scan.

To use Network Diagnostics, perform the following tasks:

1. Click Start and click Help and Support.

2. From the list of Support Tasks, click Tools.

3. Select Help and Support Center Tools.

4. Select Network Diagnostics (see Figure 6.10).

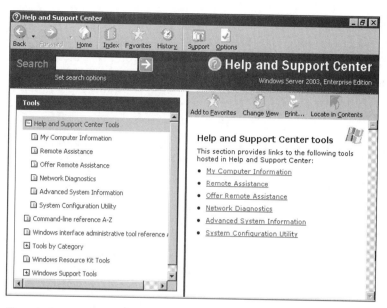

Figure 6.10   Help and Support Center tools.

5. Click Scan Your System. Network Diagnostics gathers information about hardware, software, and network connections on the local computer and displays the results (see Figure 6.11).

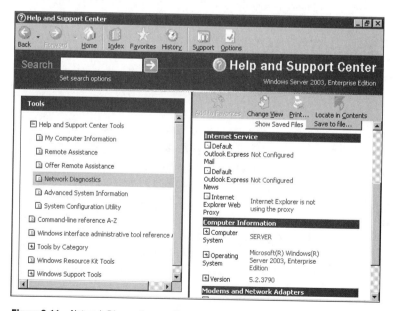

Figure 6.11   Network Diagnostics results.

The **Netdiag** Command

After the Windows Server 2003 Support Tools are installed, you can use the Netdiag.exe command-line utility to troubleshoot networking and connectivity problems. Netdiag performs a series of tests to determine the status of the network client. The information can be used by administrators and support personnel to isolate and troubleshoot network problems.

To install the Windows Server 2003 Support Tools, open the Support\Tools directory located on the Windows Server 2003 CD-ROM and double-click the **suptools.msi** file.

Netsh Command

Netsh is a command-line utility that enables you to modify the network configuration of the local computer or a remote computer. Netsh in Windows Server 2003 now introduces a set of diagnostic commands that can be used for troubleshooting. Table 6.1 summarizes some of the context commands that can be useful when troubleshooting Internet connectivity.

Table 6.1 Netsh diag Command Contexts	
Command Context	**Description**
Connect ieproxy	Establishes, verifies, and drops a connection with the proxy listed in the properties of Internet Explorer.
Connect iphost	Establishes, verifies, and drops a connection with a specified host using a specified port.
Connect mail	Establishes, verifies, and drops a connection with the host specified as the mail server within Outlook Express.
PING	Verifies connectivity with the remote host specified.
PING *adapter*	Verifies connectivity through a specified adapter. If used without parameters, it tests connectivity through all installed adapters.
PING gateway	Verifies connectivity with the default gateways listed in the TCP/IP properties for the specified adapter. If no adapter is specified, connectivity is verified through all installed adapters.
PING DNS	Verifies connectivity with DNS servers listed in the TCP/IP properties for the specified adapter. If no adapter is specified, connectivity to DNS servers is tested through all installed adapters.
PING ieproxy	Verifies connectivity with the proxy server listed in the properties of Internet Explorer.
PING iphost	Verifies connectivity with a local or remote host.

(continued)

Table 6.1	Netsh diag Command Contexts *(continued)*
Command Context	Description
PING mail	Verifies connectivity with the mail server configured in Outlook Express.
Show *modem*	Lists information about the specified modem.
Show gateway	Lists all Internet gateways for the specified adapter.
Show ieproxy	Lists all Internet Explorer proxy servers for the specified adapters.
Show mail	Shows the Outlook Express mail server configured on the local computer.

IPCONFIG

If you are experiencing network connectivity problems, one of the first actions you should perform is to verify the IP configuration on the client or server that is reporting the error. By doing so, you can verify that incorrect IP parameters configured on the computer are not causing the problem. You can use the IPCONFIG utility from the command prompt to verify a computer's IP configuration. You can view detailed IP configuration information for all interfaces, including modems (see Figure 6.12). Table 6.2 summarizes the available switches.

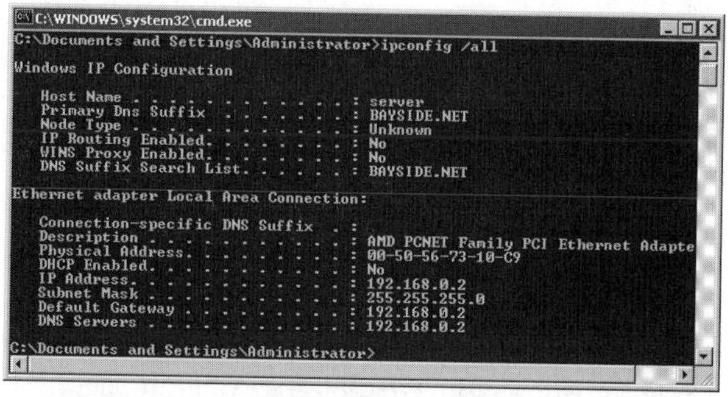

Figure 6.12   Using the **IPCONFIG /ALL** command.

Table 6.2	IPCONFIG Command-line Switches
Switch	Description
/all	Displays full configuration information
/release	Releases the IP address assigned to the specified adapter
/renew	Renews the IP address for the specified adapter
/flushdns	Purges the DNS resolve cache
/registerdns	Refreshes all DHCP leases and re-registers DNS names

PING

Use the PING command to verify connectivity with other hosts on a TCP/IP network or on the Internet. Connectivity is verified by sending Internet Control Message Protocol (ICMP) echo requests and replies. When the PING command is issued, the source computer sends echo request messages to another TCP/IP host. If reachable, the remote host then responds with four echo replies. The PING command is also issued at the command prompt, along with the TCP/IP address or domain name of the other TCP/IP host, as follows:

```
C:> PING 124.120.105.110
C:> PING www.bayside.net
```

 To determine whether TCP/IP is initialized on the local computer, issue the **PING** command and specify the loopback address of 127.0.0.1.

The general steps for troubleshooting TCP/IP using the PING command are as follows:

1. PING the loopback address of 127.0.0.1 to ensure that TCP/IP is initialized on the local computer.

2. If successful, PING the IP address assigned to the local computer.

3. Next, PING the default gateway's IP address. If this fails, verify that the default gateway's IP address is correct and that the gateway is operational.

4. Next, PING the IP address of a host on a remote network. If this is unsuccessful, verify that the remote host is operational, verify the IP address of the remote host, and verify that all routers and gateways between the local computer and remote computer are operational.

 A quick way to verify TCP/IP connectivity is to complete step 4 in the preceding steps first. If you can successfully **PING** the IP address of a remote host, steps 1 through 3 will be successful.

TRACERT and PATHPING

Two other utilities that can be used for TCP/IP troubleshooting are TRACERT and PATHPING. The TRACERT command determines the route that is taken to a specific destination. You might want to use the TRACERT command if you cannot successfully PING the IP address of a remote host. The results of the TRACERT command indicate whether there is a problem with a router or gateway between the local computer and the remote destination.

The PATHPING command is basically a combination of the PING and TRACERT commands. When the command is issued, packets are sent to each router between the local computer and a remote computer. The output can display the degree of packet loss at each router, and the results determine which routers and gateways might be causing problems on the network.

Troubleshooting Server Services

A *service* is an application that runs on a computer providing an operating system feature, such as event logging or error reporting.

Diagnose and Resolve Issues Related to Service Dependency

Service dependencies can be very complex. Some services have no dependencies, meaning that you can start and stop them without worrying whether it will affect other services. However, many services have dependencies, so starting them depends on whether other specific services are first running, and stopping them might cause other services to fail. For example, consider the IPSec service shown in Figure 6.13. The Clipbook service does not have any other services that depend upon it. However, several services must be running before it can be started.

Service Dependency

Services that run on a computer might depend on other services. In other words, one service might not be capable of starting unless another service is running. Windows Server 2003 provides administrators with a quick way of determining those services upon which another is dependent, or vice versa. In other words, you can view services that the service depends on and services that depend on it to start. You can verify a service's dependencies using the Services console using the following steps:

1. Click Start, point to Administrative Tools, and click Services. This opens the Services console (see Figure 6.14).

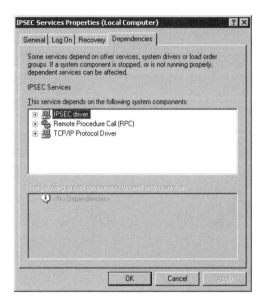

Figure 6.13 Dependencies of the IPSec service.

Figure 6.14 The Services console.

2. Right-click the appropriate service and click Properties.

3. From the service's properties window click the Dependencies tab (see Figure 6.15). The Dependencies tab lists those services upon which the service depends and the services that depend upon it.

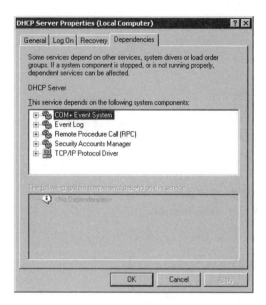

Figure 6.15   Using a service's Dependencies tab.

Before you attempt to stop a service, it is a good idea to verify which services depend upon it, to determine whether any other services will be affected.

Use Service Recovery Options to Diagnose and Resolve Service-Related Issues

Windows 2000 introduced service recovery options. They enable you to specify what actions should be taken when a service fails. For example, if a service fails upon restart or while the server is running, you can attempt to have the service automatically restarted.

Four different recovery options are available. The default is not to take action when a service fails to start. You can also choose from one of the following three recovery actions. Now if a service fails, action can be taken to restart the service without direct administrative intervention.

➤ Restart the service.

➤ Run a program.

➤ Restart the computer.

You can also specify when you want these actions to occur. A recovery action can be performed when the service initially fails, when it fails for a second time, and for any subsequent failures.

Service recovery options are available only on computers running Windows 2000, Windows XP, and Windows Server 2003.

Configuring Service Recovery Options

To configure recovery options, perform the following steps:

1. Click Start, point to Administrative Tools, and click Services.

2. Right-click the service for which you want to configure recovery options and click Properties.

3. From the properties window, click the Recovery tab (see Figure 6.16).

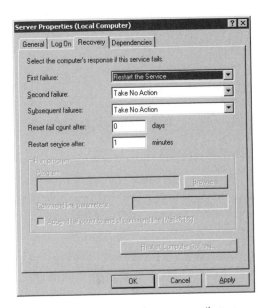

Figure 6.16 Configuring service recovery options.

4. To configure a recovery action, click the arrow beside First Failure. Select one of the available options. If you select to run a program, specify the program to run, as well as any command-line parameters.

5. Repeat step 4 to configure recovery actions for second and subsequent failures.

6. Click OK.

Other Troubleshooting Tools

Windows Server 2003 includes a number of other tools that can be used to diagnose and troubleshoot problems as they arise. Some of these tools include

➤ Task Manager

➤ System Information

➤ Event Viewer

➤ Shutdown Event Tracker

Task Manager

Task Manager can be used to view a variety of information about the local computer. You can launch the tool by right-clicking the task bar and selecting the Task Manager option (see Figure 6.17). Using Task Manager, you can view the following information:

➤ Programs currently running

➤ Processes currently running

➤ Dynamic performance of the local computer

➤ Network status

➤ Users currently connected to the computer

Table 6.3 summarizes the available tabs.

Table 6.3 Tabs Available Through Windows Task Manager	
Tab	**Description**
Applications	Lists all the applications currently running on the computer
Processes	Lists all the processes currently running on the computer
Performance	Displays real-time performance information
Networking	Displays real-time performance information for the local area connection
Users	Lists the users currently connected to the local computer

Figure 6.17 Using Task Manager.

System Information

The System Information tool provides configuration information about the local computer or a remote computer. You can use the tool to quickly locate configuration information for a computer. You can open the System Information tool by selecting Start, All Programs, Accessories, System Tools, System Information. The tool provides the following information:

➤ *System Summary*—Displays general information about the computer

➤ *Hardware Resources*—Provides information about resource usage

➤ *Components*—Provides information about the components installed on the computer

➤ *Software Environment*—Provides system configuration information

➤ *Internet Settings*—Provides information about the Internet settings configured on the computer

Event Viewer

You can use Event Viewer to view the contents of the Windows Server 2003 event log files. Every computer running Windows Server 2003 has three log files: Application, Security, and System. Additional log files might be present depending on the configuration of the computer. For example, a computer running DNS will have a DNS server log. The contents of the log files can be used to track events and troubleshoot problems as they arise.

Shutdown Event Tracker

The Shutdown Event Tracker option enables an administrator to monitor why users shut down or restart their computers. This feature is enabled by default on all computers running Windows Server 2003 and is disabled on Windows XP Professional workstations. When Shutdown Event Tracker is enabled, users are prompted to provide a reason as to why they are shutting down or restarting a computer. The information is then recorded in the system log.

Exam Prep Questions

Question 1

John has just captured a large amount of network traffic using Network Monitor. He wants to limit the captured information to display only traffic containing the SMB protocol. What should he do?

○ A. Configure a trigger.

○ B. Configure a capture filter.

○ C. Configure a display filter.

○ D. Configure a packet filter.

Answer C is correct. By configuring a display filter within Network Monitor, you can filter captured data to display only specific types of information. Answer A is incorrect because triggers enable actions to be performed based on a set of conditions that must first be met. Answer B is incorrect because capture filters are configured to specify the type of information that is captured. Answer D is incorrect because packet filters are configured to specify the type of inbound and outbound traffic a computer can accept.

Question 2

Mary is the network administrator. She wants to give Joe the capability to view real-time data as it is captured using System Monitor. Joe should be capable of performing this task from the server or from his workstation. What should Mary do?

○ A. Add his user account to the Performance Log Users group.

○ B. Add his user account to the Administrators group.

○ C. Add his user account to the Performance Monitor Users group.

○ D. Add his user account to the Domain Admins group.

Answer C is correct. By adding a user account to the Performance Monitor Users group, Joe will be capable of viewing performance counter data within System Monitor locally or from across the network. Answer A is incorrect because adding Joe to the Performance Log Users group will give him permission to manage logs and alerts as well. Answers B and D are incorrect because they would give Joe administrative permissions to the server.

Question 3

Bob has been running Network Monitor to analyze specific types of network traffic. He wants to configure Network Monitor to gather only information pertaining to specific protocols and traffic types. What should he do?

○ A. Configure a display filter.

○ B. Configure a capture filter.

○ C. Configure a packet filter.

○ D. Configure an alert.

Answer B is correct. Configuring a capture filter instructs Network Monitor to capture only data that meets the criteria you specify. Answer A is incorrect because display filters are used to filter data that has already been captured. Answer C is incorrect because packet filters are configured to control inbound and outbound traffic. Answer D is incorrect because alerts are used to notify an administrator when certain events occur.

Question 4

Susan is putting together a performance report for her managers. She wants to gather statistics about the total amount of TCP/IP traffic on the local computer. Which of the following counters should she monitor?

○ A. Packet Outbound Errors

○ B. TCP Segments/Sec

○ C. IP Datagrams/Sec

○ D. Logons/Sec

Answer C is correct. By monitoring IP Datagrams/Sec, you can monitor the total number of IP datagrams sent and received by the computer per second. Answer A is incorrect because this is the number of outbound packets that could not be transmitted because of errors. Answer B is incorrect because this counter monitors only the number of TCP segments sent per second. Answer D is incorrect because this counter monitors the number of logon requests received per second by the computer.

Question 5

You are having trouble connecting to your ISP using a dialup connection. Which command should you use to verify the TCP/IP configuration on the local computer?

- ○ A. **IPCONFIG**
- ○ B. **PING**
- ○ C. **TRACERT**
- ○ D. **PATHPING**

Answer A is correct. The IPCONFIG command can be used to verify the TCP/IP configuration of a computer. Answer B is incorrect because the PING command is used to verify connectivity with a remote host. Answer C is incorrect because TRACERT is used to trace the route a packet takes to reach a remote host. Answer D is incorrect because PATHPING is a combination of PING and TRACERT used to determine which routers and gateways between two hosts might not be functioning.

Question 6

A computer running Windows Server 2003 connects to the Internet through a dialup connection. You are having problems establishing a connection and want to verify that the modem is working. Which of the following utilities can you use to verify the status of the modem?

- ○ A. System Monitor
- ○ B. Network Monitor
- ○ C. **PING**
- ○ D. Device Manager

Answer D is correct. Device Manager can be used to verify that a hardware device is functioning properly. Answer A is incorrect because System Monitor is to used monitor the performance. Answer B is incorrect because Network Monitor is used to capture and analyze network traffic. Answer C is incorrect because PING is a command-line utility used to verify network connectivity.

Question 7

Mary is gathering network-performance statistics on a Windows Server 2003 domain controller. She wants to determine the number of logons the domain controller has received since the last time it was restarted. Which counter should she monitor?

- ○ A. Total Logons Received
- ○ B. Logon Total
- ○ C. Logons Received/Sec
- ○ D. Logons/Sec

Answer B is correct. The Logon Total counter determines the number of logon requests that the domain controller has received since the last time it was restarted. Answers A and C are incorrect because there are no such counters within System Monitor. Answer D is incorrect because this counter determines the number of logon requests received per second.

Question 8

Clients on the network cannot obtain an IP address from the DHCP server on the network. You soon discover that the DHCP service on the server has failed to start. You reboot the server, and the service still does not start. What should you do?

- ○ A. Continue to reboot the server until the service starts.
- ○ B. Verify that any services DHCP is dependent on are started using the Services console.
- ○ C. Use the DHCP console to start the service.
- ○ D. Reinstall the DHCP service.

Answer B is correct. If the service will not start, use the Services console to verify that any services that DHCP is dependent upon are also started. Therefore, answer A is incorrect. Answer C is incorrect because if the service fails to start, attempting to start it within the DHCP console will make no difference. Answer D is incorrect because this should be a last resort in terms of troubleshooting.

Question 9

Bill is configuring the service recovery options for the server service on a Windows Server 2003 domain controller. If a service fails to start, which of the following actions can be performed? (Choose all correct answers.)

❑ A. The computer can attempt to restart the service.

❑ B. The computer can be rebooted.

❑ C. The services that it is dependent upon can be restarted.

❑ D. An email message can be sent to the network administrator.

Answers A and B are correct. If a service fails to start, you can configure the computer to automatically attempt to restart the service, or you can have the computer automatically reboot. The third option is to have a specific program run. Answers C and D are incorrect because recovery actions do not include the capability to automatically restart the failed service's dependencies or to send an email to the network administrator.

Question 10

A new network service is added to the existing infrastructure. You want to determine how much more traffic has been generated since its installation. Which of the following tools can be used to capture and analyze network traffic?

○ A. Task Manager

○ B. Network Diagnostics

○ C. Network Monitor

○ D. Event Viewer

Answer C is correct. Network Monitor can be used to capture and analyze network traffic. Answer A is incorrect because Task Manager is used to view the programs and process running on a computer, as well as the performance statistics. Answer B is incorrect because Network Diagnostics is used to gather information about the hardware, software, and services running on a local computer. Answer D is incorrect because Event Viewer is used to view the contents of the various event logs.

Need to Know More?

 Search the online version of TechNet and the *Windows 2003 Server Resource Kit* using keywords such as "System Monitor," "Network Monitor," and "Service Dependencies."

 Minasi, Mark. *Mastering Windows Server 2003*. Alameda, CA: Sybex Press, 2003.

 Russel, Charlie, Sharon Crawford, and Jason Gerend. *Microsoft Windows Server 2003 Administrator's Companion*. Redmond, WA: Microsoft Press, 2003.

Practice Exam #1

Do not read Chapters 8–10 until you have learned and practiced all the material presented in the preceding chapters of this book. These chapters serve a special purpose; they are designed to test whether you are ready to take Exam 70-291, "Implementing, Managing, and Maintaining a Windows Server 2003 Network Infrastructure." In these chapters, you will find two self-tests. Each self-test is followed by an answer key and a brief explanation of the correct answers, along with an explanation of why the other answers are incorrect. Reading these chapters before the other chapters is like reading the climax of a story and then going back to find out how the story arrived at that ending. Of course, you don't want to spoil the excitement, do you?

How to Take the Practice Tests

Each self-test in this book consists of 60 questions; you should complete each test within 120 minutes. The number of questions and the time duration in the actual exam might vary but should be close to this number.

After you have studied the material presented in the preceding chapters of this book, you should take Practice Exam #1 to check how well you are prepared. After the self-test is complete, evaluate yourself using the answer key in Chapter 8, "Answer Key for Practice Exam #1." When you evaluate yourself, note the questions and which ones you answered incorrectly, identify the corresponding chapters in the book, and then read and understand that material before taking Practice Exam #2. After taking the second exam, evaluate yourself again and reread the material corresponding to any incorrect answers. Finally, take both tests again until you have correctly answered all of the questions. The information presented in the following sections should help you prepare for the exams.

Exam-taking Tips

Take these exams under your own circumstances, but I strongly suggest that when you take them, you treat them just as you would treat the actual exam at the test center. Use the following tips to get maximum benefit from the exams:

➤ Before you start, create a quiet, secluded environment where you are not disturbed for the duration of the exam.

➤ Provide yourself a few empty sheets of paper before you start. Use some of these sheets to write your answers, and use the others to organize your thoughts. At the end of the exam, use your answer sheet to evaluate your exam with the help of the answer key that follows the sample exam.

➤ Don't use any reference material during the exam.

➤ Some of the questions might be vague and require you to make deductions to come up with the best possible answer from the choices given. Others might be verbose, requiring you to read and process a lot of information before you reach the actual question.

➤ As you progress, keep track of the elapsed time and make sure that you'll be able to answer all the questions in the given time limit.

Practice Exam

Question 1

You have been using Network Monitor to capture and analyze DHCP-related traffic. You notice a large amount of traffic from IP address lease requests, and the frequency of the requests is high. You verify that the number of IP addresses within the scope exceeds the number of DHCP clients on the network. How can you reduce the amount of traffic being generated by IP address lease requests?

- ○ A. Configure half of the clients with static IP addresses.
- ○ B. Increase the lease duration for the scope.
- ○ C. Configure another DHCP server on the network.
- ○ D. Decrease the lease duration for the scope.

Question 2

John is responsible for administering a small network consisting of three subnets. He implements DHCP and places a server on each network. He confirms that clients in subnet1 have obtained IP addresses but cannot access any resources outside of the local subnet. He confirms this to be an issue on all subnets. What should he do?

- ○ A. Activate the scopes on all servers.
- ○ B. Configure the properties of TCP/IP on each workstation, and configure the IP address of the gateway.
- ○ C. Authorize the DHCP servers within Active Directory.
- ○ D. Configure the 003 router option on each DHCP server.

Question 3

Bob is the junior network administrator. He is assigned the task of installing a DHCP server in a test environment. He successfully installs the DHCP service on a member server and configures a scope, but he soon discovers that the service is constantly being shut down. What is causing the problem?

- ○ A. Bob did not activate the scope.
- ○ B. Bob must install the DHCP service on a domain controller.
- ○ C. Bob did not authorize the DHCP server.
- ○ D. Bob configured the server with incorrect scope information.

Question 4

You are the network administrator of a Windows Server 2003 network. You are in charge of configuring DHCP. Three servers on the network are running applications that require the servers to have static IP addresses. What can you do to accomplish this? (Select two.)

❑ A. Manually assign the servers IP addresses. Exclude the IP addresses that will be used for the servers from the scope.

❑ B. Configure the 003 client scope option on the DHCP server.

❑ C. Configure a client reservation for each of the servers.

❑ D. Configure a superscope and add to it the IP addresses that will be assigned to the servers.

Question 5

DHCP is deployed on the network, and all clients are configured to automatically obtain an IP address. If the DHCP server is unavailable, clients will use an IP address from which of the following address ranges?

○ A. 192.168.0.1 to 192.168.255.254.

○ B. 192.168.0.1 to 192.168.0.254

○ C. 127.0.0.1 to 127.255.255.154

○ D. 169.254.0.0 to 169.254.255.255

Question 6

Sean is responsible for implementing DHCP on the network. The network consists of multiple subnets. A single DHCP server is installed along with DHCP relay agents. The configuration is tested, and all clients are successfully leasing IP addresses. However, you soon discover that only users on subnet B can communicate outside of their local subnet. What is causing the problem?

○ A. Sean did not configure a separate scope for each subnet.

○ B. Sean configured the 003 router option but did not activate it.

○ C. Sean did not activate the DHCP server.

○ D. Sean configured the 003 router option at the server level.

Question 7

Dan is the junior network administrator for FKB International. He is installing and configuring an existing Windows Server 2003 member server as a DHCP server in a test environment. He configures and activates a scope. When he attempts to authorize the DHCP server, he receives an access denied error message. What is causing the problem?

○ A. The user must be a member of the DNSUpdateProxy group to authorize a DHCP server.

○ B. The user must be a member of the Enterprise Admins group to authorize a DHCP server.

○ C. The user must be a member of the Domain Admins group to authorize a DHCP server.

○ D. The user must be a member of the Administrators group to authorize a DHCP server.

Question 8

Mike is the junior network administrator for a medium-size network. The network has multiple subnets. He is trying to recall the order in which scope options are configured. Which of the following answers are correct?

○ A. Server, scope, class, client

○ B. Server, class, scope, client

○ C. Server, scope, client, class

○ D. Scope, server, client, class

Question 9

Three servers on the network are configured with the following static IP addresses: 192.168.0.10, 192.168.0.11, and 192.168.0.12. You install a DHCP server on the network and configure a scope of 192.168.0.1 to 192.168.0.254. What else must you do to ensure that there are no address conflicts on the network?

○ A. Configure client reservations for the three servers.

○ B. Exclude the three IP addresses from the scope.

○ C. Place the servers on a separate subnet.

○ D. Create a superscope for the three static IP addresses.

Question 10

There are two subnets on the network. A DHCP server is placed on each one. How can you implement fault tolerance between the two DHCP servers?

- ○ A. Within the DHCP console, configure the two servers to replicate scope information.
- ○ B. Configure each DHCP server with a scope for each subnet.
- ○ C. Configure a DHCP relay agent on each subnet.
- ○ D. Configure DHCP clients with the IP address of both DHCP servers using the TCP/IP Properties window.

Question 11

During which phase of the IP address lease process has the client officially been leased an IP address?

- ○ A. DHCPDISCOVER
- ○ B. DHCPOFFER
- ○ C. DHCPREQUEST
- ○ D. DHCPACK

Question 12

Mary is the network administrator for a Windows Server 2003 network. She has just installed a new DHCP server. The scope has been configured, and the server now needs to be authorized. Which administrative console can be used to authorize a DHCP server within Active Directory?

- ○ A. DHCP console
- ○ B. Active Directory Sites and Services
- ○ C. Active Directory Users and Computers
- ○ D. Active Directory Domains and Trusts

Question 13

There is a DHCP server and a DNS server on the network. Workstations are running a variety of different platforms. When configuring DHCP for DNS integration, which of the following clients can perform the updates on their own? (Choose all correct answers.)

❏ A. Windows 95

❏ B. Windows Me

❏ C. Windows 2000

❏ D. Windows XP

❏ E. Windows 98

Question 14

A workstation on the network cannot communicate with other clients. You want to verify that the workstation is receiving an IP address from a DHCP server. Which of the following steps can you take to verify this?

○ A. Verify through the properties of TCP/IP that the workstation is configured with the IP address of the DHCP server.

○ B. Ping the IP address of the DHCP server.

○ C. Use the **IPCONFIG /ALL** command to verify the workstation's IP address.

○ D. Use the properties of TCP/IP to verify the workstation's IP address.

Question 15

Bob wants to change the default interval at which the DHCP database is backed up. How should he proceed?

○ A. Make the change within the DHCP console.

○ B. Make the change within the Windows Registry.

○ C. Make the change within the Windows Backup program.

○ D. The default interval cannot be changed.

Question 16

Felicia is planning the implementation of DHCP for a network that consists of a single subnet. Her manager is concerned that clients will not be able to access the company database server if the DHCP server is unavailable. All clients and servers are configured as DHCP clients. The workstations are running a number of different platforms. Felicia informs her manager that the computers will use Automatic Private IP Addressing (APIPA) if a DHCP server is unavailable. Which of the following platforms will support Automatic Private IP Addressing? (Choose all correct answers.)

❑ A. Windows 95

❑ B. Windows 98

❑ C. Windows Me

❑ D. Windows XP

❑ E. Windows NT 4.0

Question 17

All clients currently lease IP addresses from a DHCP server. The DHCP server has now been configured to perform DNS updates on behalf of DHCP clients. The zone is configured for secure updates only. What else must you do for the DHCP server to perform the updates?

○ A. Authorize the DHCP server.

○ B. Configure the zone for dynamic updates.

○ C. Configure the dynamic update credentials.

○ D. Configure static IP addresses for all clients.

Question 18

Greg is the administrator of a Windows Server 2003 network that has a DHCP server and a DNS server. The zone is configured for dynamic updates. The DHCP server is configured with the default settings. All workstations are running Windows 95, Windows 2000, and Windows XP. Which of the following statements are true? (Select two.)

❑ A. Clients will update their own PTR records and A records.

❑ B. The DHCP server will update PTR records for Windows 2000 and Windows XP clients.

❏ C. The DHCP server will update A records and PTR records on behalf of all clients.

❏ D. Windows 2000 and Windows XP clients will update their own A records.

❏ E. The DHCP server will update A and PTR records on behalf of Windows 95 clients.

Question 19

There are currently two DNS servers on the network. Both are configured as member servers and upgraded to domain controllers. One server is configured as the primary DNS server. The other is configured as a secondary DNS server. You want to store the zone within Active Directory. How should you proceed?

○ A. From the Properties window for the DNS server, select the General tab and click the Change button beside the Zone Type option. Select the option to store the zone in Active Directory.

○ B. From the Properties window for the zone, select the Security tab and click the Change button. Select the option to store the zone in Active Directory.

○ C. From the Properties window for the DNS server, select the Security tab and click the Change button. Select the option to store the zone in Active Directory.

○ D. From the Properties window for the zone, select the General tab and click the Change button beside the Zone Type option. Select the option to store the zone in Active Directory.

Question 20

A mail server has just been added to the network, but mail is not getting delivered properly. You suspect that the mail is not getting routed to the proper server because its name might be unknown to the Unix DNS server. What should you ask the Unix DNS administrator to check?

○ A. Verify that the appropriate MX record exists.

○ B. Verify that the Unix server is configured for dynamic updates.

○ C. Verify that clients have been configured with the IP address of the mail server through the properties of TCP/IP.

○ D. Verify that a CNAME record exists for the mail server.

Question 21

John has been asked to increase the availability of DNS on the network. There is currently a single DNS server configured as a member server. It is a primary DNS server. To add fault tolerance so that clients can still resolve names if the primary DNS server goes offline, what type of server should John add to the network?

- ○ A. Caching-only
- ○ B. Primary DNS server
- ○ C. Secondary DNS server
- ○ D. Active Directory DNS server

Question 22

A network currently has multiple DNS servers within the head office. There are also several branch offices. Name-resolution response time is reportedly slow because the branch offices are connected by slow links. The budget allows you to place a DNS server within each location. However, you do not want any more traffic generated from zone transfers. Which DNS server role should be configured within each branch office location?

- ○ A. Primary
- ○ B. Secondary
- ○ C. Caching-only
- ○ D. Master name server

Question 23

Bill is using the **nslookup** command to determine the hostname associated with the IP address of 192.168.0.35. He knows that the IP address is assigned to Computer1. He can successfully resolve other IP addresses to hostnames using the command. What is causing the problem?

- ○ A. There is no A record for Computer1.
- ○ B. The DNS server is not online.
- ○ C. There is no MX record for Computer1.
- ○ D. The PTR record has not been created for Computer1.

Question 24

John is trying to configure his DNS server to accept only secure updates. However, the Secure Updates option is not available. What is causing the problem?

- ○ A. The DNS service is installed on a member server.
- ○ B. The zone is not configured to accept dynamic updates.
- ○ C. The DHCP server has not been configured with dynamic update credentials.
- ○ D. John does not have permission to configure secure updates.

Question 25

The Bayside organization currently hosts a single primary DNS server. The server is running Active Directory. Mary wants to increase security by specifying which users and groups can perform dynamic updates. What should she do?

- ○ A. From the Properties window for the DNS server, select the General tab and change the Dynamic Updates option to Secure Only.
- ○ B. From the Properties window for the zone, select the General tab and change the Dynamic Updates option to Secure Only.
- ○ C. From the Properties window for the DNS server, select the Security tab and change the Dynamic Updates option to Secure Only.
- ○ D. From the Properties window for the zone, select the Security tab and change the Dynamic Updates option to Secure Only.

Question 26

A primary DNS server exists within the head office of the Riverside Corporation. The branch offices are configured with secondary DNS servers. The budget allows for another DNS server to be placed within each of the sites. The links are already slow and heavily utilized. There should be no more traffic on these links from DNS zone transfers. How should you proceed?

- ○ A. Configure the existing secondary DNS servers as the master name servers for the new secondary DNS servers.
- ○ B. Increase the refresh interval.
- ○ C. Configure the new secondary DNS servers to receive zone transfers from the primary DNS server in the head office.
- ○ D. Configure the new secondary servers as forwarders.

Question 27

> Changes have recently been made to the records within the zone file. One of the
> clients now reports name-resolution errors. You suspect that the client resolver
> cache has incorrect entries. What command can you use to clear the contents
> of the cache?
>
> ○ A. **ipconfig /all**
>
> ○ B. **ipconfig /renew**
>
> ○ C. **ipconfig /displaydns**
>
> ○ D. **ipconfig /flushdns**

Question 28

> The primary and secondary DNS servers are connected by slow links that are
> already heavily utilized. Jen wants to increase the interval at which the second-
> ary DNS server will poll the primary DNS server for changes. Which of the fol-
> lowing parameters should she configure?
>
> ○ A. TTL
>
> ○ B. Refresh interval
>
> ○ C. Retry interval
>
> ○ D. Serial number

Question 29

> Mike is concerned about DNS fault tolerance on the network. There is currently
> a single primary DNS server. Users should still be able to resolve hostnames if
> the server goes offline unexpectedly or for maintenance. What can Mike do to
> ensure that users can still resolve hostnames in case the primary DNS server
> goes offline?
>
> ○ A. A secondary DNS server should be added to the network.
>
> ○ B. A caching-only server should be added to the network.
>
> ○ C. DNS forwarding should be configured.
>
> ○ D. A master name server should be added to the network.

Question 30

A merger has just occurred between the Bayside and Riverside corporations. Each network maintains its own DNS servers. You want the DNS servers in Bayside to send all queries for hosts in the Riverside organization directly to the Riverside DNS servers. How should you proceed?

○ A. Using the Forwarders tab from the zone's Properties window, configure the Bayside DNS server to forward all name-resolution requests to the Riverside DNS servers.

○ B. Using the Forwarders tab from the DNS server's Properties window, configure the Bayside DNS server to forward all name-resolution requests to the Riverside DNS servers.

○ C. Using the Forwarders tab from the DNS server's Properties window, configure the Bayside DNS server to forward all name-resolution requests for clients in the Riverside domain to the Riverside DNS servers.

○ D. Using the Forwarders tab from the zone's Properties window, configure the Bayside DNS server to forward all name-resolution requests for clients in the Riverside domain to the Riverside DNS servers.

Question 31

Dana is the junior network administrator of a Windows Server 2003 network. The senior network administrator has assigned her the task of installing and configuring DNS. Dynamic updates will be used. The senior network administrator also wants the ability to control who can perform dynamic updates. How should Dana proceed?

○ A. Install the DNS service on a Windows Server 2003 domain controller.

○ B. Install the DNS service on a Windows Server 2003 member server.

○ C. Install the DNS service on a Windows Server 2003 standalone server.

○ D. Install the DNS service on a Windows XP Professional workstation.

Question 32

Don has just finished installing and configuring a DNS server for his organization. The DNS server is still in the test environment. Don wants to ensure that the DNS server is functioning before placing it on the network. He specifically wants to test the configuration to ensure that the DNS server can resolve hostnames. What should he do?

- ○ A. Ping the IP address of the DNS server.
- ○ B. Check the Event Viewer for any DNS-related events.
- ○ C. Use the Monitoring tab from the DNS server's Properties window to test the configuration.
- ○ D. Verify that the appropriate records exist within the zone file.

Question 33

Your network consists of Unix hosts that use only DNS. There are also legacy clients on the network that use NetBIOS. The Unix hosts cannot resolve the NetBIOS names of the legacy clients. What should you do?

- ○ A. Enable DNS for WINS lookup.
- ○ B. Configure replication between DNS and WINS.
- ○ C. Install a WINS proxy agent on the network.
- ○ D. Configure DHCP to register NetBIOS names with the DNS server.

Question 34

Mark is the administrator of a Windows Server 2003 network. Currently, there is only a single DNS server. A recent mishap caused the DNS server to go offline unexpectedly. For increased fault tolerance, Mark wants to install the DNS service on an existing domain controller. He logs on to the domain controller. How should he proceed? (Choose all correct answers.)

- ❑ A. Run the **DCPROMO** command.
- ❑ B. Install DNS using the Add or Remove Programs applet.
- ❑ C. Install DNS using the Configure Your Server Wizard.
- ❑ D. Install DNS through the DNS management console.
- ❑ E. Install DNS using Software Update Services.

Question 35

Which of the following record types must exist before you can use the **nslookup** command to resolve an IP address to a hostname?

○ A. PTR

○ B. MX

○ C. A

○ D. CNAME

Question 36

David is the administrator of a Windows Server 2003 network. The head office hosts a primary DNS server that is also used by the branch office. David wants to place a DNS server within the branch office location without increasing the network traffic on the WAN link. What should he do?

○ A. Configure another primary DNS server in the branch office location.

○ B. Configure a secondary DNS server in the branch office location, but do not configure a master name server.

○ C. Configure a caching-only DNS server in the branch office location.

○ D. Configure a master name server in the branch office location.

Question 37

There are a number of DNS servers on the network. You want to limit which secondary servers are permitted to receive zone updates from DNS01. What should you do?

○ A. Use the Security tab from the zone's Properties window to list servers that can receive updates.

○ B. Use the Zone Transfers tab from the zone's Properties window to list servers that can receive updates.

○ C. Use the Security tab from the DNS server's Properties window to list servers that can receive updates.

○ D. Enable zone transfers to all servers using the Zone Transfers tab from the zone's Properties window.

Question 38

A single DNS server is being added to the network. Dynamic updates are not configured. Jim, the network administrator, is configuring the zone file. Clients must be capable of resolving hostnames. Network administrators must be able to use the **nslookup** command to troubleshoot DNS problems. Which of the following must exist within the zone file to meet these requirements? (Select two.)

❑ A. PTR

❑ B. A

❑ C. MX

❑ D. CNAME

Question 39

John has configured the IPSec policy for the company Web server. He wants to monitor and view IPSec statistics to ensure that secure communications are taking place. Which of the following tools can be used to view IPSec statistics?

○ A. IP Security Policy management console

○ B. Network Monitor

○ C. IP Security Monitor

○ D. System Monitor

Question 40

FKB International is implementing Software Update Services to streamline the process of applying updates to computers on the network. Mary, the network administrator, needs to install Software Update Services on an existing server. Before performing the installation, which of the following must be configured on the server? (Choose all correct answers.)

❑ A. Internet Explorer 5.0 or later

❑ B. IIS 5.0 or later

❑ C. NTFS system partition

❑ D. Service Pack 1

Question 41

Mike is the network administrator configuring automatic updates for a group of workstations on the network. He creates a new Group Policy Object (GPO) for the appropriate OU. When he opens the GPO to edit the automatic update settings, they are not available. What is causing the problem?

○ A. Mike does not have sufficient privileges to edit the policy settings.

○ B. Software Update Services has not been installed yet.

○ C. Mike must configure the settings on each workstation.

○ D. The Automatic Updates ADM file has not been loaded.

Question 42

Mary has just finished installing Software Update Services. The server is configured and ready to be placed on the network. She now needs to install the updated version of Automatic Updates on the client computers. The computers are running a variety of platforms, all of which will not support the new software. On which computers should Mary perform the update? (Choose all correct answers.)

❑ A. Windows 2000

❑ B. Windows 95

❑ C. Windows Me

❑ D. Windows XP

❑ E. Windows 98

Question 43

John is the administrator of a Windows Server 2003 network. He has created a security template that is applied to all new servers. He notices that the account lockout threshold on one of the network servers has been changed. He is concerned that several other settings might have been changed. John wants to determine which settings were changed by comparing the existing settings against those within the original template. What tool can he use?

○ A. Security Templates

○ B. System Monitor

○ C. Security Configuration and Analysis

○ D. IP Security Monitor

Question 44

There are six servers on the network. Jim wants to implement a standard set of security settings to apply to all six servers. What would be the easiest way for him to proceed?

○ A. Configure the security settings on each server.

○ B. Configure a security template and import it on each server.

○ C. Configure a security template and deploy it through a GPO.

○ D. Configure a security template and deploy it using SUS.

Question 45

You want to configure a Windows XP client to use an SUS server for automatic updates. Which Registry value should you configure to enable SUS for automatic updates?

○ A. **UseWUServer**

○ B. **AUOptions**

○ C. **WUServer**

○ D. **WUStatusServer**

Question 46

You have enabled Automatic Updates on a Windows XP workstation to use SUS. You now want to specify which SUS server the workstation will download options from. Which Registry value should you configure?

○ A. **UseWUServer**

○ B. **AUOptions**

○ C. **WUServer**

○ D. **WUStatusServer**

Question 47

The IPSec policies are no longer behaving normally. You suspect that a junior network administrator made some policy changes, but you need to verify this. What tool can you use?

○ A. Event Viewer

○ B. Network Monitor

○ C. Active Directory Users and Computers

○ D. IP Security Monitor snap-in

Question 48

John wants to view IPSec statistics using the IP Security Monitor. He has recently upgraded from Windows 2000 to Windows Server 2003. John recalls the command used to launch the utility in Windows 2000. How can he open the IP Security Monitor utility in Windows Server 2003?

○ A. Using Administrative Tools located on the Start menu

○ B. Using the IP Security Monitor icon within the Control Panel

○ C. Using the **run** command and typing **ipsecmon.exe**

○ D. Using the Microsoft Management Console and adding the IP Security Monitor snap-in

Question 49

The internal network is using the private IP address range of 192.168.0.0/24. DHCP is being implemented. Two servers will continue to use static IP addresses. What should you do to ensure that there are no address conflicts on the network?

○ A. Configure client reservations for both servers.

○ B. Exclude the static IP addresses from the scope.

○ C. Place the static IP addresses within a separate scope.

○ D. Configure the scope options on the DHCP server.

Question 50

IP Security Monitor will be used to monitor IPSec communications on several servers. Your organization is still in the process of migrating to Windows Server 2003, so some of the servers are still running Windows 2000. You use the IP Security Monitor snap-in from your computer to monitor the servers across the network. However, you discover that you can monitor only computers running Windows Server 2003. What is causing the problem?

○ A. You do not have administrative permissions on the servers running Windows 2000.

○ B. IP Security Monitor cannot be used to monitor computers running Windows 2000.

○ C. The Windows 2000 servers are not members of the local domain.

○ D. The Network Monitor driver is not installed on the Windows 2000 servers.

Question 51

Which of the following utilities can be used to view IPSec statistics? (Choose two.)

❑ A. **netdiag**

❑ B. IP Security Monitor

❑ C. **ping**

❑ D. **netsh**

Question 52

You are trying to install Software Update Services on a computer running Windows Server 2003. The installation of the software continually fails. You verify that the computer meets the hardware requirements. The server is also running IIS 5.0 and Internet Explorer 6.0, and all partitions except the system partition are formatted with FAT. What could be causing the problem?

○ A. Service Pack 1 is not installed.

○ B. The partition storing the updates is not formatted with FAT.

○ C. IIS must be uninstalled.

○ D. The system partition must be formatted with NTFS.

Question 53

Mark is in charge of implementing DHCP in a new branch office. There is an existing DHCP server in the head office. Fault tolerance is a concern, and clients in the branch office should be able to obtain an IP address if the local DHCP server goes offline or if the WAN link to the head office becomes unavailable. What should he do? (Select three.)

- ❑ A. Place a DHCP server in the branch office location.
- ❑ B. Configure the local DHCP server with 80% of the available IP address-es. Configure the DHCP server within the head office with the remaining 20% of the IP addresses.
- ❑ C. Enable the DHCP Relay Agent on a server within the branch office.
- ❑ D. Configure all clients with the IP address of both DHCP servers.

Question 54

Bob's network consists of Windows XP workstations and a few workstations still running Windows 95. He notices that the Windows 95 clients are not dynamically updating their host records with the DNS server. What should he do?

- ○ A. Configure DNS for dynamic updates.
- ○ B. Configure the properties of TCP/IP on the Windows 95 workstations, and enable them for dynamic updates.
- ○ C. Configure the DHCP server to perform updates for legacy clients.
- ○ D. Place a DHCP relay agent on the network.

Question 55

Don is the junior network administrator. His boss has asked him to install DHCP on an existing standalone server. Don installs the service and configures the scope. When he attempts to authorize the DHCP server within Active Directory, the Authorize option is not available within the DHCP console. What is causing this to occur?

- ○ A. Don is not a member of the DHCP Administrators group.
- ○ B. Don is not a member of the Enterprise Admins group.
- ○ C. DHCP has been installed on a standalone server and, therefore, does not need to be authorized.
- ○ D. Don must authorize the DHCP server using the Active Directory Users and Computers snap-in.

Question 56

You have delegated sales.bayside.net to another DNS server on the network. You want to ensure that the name server for bayside.net is notified any time a new authoritative name server is added to the sales.bayside.net zone. What should you do?

- ○ A. Using the Name Servers tab from the sales.bayside.net zone, configure the DNS server to notify the DNS server in the parent domain of any changes.
- ○ B. Configure a stub zone on the DNS server within the parent domain.
- ○ C. Configure a DNS server within the bayside.net zone to be a secondary server to the sales.bayside.net zone.
- ○ D. Configure all zones to store information within Active Directory.

Question 57

All of the DNS servers on your network are also configured as domain controllers. Zone information is stored within Active Directory. You want to verify that replication between DNS servers is occurring as it should. Which tool can you use to verify this?

- ○ A. System Monitor
- ○ B. Replication Monitor
- ○ C. DNS management console
- ○ D. DNS Monitor

Question 58

Your company has recently moved its Web site to another server. Clients report that they no longer can view the site. Upon further examination, you discover that the DNS server is providing clients with the IP address of the old Web server. You suspect a problem with the cache. What should you do?

- ○ A. Uninstall the DNS server service.
- ○ B. Delete the cache.dns file.
- ○ C. Use the Clear Cache option from the DNS server's Properties window.
- ○ D. Use the Clear Cache option from the Action menu.

Question 59

Mary is using Software Update Services within a test environment on two computers before implementing the service in the production environment. She installs Software Update Services on a standalone server. She has a Windows XP workstation to use to perform testing. She wants to configure automatic updates so that the local administrator is notified of downloads and installations. How should she proceed?

○ A. Edit the Registry and configure the **UseWUServer** Registry value.

○ B. Edit the Registry and configure the appropriate value for the **AUOptions** entry.

○ C. Install the Automatic Updates ADM file. Configure the **WUServer** option within a Group Policy.

○ D. Install the Automatic Updates ADM file. Configure the **SUSServer** option through a Group Policy.

Question 60

Dan is the network administrator of a Windows Server 2003 network. The company has recently opted to host a Web server on the private network. Dan wants to monitor and log network activity coming to and going from the Web server. Which of the following tools should he use? (Select two.)

❑ A. System Monitor

❑ B. IP Security Monitor

❑ C. Network Monitor

❑ D. Event Viewer

Answer Key for Practice Exam #1

1. B	**16.** C, D	**31.** A	**46.** C
2. D	**17.** C	**32.** C	**47.** A
3. C	**18.** B, D	**33.** A	**48.** D
4. A, C	**19.** D	**34.** B, C	**49.** B
5. D	**20.** A	**35.** A	**50.** B
6. D	**21.** C	**36.** C	**51.** B, D
7. B	**22.** C	**37.** B	**52.** D
8. A	**23.** D	**38.** A, B	**53.** A, B, C
9. B	**24.** A	**39.** C	**54.** C
10. B	**25.** B	**40.** A, B, C	**55.** C
11. D	**26.** A	**41.** D	**56.** B
12. A	**27.** D	**42.** A, D	**57.** B
13. C, D	**28.** B	**43.** C	**58.** D
14. C	**29.** A	**44.** C	**59.** B
15. B	**30.** C	**45.** A	**60.** A, C

1. Answer B is correct. By increasing the lease duration, clients will not have to renew their IP address leases with the DHCP server as often. Answer A is incorrect because, although this would reduce the amount of DHCP traffic, it does not really address the problem at hand and decentralizes IP address administration. Answer C is incorrect because placing a second DHCP server on the network would provide load balancing but would not address the amount of traffic being generated. Answer D is incorrect because decreasing the existing lease time would only further increase traffic.

2. Answer D is correct. For clients to communicate outside of their local subnet, they must be configured with the IP address of the default gateway. This can be done by configuring the 003 router option on each DHCP server. Answers A and C are incorrect because the clients can successfully lease IP addresses. Answer B is incorrect because the clients are configured for DHCP, so the gateway option can be assigned dynamically when the clients are assigned an IP address.

3. Answer C is correct. If a DHCP server is not authorized in Active Directory, the service will be shut down when it attempts to start. Answer A is incorrect because an inactive scope will not cause the service to fail. Answer B is incorrect because the DHCP service can be installed on a member server, domain controller, or a standalone server. Answer D is incorrect because misconfigured scope information would not cause the DHCP service to fail.

4. Answers A and C are correct. You can manually configure IP addresses for the servers or leave them as DHCP clients. If you manually configure IP addresses, those addresses must be excluded from the scope. The other option is to configure client reservations. By configuring a client reservation for each server, the servers can remain as DHCP clients but will always be assigned the same IP address. Answer B is incorrect because scope options are used to configure DHCP clients with optional parameters. The 003 option also is used to assign clients the IP addresses of network routers. Answer D is incorrect because superscopes are used to organize existing scopes.

5. Answer D is correct. If a DHCP server is unavailable, clients will use Automatic Private IP Addressing and will use an IP address in the range of 169.254.0.0 to 169.254.255.255. Therefore, answers A, B, and C are incorrect.

6. Answer D is correct. For all clients to be able to communicate outside of the local subnet, the 003 router option must be configured at the scope level. Answers A and C are incorrect because all clients are successfully leasing IP addresses. Answer B is incorrect because optional parameters are not activated; scopes are activated.

7. Answer B is correct. To authorize the DHCP servers, a user must be a member of the Enterprise Admins group. Answers A, C, and D are incorrect because these groups have insufficient privileges to perform the operation.

8. Answer A is correct. Scope options are applied in the following order: server, scope, class, and client. Therefore, answers B, C, and D are incorrect.

9. Answer B is correct. To ensure that there are no address conflicts on the network, you must exclude the IP addresses already assigned to the three servers from the scope. Therefore, answers C and D are incorrect. Answer A is incorrect because client reservations ensure that certain DHCP clients are always assigned the same IP address.

10. Answer B is correct. To add fault tolerance to the DHCP server implementation, configure each DHCP server with a scope for each subnet. DHCP servers do not share information, so make sure that the scopes do not overlap. Answer A is incorrect because DHCP servers cannot be configured to replicate scope information. Answer C is incorrect because configuring a DHCP relay agent does not add fault tolerance, although it might be required for clients to obtain an IP address from a DHCP server on another subnet. Answer D is incorrect because clients are not configured with the IP address of a DHCP server. DHCP servers are located on the network by performing a broadcast.

11. Answer D is correct. During the final phase of the IP address lease process, the client receives a DHCPACK from the DHCP server. At this point, the client has successfully leased an IP address from the DHCP server. Therefore, answers A, B, and C are incorrect.

12. Answer A is correct. The DHCP console is used to authorize a DHCP server within Active Directory. Therefore, answers B, C, and D are incorrect.

13. Answers C and D are correct. Both Windows 2000 and Windows XP clients can update their own records with the DNS server. Answers A, B, and E are incorrect because these clients do not support the dynamic update feature; in such cases, the DHCP server can be configured to update the records on their behalf.

14. Answer C is correct. The IPCONFIG /ALL command can be used to view detailed information about TCP/IP parameters on a computer, including whether the IP address is being leased from a DHCP server. Answer A is incorrect because you cannot configure a client with the IP address of a DHCP server. Answer B is incorrect because the PING command is used to test connectivity, and it has already been determined that the client cannot communicate on the network. Answer D is incorrect because if the client is configured to dynamically obtain an IP address, it will not be listed in the TCP/IP Properties window.

15. Answer B is correct. The default interval at which the DHCP database is backed up must be changed through the Registry by editing the HKEY_LOCAL_MACHINE\SYSTEM\Currentcontrolset\services\DHCPServer\ Parameters Registry key. Therefore, answers A, C, and D are incorrect.

16. Answers C and D are correct. Of the platforms listed, only Windows Me and Windows XP support Automatic Private IP Addressing. Therefore, answers A, B, and E are incorrect.

17. Answer C is correct. If the zone is configured to accept only secure updates, you must configure the dynamic update credentials on the DHCP server. This is the username and password under which the DHCP server will perform the updates to the DNS database. Answer A is incorrect because clients are already leasing IP addresses. If the DHCP server is not authorized, the service will fail to start. Answer B is incorrect because the question already states that the zone is configured for secure updates. Answer D is incorrect because if clients are configured with static IP addresses, dynamic updates would not be required, nor would DHCP.

18. Answers B and D are correct. By default, Windows 2000 and Windows XP clients will dynamically register their own A records. Answer A is incorrect because the DHCP server will register the PTR records for clients. Answer C is incorrect because the DHCP server will not update A records unless requested to do so. Answer E is incorrect because a DHCP server will not update any records on behalf of legacy clients unless it is configured to do so.

19. Answer D is correct. A zone type can be changed using the General tab from the zone's Properties window. Select the option to store the zone in Active Directory. Answer B is incorrect because the Security tab is used to configure permissions to the zone file. Answers A and C are incorrect because a zone type cannot be changed from the DNS server's properties window.

20. Answer A is correct. MX records are used to identify mail servers. Answer B is incorrect because some versions of Unix support dynamic updates. However, there is no mention of what version of Unix is being used, so you can assume that dynamic updates are not configured. Answer C is incorrect because you cannot configure the IP address of a mail server through the properties of TCP/IP. Answer D is incorrect because CNAME records are used to assign alias names to an existing host.

21. Answer C is correct. A secondary DNS server maintains a copy of the zone file. If the primary DNS server goes offline, clients can still resolve hostnames using the secondary DNS server. Answer A is incorrect because caching-only DNS servers do not maintain zone information; they only cache records. Answer B is incorrect because a primary server already exists. Answer D is incorrect because there is no such DNS role.

22. Answer C is correct. Because caching-only servers do not maintain any zone information, no traffic is generated from zone transfers. As the server builds up, the contents of the cache response time will be decreased for DNS clients. Answers A and B are incorrect because primary and secondary DNS servers will generate zone-replication traffic. Answer D is incorrect because a master name server is the DNS server from which a secondary DNS server gets zone updates.

23. Answer D is correct. To use the `nslookup` command to resolve the hostname associated with an IP address, the appropriate PTR record must exist within the reverse lookup file. Answer A is incorrect because the A record is not used to resolve the hostname associated with an IP address. Answer B is incorrect because the `nslookup` command returns results for other queries. Answer C is incorrect because MX records are used to identify mail servers.

24. Answer A is correct. The Secure Updates option is available only if the DNS service is installed on a domain controller. Answers B and C are incorrect because these would not cause the Secure Updates option to not be available. Answer D is incorrect because the user already has the required permission if the user can navigate through the DNS management console.

25. Answer B is correct. To specify which users and groups can update the zone file, the zone must be configured for secure updates. This can be done through the zone's Properties window using the General tab. Answers A and C are incorrect because a zone cannot be configured for secure updates from the DNS server's properties window. Answer D is incorrect because the Security tab is used to configure users and groups that have permission to update the zone file.

26. Answer A is correct. By configuring the existing secondary DNS servers as the master name servers for the new secondary DNS servers, zone replication for the new servers can occur locally instead of across the slow link. Answer B is incorrect because the refresh interval defines only how often a secondary server will poll for updates. Answer C is incorrect because this will result in more replication traffic. Answer D is incorrect because forwarders are configured to tell a DNS server where to forward name-resolution requests.

27. Answer D is correct. The `ipconfig /flushdns` command clears the contents of the client resolver cache. Answer A is incorrect because this command displays the IP configuration for the computer. Answer B is incorrect because this command renews the IP address lease. Answer C is incorrect because this command displays the contents of the client resolver cache.

28. Answer B is correct. The refresh interval defines how often a secondary server will poll its master name server for updates to the zone file. Answer A is incorrect because the TTL defines how long records can remain within the cache before they must be purged. Answer C is incorrect because this defines how often the secondary server will continue to poll for updates if the master name server does not respond. Answer D is incorrect because the serial number is used to determine whether the zone file has changed.

29. Answer A is correct. A secondary server maintains a copy of the zone file. DNS clients can resolve hostnames using the secondary server if the primary DNS server goes offline. Answer B is incorrect because a caching-only server caches results only as the hostnames are resolved. Answer C is incorrect because forwarders are configured to tell a DNS server where to send name-resolution requests. Answer D is incorrect because a master name server is the DNS server from which a secondary server retrieves zone updates.

30. Answer C is correct. Using the Forwarders tab from the DNS server's Properties window, configure the DNS server to forward all name-resolution requests for clients in the Riverside organization to the Riverside DNS servers. Answers A and D are incorrect because forwarders cannot be configured from the zone's properties window. Answer B is incorrect because you do not want all name-resolution requests forwarded to the Riverside DNS servers.

31. Answer A is correct. To use secure updates, the DNS service must be running on a domain controller. Answers B and C are incorrect because when the DNS service is installed on a member server or standalone server, secure updates are not available. Answer D is incorrect because DNS cannot be installed on Windows XP.

32. Answer C is correct. Using the Monitoring tab, you can perform simple queries against the DNS server to test the configuration. Therefore, answers A, B, and D are incorrect.

33. Answer A is correct. If the Unix hosts do not support NetBIOS, WINS lookup can be enabled on the DNS server. The DNS server can query the WINS server if it cannot resolve the hostname. Answer B is incorrect because you cannot configure replication between DNS and WINS. Answer C is incorrect because a WINS proxy forwards NetBIOS broadcasts to a WINS server. Answer D is incorrect because a DHCP server cannot update NetBIOS names with a DNS server.

34. Answers B and C are correct. The DNS service can be installed using the Add or Remove Programs applet or the Configure Your Server Wizard. Answer A is incorrect because this would require uninstalling Active Directory. Answer D is incorrect because the DNS management console is available only after the DNS service is installed. Answer E is incorrect because Software Update Services is used only for deploying software updates.

35. Answer A is correct. PTR records must exist before you can use the nslookup command to resolve IP addresses to hostnames. Therefore, answers B, C, and D are incorrect.

36. Answer C is correct. Caching-only DNS servers do not maintain any zone information; therefore, no additional traffic would exist on the WAN link. Answer A is incorrect because a primary DNS server already exists for the zone. Answers B and D are incorrect because they maintain zone information and would result in zone transfers.

37. Answer B is correct. Using the Zone Transfers tab, you can specify which secondary servers can receive zone updates. Answer A is incorrect because the Security tab is used to configure users and groups that can perform updates. Answer C is incorrect because you must configure this at the zone level. Answer D is incorrect because you do not want all secondary DNS servers to be capable of requesting updates.

38. Answers A and B are correct. A records are used to resolve hostnames to IP addresses. PTR records are required to perform reverse lookups. Therefore, answers C and D are incorrect.

39. Answer C is correct. The IP Security Monitor utility can be used to view IPSec statistics. Therefore, answers A, B, and D are incorrect.

40. Answers A, B, and C are correct. Software Update Services requires Internet Explorer 5.0 (or later) and IIS 5.0 (or later), and the system partition must be NTFS. Answer D is incorrect because Service Pack 1 is required only to install SUS on Windows 2000.

41. Answer D is correct. To configure Automatic Updates settings through a Group Policy Object, the Automatic Updates ADM file must be loaded. Answer A is incorrect because the user is already an administrator. Answer B is incorrect because installing the SUS software does not automatically add the Automatic Updates settings into a Group Policy Object. Answer C is incorrect because settings can be configured locally or through a Group Policy.

42. Answers A and D are correct. Windows 2000 and Windows XP support the updated version of Automatic Updates. Therefore, answers B, C, and E are incorrect.

43. Answer C is correct. The Security Configuration and Analysis tool enables you to compare current security settings against those in a template. Answer A is incorrect because the Security Templates snap-in is used to configure existing templates and create new ones. Answer B is incorrect because System Monitor is used to monitor the real-time performance of various components and services. Answer D is incorrect because IP Security Monitor is used to monitor and troubleshoot IPSec communications.

44. Answer C is correct. The simplest way to configure the same security settings on each server is to configure a security template and deploy it through a GPO. Answers A and B are incorrect because these options would require visiting each of the servers. Answer D is incorrect because SUS cannot be used to deploy security settings.

45. Answer A is correct. This parameter specifies that Automatic Updates uses an SUS server. Answer B is incorrect because this option specifies how updates are downloaded and installed. Answer C is incorrect because this option specifies which SUS server updates are downloaded from. Answer D is incorrect because this option specifies which server the client will send status information to.

46. Answer C is correct. This option specifies which SUS server updates will be downloaded from. Answer A is incorrect because this option enables only Automatic Updates to use an SUS server. Answer B is incorrect because this option specifies how updates are downloaded and installed. Answer D is incorrect because this option specifies which server the client will send status information to.

47. Answer A is correct. As long as auditing of policy changes has been enabled, you can monitor when changes are made to an IPSec policy using the Event Viewer. Therefore, answers B, C, and D are incorrect.

48. Answer D is correct. The IP Security Monitor utility can be opened from the Microsoft Management Console. Therefore, answers A and B are incorrect. Answer C is incorrect because this is the command used in Windows 2000 to launch IPSec Monitor.

49. Answer B is correct. The static IP addresses assigned to the servers must be excluded from the scope configured on the DHCP server. Therefore, answers C and D are incorrect. Answer A is incorrect because client reservations are created for DHCP clients that are required to lease the same IP address.

50. Answer B is correct. The IP Security Monitor included with Windows Server 2003 cannot be used to monitor computers running Windows 2000. Therefore, answers A, C, and D are incorrect.

51. Answers B and D are correct. The netsh command-line utility and IP Security Monitor can be used to view IPSec statistics. Answer A is incorrect because this command-line utility is no longer used to view IPSec-specific statistics. Answer C is incorrect because ping is used to test TCP/IP connectivity.

52. Answer D is correct. Software Update Services requires that the system partition be formatted with NTFS along with the partition on which the software will be installed. Answer A is incorrect because no service pack is required. Answer B is incorrect because the partition on which SUS is installed must be NTFS as well. Answer C is incorrect because IIS 5.0 is required.

53. Answers A, B, and C are correct. By placing a DHCP server within the branch office and configuring the remote server with 20% of the IP addresses, you can eliminate DHCP and the WAN link as points of failure. The DHCP Relay Agent is required for DHCP clients to lease an IP address from a DHCP server on a remote subnet. Answer D is incorrect because clients are not configured with the IP addresses of DHCP servers.

54. Answer C is correct. The DHCP server must be enabled to perform updates for clients that cannot update their own host records. Answer A is incorrect because DNS is already configured for dynamic updates because the Windows XP clients are successfully performing updates. Answer B is incorrect because Windows 95 clients cannot be configured to perform dynamic updates. Answer D is incorrect because a DHCP relay agent forwards IP address lease requests to a DHCP server.

55. Answer C is correct. A standalone server is not authorized in Active Directory. The Authorize option is not available on a standalone server. Therefore answers A, B, and D are incorrect.

56. Answer B is correct. By configuring an authoritative DNS server within bayside.net to host a stub zone for the sales.bayside.net zone, any updates made to the authoritative name server resource records will be updated within the parent zone as well. Therefore, answers A, C, and D are incorrect.

57. Answer B is correct. If the support tools have been installed, you can use Replication Monitor to ensure that replication between DNS servers is occurring on a regular basis. Answer A is incorrect because System Monitor is used to monitor the real-time performance of a DNS server. Answer C is incorrect because the DNS management console is used to configure and manage a DNS server but cannot be used to monitor DNS replication. Answer D is incorrect because there is no such tool as the DNS Monitor.

58. Answer D is correct. Using the Clear Cache option from the Action menu within the DNS management console allows you to delete the contents of the cache file. Although uninstalling the service would clear the contents of the cache, it's not the easiest way to perform the task; therefore, answer A is incorrect. Answer B is incorrect because deleting the file completely removes it. Answer C is incorrect because there is no Clear Cache option available from the server's Properties window.

59. Answer B is correct. This option enables you to configure how updates are downloaded and installed. Because Active Directory is not installed, the Automatic Updates settings must be configured through the Registry, not a Group Policy. Answer A is incorrect because this option enables Automatic Updates to use SUS. Answer C is incorrect because this option specifies the SUS server that updates are downloaded from. Answer D is incorrect because this option specifies which SUS server the client will send status information to.

60. Answers A and C are correct. Network Monitor can be used to monitor and log network activity. System Monitor can also be used to monitor various network components. Therefore, answers B and D are incorrect.

Practice Exam #2

Question 1

Some of the users in your organization have home offices, where they work during the weekdays. They require access to network resources, and all users can dial directly into the RAS server. Users currently have access 24 hours a day, 7 days a week. For security purposes, you want to limit the dial-in hours from 8 a.m. to 6 p.m. How should you proceed?

- O A. Configure the properties of each user account.
- O B. Configure the properties of the RAS server.
- O C. Configure the conditions of the remote access policy.
- O D. Configure the port properties.

Question 2

John is the administrator of a Windows Server 2003 network. One of the users is reporting problems when attempting to dial into a remote access server. John suspects a conflict with the remote access policies. He cannot recall the order in which elements are applied. Which of the following correctly identifies the order in which remote access policy elements are evaluated?

- O A. Permissions, conditions, profile
- O B. Conditions, permissions, profile
- O C. Conditions, properties, permissions
- O D. Profile, permissions, conditions

Question 3

You configured Windows Server 2003 as a remote access server. While enabling the service, you chose to use DHCP for IP address assignment. You are still using WINS on the internal network because you are still in the process of upgrading. Clients report that they can successfully connect but cannot access network resources using the UNC path. What must you do to resolve the problem?

- O A. You must configure a range of IP addresses on the RAS server, as well as assign any optional IP parameters to clients.
- O B. You must manually configure the IP settings on the remote access clients.
- O C. You must install the DHCP Relay Agent on the DHCP server.
- O D. You must install the DHCP Relay Agent on the RAS server.

Question 4

John made changes to a group policy object and he wants to manually refresh all settings regardless of whether they have been changed. What command should he use?

- ○ A. **secedit /refresh**
- ○ B. **gpupdate /force**
- ○ C. **gpupdate /target:computer**
- ○ D. **gpupdate /refreshpolicy**
- ○ E. **secedit /refreshpolicy**

Question 5

You have multiple RAS servers on your network. You want to centralize the authentication of remote access clients and accounting information. Which of the following services should you install?

- ○ A. IAS
- ○ B. IIS
- ○ C. RADIUS
- ○ D. RRAS

Question 6

For security purposes, smart cards are being implemented for all remote access users. Which of the following protocols is required to support smart card authentication?

- ○ A. PAP
- ○ B. EAP
- ○ C. MS-CHAP
- ○ D. SPAP

Question 7

David is the network administrator of a Windows Server 2003 network. He is configuring demand-dial routing between a server in the head office and a server within a branch office. Both servers are running Windows Server 2003. David is configuring the user account on the answering router. Which of the following statements is true?

○ A. Any user account name can be used.

○ B. The user account name should match the demand-dial interface name of the answering router.

○ C. The user account name should match the demand-dial interface name of the calling router.

○ D. The user account name must match the computer name of the answering router.

Question 8

Your internetwork consists of seven subnets. All subnets are connected using Windows Server 2003 RRAS servers. Nonpersistent demand-dial connections have been configured. You do not want to be burdened with updating the routing tables, and you want any changes to the network topology to be propagated immediately. Which of the following routing options should you implement?

○ A. Static routes

○ B. ICMP

○ C. OSPF

○ D. RIPv2

Question 9

Mary is the administrator of a Windows Server 2003 network. She added a new subnet to the existing network infrastructure. She needs to add a static route to the routing table to reach the new subnet. The subnet ID in use is 192.168.126.0. Which of the following commands would add a static route to the routing table?

○ A. **route -p 192.168.126.0 mask 255.255.255.0 192.168.125.1 metric 2**

○ B. **route add 192.168.126.0 mask 255.255.255.0 192.168.125.1 metric 2**

○ C. **route add 192.168.126.0 255.255.255.0 192.168.125.1 metric 2**

○ D. **route add 192.168.126.0 mask 255.255.255.0 gateway 192.168.125.1 metric 2**

Question 10

Brandon is configuring IP security for his network. He wants all data to be encrypted but still wants clients that do not support IPSec to be capable of authenticating with the server. What should he do?

○ A. Within the IP Security Monitor snap-in, assign the Secure Server (Require Security) policy.

○ B. Configure the settings of the appropriate group policy object and assign the Client (Respond Only) policy.

○ C. Configure the Properties of TCP/IP and assign the Secure Server (Require Security) policy.

○ D. Edit the appropriate group policy object and assign the Server (Request Security) policy.

Question 11

You are configuring IPSec between two servers in a workgroup. You assign Client (Respond Only) to each of the servers, but you notice that IP packets being sent between the two servers are not being secured. What is causing the problem?

○ A. Both are configured with the Client (Respond Only) policy.

○ B. You can use IPSec only with Active Directory.

○ C. One of the servers must be configured as an IPSec client.

○ D. The servers cannot be members of the same workgroup.

Question 12

You updated the policy settings and you want to apply changes immediately. Which of the following commands can you use?

○ A. **secedit**

○ B. **gpupdate**

○ C. **dcgpofix**

○ D. **gpresult**

Question 13

Mike is planning a VPN solution for his company network. Which of the following protocols can you use to establish a VPN tunnel with a Windows Server 2003 VPN server? (Choose all correct answers.)

- ❏ A. PPP
- ❏ B. PPTP
- ❏ C. SLIP
- ❏ D. L2TP

Question 14

John has enabled Routing and Remote Access on a computer running Windows Server 2003. Several clients establish VPN connections with the server from home offices. There are 20 clients that will be accessing the VPN server. John needs to increase the number of available PPTP ports. How can he accomplish this task?

- ○ A. From the Properties window for the server, select the Ports tab.
- ○ B. Using the Edit Profile button within the properties window for the policy, select the Ports tab.
- ○ C. Use the Properties window for the Ports option.
- ○ D. Use the PPTP tab from the Ports Properties window.

Question 15

RRAS is installed on Server1. All remote access clients are running Windows XP Professional. You want to configure the most secure authentication protocol. Which of the following should you enable?

- ○ A. PAP
- ○ B. CHAP
- ○ C. MS-CHAP version 1
- ○ D. MS-CHAP version 2

Question 16

Your network consists of three subnets: Subnet A, Subnet B, and Subnet C. There is a RRAS server on Subnet C configured with a range of IP addresses to assign to remote access clients. There are two DNS servers on the network, DNS01 and DNS02. You want remote access clients to use DNS02. What should you do?

- ○ A. Configure the RRAS server to use DHCP. Install a DHCP server on Subnet C. Configure a scope on the DHCP server for the remote access clients. Configure the DHCP relay agent on the DNS server.

- ○ B. Install a DHCP server on the network and configure the RRAS server to use DHCP for IP address assignment. Configure a scope on the DHCP server for the remote access clients.

- ○ C. Install a DHCP server on the network. Configure a scope on the DHCP server for remote access clients. Configure RRAS to use DHCP. Configure the relay agent on the DHCP server.

- ○ D. Install a DHCP server on Subnet C. Configure a scope on the DHCP server for remote access clients. Configure RRAS to use DHCP. Configure the relay agent on the RRAS server.

Question 17

Joe is the administrator of a Windows Server 2003 network. He has configured a remote access server. Because of the security requirements of the company, he creates multiple remote access policies. User A attempts to gain remote access. The connection attempt does not meet the conditions of the first remote access policy. Which of the following statements is true?

- ○ A. The connection attempt is denied.
- ○ B. The properties of the user's account are evaluated.
- ○ C. The next policy in the list is evaluated.
- ○ D. The profile settings are evaluated.

Question 18

Dayton Distributing plans to use Routing and Remote Access to give users the ability to access resources from other locations while still maintaining a high level of security. Specifically, the company president needs to be able to access resources from his home office and other locations. Network administrators also require remote access when they are working from home. You add a Windows Server 2003 server to the network and configure it as a remote access server. When configuring the dial-in properties of user accounts, how should you configure them for callback?

- ○ A. Choose No Callback for the president's account and Set by Caller for the network administrators' accounts.
- ○ B. Choose Set by Caller for the president's account and No Callback for the network administrators' accounts.
- ○ C. Choose Always Callback To for the president's account and Set by Caller for the network administrators' accounts.
- ○ D. Choose Set by Caller for the president's account and Always Callback To for the network administrators' accounts.

Question 19

Your junior network administrator was responsible for installing and configuring a remote access server. Certain users need to be able to dial directly into the server to access network resources. To test the configuration, you attempt to connect to the server but are unsuccessful. When you open the Routing and Remote Access snap-in, you notice that the default remote access policy has been deleted. What should you do?

- ○ A. Disable Routing and Remote Access and then re-enable the service.
- ○ B. Create a remote access policy.
- ○ C. Configure the dial-in properties of the user accounts.
- ○ D. Configure the remote access profile settings.

Question 20

Jim has configured two remote access policies. The profile settings of Policy A are configured so that remote access is permitted only during the hours of 8 a.m. and 5 p.m. This policy is applied to the Sales group. Policy B has no dial-in restrictions configured, and it is applied to the Managers group. Policy A is listed first. Mike is a member of the Sales and Managers groups. He attempts to dial into the remote access server at 6 p.m. Which of the following statements is true?

○ A. Mike will be permitted remote access.

○ B. Because the connection attempt does not match the profile settings of Policy A, Policy B is evaluated.

○ C. The connection attempt is denied.

○ D. The dial-in restrictions configured for Mike's user account determine whether he has remote access permission.

Question 21

You are in the process of configuring profile settings for a remote access policy. You configure the settings as shown in the following figure. Which of the following statements are true? (Choose all correct answers.)

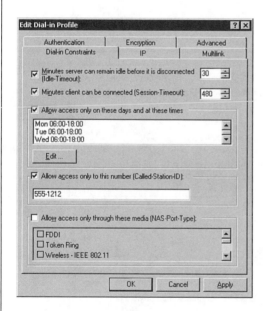

❏ A. Users will be disconnected after 8 hours of inactivity.

❏ B. Users will be disconnected after 30 minutes of inactivity.

❏ C. Users can remain connected as long as necessary.

❏ D. Users can dial in only between 6 p.m. and 6 a.m.

❏ E. Users can dial in only between 6 a.m. and 6 p.m.

❏ F. Users can dial any number for remote access.

Question 22

Mark is the administrator of a Windows Server 2003 network. A user reports that he is unable to communicate with any hosts on a remote subnet. Mark uses the **ipconfig** command to verify that TCP/IP is properly configured on the workstation. He uses the **ping** command to test whether TCP/IP is initialized on the local computer. He then pings the IP address assigned to the local workstation. Both pings have successful results. When troubleshooting the problem, what should he do next?

○ A. Ping the IP address of a local host.

○ B. Ping the IP address of the default gateway.

○ C. Ping the IP address of a remote host.

○ D. Ping the IP address of a remote router.

Question 23

John captured a large amount of network traffic using Network Monitor. He wants to limit the captured information to only display traffic containing the SMB protocol. What should he do?

○ A. Configure a trigger.

○ B. Configure a capture filter.

○ C. Configure a display filter.

○ D. Configure a packet filter.

Question 24

Mary is the network administrator. She wants to give Joe the ability to view real-time data as it is captured using System Monitor. Joe should be able to perform this task from the server or from his workstation. What should Mary do?

○ A. Add his user account to the Performance Log Users group.

○ B. Add his user account to the Administrators group.

○ C. Add his user account to the Performance Monitor Users group.

○ D. Add his user account to the Domain Admins group.

Question 25

Bob is running Network Monitor to analyze specific types of network traffic. He wants to configure Network Monitor to only gather information pertaining to specific protocols and traffic type. What should he do?

- ○ A. Configure a display filter.
- ○ B. Configure a capture filter.
- ○ C. Configure a trigger.
- ○ D. Configure an IP packet filter.

Question 26

Susan is putting together a performance report for her managers. She wants to gather statistics about the total amount of TCP/IP traffic on the local computer. Which of the following counters should she monitor?

- ○ A. Packet Outbound Errors
- ○ B. TCP Segments/sec
- ○ C. IP Datagrams/sec
- ○ D. Logons/sec

Question 27

You are having trouble connecting to your ISP using a dial-up connection. You want to verify the TCP/IP configuration on the local computer. Which utility should you use?

- ○ A. **ipconfig**
- ○ B. **ping**
- ○ C. **tracert**
- ○ D. **pathping**

Question 28

A computer running Windows Server 2003 connects to the Internet through a dial-up connection. You are having problems establishing a connection and you want to verify that the modem is working. Which of the following can you use to verify the status of the modem?

○ A. System Monitor

○ B. Network Monitor

○ C. **ping**

○ D. Device Manager

Question 29

Mary is gathering network-performance statistics on a Windows Server 2003 domain controller. She wants to determine the number of logons the domain controller has received since the last time it was restarted. Which counter should she monitor?

○ A. Logons Received Total

○ B. Logon Total

○ C. Logons Received/sec

○ D. Logons/sec

Question 30

Clients on the network are unable to obtain an IP address from the DHCP server on the network. You soon discover that the DHCP service on the server has failed to start. You reboot the server and the service still does not start. What should you do?

○ A. Continue to reboot the server until the service starts.

○ B. Verify that any services DHCP depends on are started using the Services console.

○ C. Use the DHCP console to start the service.

○ D. Reinstall the DHCP service.

Question 31

Bill is configuring the service-recovery options for the server service on a Windows Server 2003 domain controller. If a service fails to start, which of the following actions can he perform? (Choose all correct answers.)

❑ A. The computer can attempt to restart the service.

❑ B. He can reboot the computer.

❑ C. He can restart the services that it depends on.

❑ D. He can send an email message to the network administrator.

Question 32

A new network service is added to the existing infrastructure. You want to determine how much more traffic is generated since it was installed. Which of the following tools can you use to capture and analyze network traffic?

○ A. Network Performance

○ B. Network Diagnostics

○ C. Network Monitor

○ D. Network Manager

Question 33

Which of the following command-line utilities can you use to view a list of all the routers a packet passes through to reach a specific destination host?

○ A. **ping**

○ B. **tracert**

○ C. **arp**

○ D. **ipconfig**

Question 34

A new service pack has just been released for Windows Server 2003. You download the service pack. What should you do before installing it?

- ○ A. Notify users that the server will be down.
- ○ B. Take all production servers offline.
- ○ C. Install the service pack in a test environment.
- ○ D. You need do nothing but proceed with the installation.

Question 35

Diane finished installing Windows Server 2003. She is in the process of performing some basic steps to secure the operating system. She wants to implement the principle of least privilege. What should she do?

- ○ A. Create a new user account for herself and add it to the local Administrators group so that she can perform administrative tasks at any time.
- ○ B. Nothing. She should always log on with the Administrators account.
- ○ C. Create a new group and add the group to the local Administrators group. Create a user account for herself and add it to the new group.
- ○ D. Create two user accounts: one with restrictive permissions for performing daily tasks and the other with additional privileges for performing administrative tasks.

Question 36

Sean finished running the Security Configuration and Analysis utility on a domain controller. He notices that several of the results appear with a red X beside them. What does this red X indicate?

- ○ A. It indicates that the system settings correspond with those in the template.
- ○ B. It indicates that the configured system settings do not match those in the template.
- ○ C. It indicates that these values do not need to be configured based on the server role.
- ○ D. It indicates that these settings have not been configured.

Question 37

Joe has just made changes to the security settings on a domain controller. He is concerned that the changes will not be automatically updated. What is the default interval at which security settings are automatically refreshed on a domain controller?

- ○ A. 24 hours
- ○ B. 60 minutes
- ○ C. 5 minutes
- ○ D. 60 seconds

Question 38

Mary is testing the impact of various security settings within a test environment. She makes several changes to the security settings on a standalone server. What is the default interval at which security settings are automatically refreshed on a workstation or server?

- ○ A. 24 hours
- ○ B. 12 hours
- ○ C. 120 minutes
- ○ D. 90 minutes

Question 39

Auditing is enabled for the Bayside network. Tony is the senior network administrator and suspects that one of the junior network administrators has made changes to some of the settings with the group policy object. Which log file should Tony use to verify his suspicions?

- ○ A. Application
- ○ B. Audit
- ○ C. Security
- ○ D. System

Question 40

Mary is planning to install SUS. Which of the following are considered to be minimum hardware requirements for installing SUS? (Choose all correct answers.)

- ❑ A. Pentium III 500MHz
- ❑ B. Pentium III 700MHz
- ❑ C. 265MB RAM
- ❑ D. 512MB RAM
- ❑ E. 4GB storage space
- ❑ F. 6GB storage space

Question 41

Which of the following correctly identifies the order of steps in which the IP address lease process occurs?

- ○ A. **DHCPAck, DHCPRequest, DHCPDiscover, DHCPOffer**
- ○ B. **DHCPRequest, DHCPAck, DHCPDiscover, DHCPOffer**
- ○ C. **DHCPDiscover, DHCPOffer, DHCPAck, DHCPRequest**
- ○ D. **DHCPDiscover, DHCPOffer, DHCPRequest, DHCPAck**

Question 42

Ryan finished configuring a new DHCP server. He installed the service and configured and activated a scope. Ryan now needs to authorize the DHCP server. Which administrative tool can he use to perform this task?

- ○ A. Active Directory Users and Computers
- ○ B. DHCP console
- ○ C. Active Directory Sites and Services
- ○ D. Service applet

Question 43

Mike is adding a new DHCP server to the network. Of the following, which steps must he complete for the DHCP server to function on the network? (Choose all correct answers.)

❏ A. Install DHCP.

❏ B. Activate a scope.

❏ C. Configure a scope.

❏ D. Authorize the DHCP server.

❏ E. Configure the scope options.

❏ F. Install Active Directory on the local server.

❏ G. Enable dynamic updates.

Question 44

Your DHCP server must support multicasting. When configuring a multicast scope, which IP address range can you use?

○ A. 192.160.0.1–192.168.0.255

○ B. 127.0.0.1–127.0.0.255

○ C. 169.254.0.1–169.254.255.254

○ D. 224.0.0.1–239.255.255.255

Question 45

Your network consists of two subnets: Subnet A and Subnet B. Each has its own DHCP server. You configure the scope on DHCP1 for Subnet A. Users are all leasing an IP address but report that they cannot access any resources outside of their own subnet. How can you most easily solve the problem?

○ A. Activate the scope on DHCP1.

○ B. Configure the default gateway on each workstation.

○ C. Configure the 003 router option on DHCP1.

○ D. Configure the 006 DNS server option on DHCP1.

Question 46

Which of the following components is responsible for negotiating security between IPSec-enabled hosts?

- ○ A. IP Security Policy Management
- ○ B. ISAKMP/OAKLEY
- ○ C. IPSec Driver
- ○ D. IPSec Policy Agent

Question 47

You use a DHCP server to assign IP addresses to clients and member servers on the network. Three of the member servers host print devices. How can you ensure that these print servers lease the same IP address from the DHCP server? (Choose all correct answers.)

- ❑ A. Exclude the IP addresses from the scope.
- ❑ B. Create a separate scope for each of the print servers.
- ❑ C. Create a client reservation for each print server.
- ❑ D. Configure the DHCP options for the scope.

Question 48

Because of security needs and the different needs of dial-in clients, you configure three remote access policies. When a remote access client attempts to connect to a remote access server, which of the following statements is true regarding policy evaluation?

- ○ A. All policies in the list are evaluated.
- ○ B. The first policy to match the conditions of the connection attempt is evaluated.
- ○ C. Only the first policy in the list is evaluated.
- ○ D. The first policy that gives the user remote access is evaluated.

Question 49

Your primary DNS server is located in the corporate head office. The five branch offices are all configured with secondary DNS servers. The WAN links between offices are extremely slow. You want to increase the interval at which secondary servers poll the primary server for updates to the zone file. Which of the following settings should you change?

○ A. Retry interval

○ B. Serial number

○ C. Refresh interval

○ D. Time to Live

Question 50

You recently deployed a DHCP server to centralize the administration of all IP addresses on the network. Prior to this step, all IP addresses were statically configured. All users are successfully leasing IP addresses but sometimes report that they cannot print to the network interface printers. The printers are not configured as DHCP clients and are still configured with static IP addresses. Upon examining the event log, you notice there are IP address conflicts. What should you do?

○ A. Define separate scopes for each of the print devices.

○ B. Create client reservations for the print devices.

○ C. Exclude the IP addresses of the print devices from the scope.

○ D. Create client exclusions for the print devices.

Question 51

FKB Consulting hosts a primary DNS server in the corporate head office. The five branch offices are all configured with secondary DNS servers. Each branch office is now being configured with a second DNS server. You do not want any more traffic generated on the WAN links or the LAN from zone transfers. How should you configure the new DNS servers?

○ A. Configure the new servers as secondary DNS servers with the existing secondary DNS servers as master name servers.

○ B. Configure the new DNS servers as caching-only servers.

○ C. Configure the new DNS servers as secondary DNS servers with the primary DNS server as the master name server.

○ D. Configure the new DNS servers as primary DNS servers.

Question 52

John is configuring a remote access server. All workstations requiring remote access are running Windows XP Professional. John wants all remote access users to authenticate using MS-CHAP version 2. What should he do?

○ A. Enable MS-CHAP version 2 through the Properties of the remote access server.

○ B. Edit the conditions of the remote access policy and enable MS-CHAP version 2.

○ C. Configure the profile of the remote access policy and enable MS-CHAP version 2.

○ D. Enable MS-CHAP version 2 through the Properties of each user account.

Question 53

Your network consists of two subnets: Subnet A and Subnet B. Subnet A has a WINS server that is used by all clients on the network to resolve NetBIOS names to IP addresses. A Windows Server 2003 DHCP server assigns IP addresses to clients. The DHCP 044 WINS/NBNS Servers option is configured at the scope level to assign clients the IP address of WINSRV A. You move the WINS server from Subnet A to Subnet B and configure the 044 WINS/NBNS option at the server level to assign clients the new IP address of the WINS server. You discover that clients are still being assigned the old IP address. What is causing the problem?

○ A. Clients must use the **ipconfig /renew** command to obtain the new WINS IP address.

○ B. The IP address of the WINS server must be statically configured on client workstations.

○ C. You must configure the 046 WINS/NBT node type.

○ D. The new 044 WINS/NBNS option must be configured at the scope level.

Question 54

You are asked to ensure that the IPSec policy put into place secures all communications while still allowing non-IPSec–aware clients to authenticate. Which of the following policies should you use?

- O A. Client (Respond Only)
- O B. Server (Request Security)
- O C. Secure Server (Require Security)
- O D. Secure Client (Respond Only)

Question 55

Users on the network require remote access. All users should have the same remote access security requirements except the Administrators group. How should you configure RRAS?

- O A. Create two groups within RRAS, one for users and one for administrators. Create two remote access policies and use the Windows Groups condition to apply each policy to the appropriate set of users.
- O B. Create two groups within Active Directory User and Computers, one for users and one for administrators. Create two remote access policies and use the Windows Groups condition to apply each policy to the appropriate set of users.
- O C. Create two groups within RRAS. Configure different settings within a single policy for each group.
- O D. Create two access policies. Using the Dial-In tab for each user account, specify which remote access policy should be applied.

Question 56

Which of the following commands allows you to clear the DNS resolver cache on a Windows XP Professional workstation?

- O A. **ipconfig /clearcache**
- O B. **ipconfig /all**
- O C. **ipconfig /flushdns**
- O D. **ipconfig /cleardns**

Question 57

You are implementing an IP security policy for your network. SRV1 requires the highest level of security because it hosts sensitive company data. SRV2 does not require this level of security but should respond to any requests for secure communication. How should you proceed? (Choose two.)

❑ A. Assign the Server (Request Security) policy on SRV1.

❑ B. Assign the Secure Server (Require Security) policy on SRV1.

❑ C. Assign the Client (Respond Only) policy on SRV2.

❑ D. Assign the Server (Request Security) policy on SRV2.

❑ E. Assign the Secure Server (Require Security) policy on SRV2.

❑ F. Assign the Client (Respond Only) policy on SRV1.

Question 58

Your internetwork consists of 10 subnets. All subnets are connected using Windows Server 2003 RRAS servers. You configured nonpersistent demand-dial connections. You do not want to manually update routing tables. You want to configure password authentication between routers. Which of the following should you implement?

○ A. Static routes

○ B. ICMP

○ C. OSPF

○ D. RIPv2

Question 59

Which of the following statements is true regarding two-way demand-dial connections?

○ A. The user account name on the answering router must match the demand-dial interface name on the calling router.

○ B. The demand-dial interface names must be identical.

○ C. The user account names on both routers must be identical.

○ D. The user account name on the answering router must be different from the interface name on the calling router.

Question 60

Which of the following parameters can you use with the **route** command to ensure that a static route is not deleted from the routing table upon restart?

○ A. **/f**

○ B. **/s**

○ C. **/r**

○ D. **/p**

Answer Key for Practice Exam #2

1. C	16. D	31. A, B	46. B
2. B	17. C	32. C	47. A, C
3. D	18. D	33. B	48. B
4. B	19. B	34. C	49. C
5. A	20. C	35. D	50. C
6. B	21. B, E	36. B	51. B
7. C	22. B	37. C	52. B
8. D	23. C	38. D	53. D
9. B	24. C	39. C	54. B
10. D	25. B	40. B, D, F	55. B
11. A	26. C	41. D	56. C
12. B	27. A	42. B	57. B, C
13. B, D	28. D	43. A, B, C, D	58. D
14. C	29. B	44. D	59. A
15. D	30. B	45. C	60. D

Question 1

Answer C is correct. You can set day and time restrictions for remote users by configuring the conditions of the remote access policy. Answer A is incorrect because day and time restrictions are no longer configured through the properties of a user account as they were in Windows NT 4.0. You cannot configure day and time restrictions by configuring the properties of the remote access server or the ports; therefore, answers B and D are incorrect.

Question 2

Answer B is correct. Policy elements are evaluated in the following order: conditions, permissions, profile. Therefore, answers A and D are incorrect. Answer C is incorrect because "properties" is not a remote access policy element.

Question 3

Answer D is correct. You need to configure the clients with the IP address of the WINS server. To do so, you must install the DHCP Relay Agent on the RAS server so that it can forward DHCPInform messages between the clients and the DHCP server. Answer A is incorrect because you cannot configure optional parameters on the RAS server. You can configure clients with the IP address of the WINS server; however, it's easier from a management perspective to centralize IP address assignment and use a relay agent instead. Therefore, answer B is incorrect. Answer C is incorrect because the DHCP Relay Agent isn't installed on a DHCP server.

Question 4

Answer B is correct. You use the gpupdate /force command to manually refresh all settings regardless of whether they have changed. Answers A and E are incorrect because secedit was the command used in Windows 2000 to refresh policy changes. Answer C is incorrect because this command refreshes only the computer settings. Answer D is incorrect because the gpupdate command does not support the /refreshpolicy switch.

Question 5

Answer A is correct. To centralize the authentication of remote access clients and accounting information, you should install the Internet Authentication Service (IAS). Answer B is incorrect because IIS is for Web hosting. Answer C is incorrect because RADIUS is the protocol used by IAS to provide authentication and accounting services. Answer D is incorrect because Routing and Remote Access Service (RRAS) is not used to centralize authentication and accounting information, but to provide a variety of services, including remote access, VPN, and routing.

Question 6

Answer B is correct. The Extensible Authentication Protocol (EAP) is required to support smart card authentication. Answers A, C, and D are incorrect because they do not support smart card authentication.

Question 7

Answer C is correct. When you create demand-dial connections, the user account name on the answering router must match the demand-dial interface name on the calling router. Therefore, answers A, B, and D are incorrect.

Question 8

Answer D is correct. To have changes propagated throughout the network when changes occur, and to reduce the administrative overhead associated with updating the routing tables, a routing protocol is required. Because you cannot use OSPF with nonpersistent connections, you must use RIPv2 (or RIPv1). Therefore, answers A and C are incorrect. Answer B is incorrect because ICMP is not a routing protocol.

Question 9

Answer B is correct. The correct syntax when adding new static routes using the `route` command is `route add <network> mask <subnetmask> <gateway> metric`. Therefore, answers A, C, and D are incorrect.

Question 10

Answer D is correct. If you assign the Server (Request Security) policy, the server always attempts secure communications. Unsecured communications are still allowed if the client is not IPSec aware. Answer A is incorrect because communications are not allowed if the client is not IPSec aware. Answer B is incorrect because Assigning Client (Respond Only) means that the server responds only to requests for secure communications but does not attempt to secure all communications. Answer C is incorrect because IPSec is not configured through the Properties of TCP/IP.

Question 11

Answer A is correct. If both servers are configured with the Client (Respond Only) policy, they respond only to requests for secure communications. You must configure both of the servers with Server (Require Security). Answer B is incorrect because you can configure IPSec through Active Directory or on the local computer. Answer C is incorrect because computers are not configured as IPSec clients. Answer D is incorrect because the workgroup membership has no impact on how servers respond to security.

Question 12

Answer B is correct. To refresh policy settings, you can use the gpupdate command. Answer A is incorrect because it was the command used in Windows 2000. Answer C is incorrect because this command restores default group policy objects to their original state. Answer D is incorrect because this command displays group policy settings for a computer.

Question 13

Answers B and D are correct. The two tunneling protocols supported by Windows Server 2003 are the Point-to-Point Tunneling Protocol (PPTP) and the Layer 2 Tunneling Protocol (L2TP). PPP and SLIP establish dial-up connections. Therefore, answers A and C are incorrect.

Question 14

Answer C is correct. To increase the number of available PPTP ports, open the Ports Properties window within the Routing and Remote Access management console. Select PPTP and click Configure. Therefore, answers A, B, and D are incorrect.

Question 15

Answer D is correct. Because all the remote access users are running Windows XP Professional, the authentication protocol should be MS-CHAP version 2. Answers B and C are incorrect because they are not as secure as MS-CHAP version 2. Answer A is incorrect because PAP sends credentials in cleartext and should only be used for non-Windows clients.

Question 16

Answer D is correct. Install a DHCP server on Subnet C and configure it with a scope for remote access clients. The scope should assign the clients the IP address of the DHCP server. Configure RRAS to use DHCP and configure it as a relay agent. This step ensures that remote users are assigned the IP address of the DNS server. Therefore, answers A, B, and C are incorrect.

Question 17

Answer C is correct. If the connection attempt does not match the conditions of the first policy in the list, the conditions of the next policy are evaluated. The permissions and profile settings of a policy are not evaluated until the connection attempt meets the conditions of a policy. Therefore, answers A, B, and D are incorrect.

Question 18

Answer D is correct. Because the president needs remote access from various locations, you should select the Set by Caller option. To limit where network administrators can dial in from, select Always Callback to. In this way, the remote access server always calls them back at the configured phone numbers, ensuring that is where they are attempting remote access. Selecting No Callback disables this feature. Therefore, answers A, B, and C are incorrect.

Question 19

Answer B is correct. If you delete the default remote access policy and no other policy exists, users will not be permitted remote access. Therefore, you must create a remote access policy to solve the problem. Answer A is incorrect because disabling and then enabling Routing and Remote Access re-creates the default policy, but it is not the easiest solution. You would have to reconfigure the remote access server afterward. Answer C is incorrect because dial-in permission can be granted through the properties of a user account, but a policy must still exist. Answer D is incorrect because you cannot configure profile settings until you create a policy.

Question 20

Answer C is correct because the connection attempt matches the conditions of the first policy. The permissions and profile settings of this policy are evaluated. The profile settings restrict dial-in access after 5 p.m., so the connection attempt is denied. Therefore, answer A is incorrect. Answer B is incorrect because if a connection attempt does not meet the profile settings of a policy, no other policies in the list are evaluated. Answer D is incorrect because day and time restrictions are not configured through the user account properties.

Question 21

Answers B and E are correct. The profile settings disconnect a session after 30 minutes of idle time, restrict the maximum session to 8 hours, allow users remote access during the hours of 6 a.m. and 6 p.m., and allow users to dial in to a specified number. Therefore, answers A, C, D, and F are incorrect.

Question 22

Answer B is correct. When troubleshooting connectivity problems using the ping command, it is recommended that you use the following steps: ping the loopback address, ping the IP address of the local computer, ping the IP address of the default gateway, and then ping the IP address of a remote host. Therefore, answers A, C, and D are incorrect.

Question 23

Answer C is correct. By configuring a display filter within Network Monitor, you can filter captured data to only display specific types of information. Answer A is incorrect because triggers enable actions to be performed based on a set of conditions that must first be met. Answer B is incorrect because capture filters specify the type of information that is captured. Answer D is incorrect because packet filters specify the type of inbound and outbound traffic a computer can accept.

Question 24

Answer C is correct. By adding his user account to the Performance Monitor Users group, Joe can view performance counter data within System Monitor locally or across the network. Answer A is incorrect because adding Joe to the Performance Log Users group gives him permission to manage logs and alerts as well. Answers A and B are incorrect because it would give Joe administrative permissions to the server. Adding his user account to the Domain Admins group would give him too many permissions; therefore, answer D is incorrect.

Question 25

Answer B is correct. If you configure a capture filter, Network Monitor only captures data that meets the criteria you specify. Answer A is incorrect because display filters filter data that has already been captured. Answer C is incorrect because triggers are configured to specify an action that should occur when certain criteria are met. Answer D is incorrect because IP packet filters are used to specify the type of traffic that is permitted to reach a computer.

Question 26

Answer C is correct. By monitoring IP Datagrams/sec, you can monitor the total amount of IP datagrams sent and received by the computer each second. Answer A is incorrect because it is the number of outbound packets that could not be transmitted because of errors. Answer B is incorrect because this counter only monitors the number of TCP segments sent each second. Answer D is incorrect because this counter monitors the number of logon requests received each second by the computer.

Question 27

Answer A is correct. You can use the ipconfig command to verify the TCP/IP configuration of a computer. Answer B is incorrect because you use the ping command to verify connectivity with a remote host. Answer C is incorrect because you use tracert to trace the route a packet takes to reach a remote host. Answer D is incorrect because pathping is a combination of ping and tracert used to determine which routers and gateways between two hosts might not be functioning.

Question 28

Answer D is correct. You can use Device Manager to verify that a hardware device is functioning properly. Answer A is incorrect because System Monitor monitors performance. Answer B is incorrect because you use Network Monitor to capture and analyze network traffic. Answer C is incorrect because ping is a command-line utility used to verify network connectivity.

Question 29

Answer B is correct. The Logon Total counter determines the number of logon requests the domain controller has received since the last time it was restarted. Answers A and C are incorrect because there are no such counters within System Monitor. Answer D is incorrect because this counter determines the number of logon requests received each second.

Question 30

Answer B is correct. If the service does not start, use the Services console to verify that any services that DHCP depends on are also started. Therefore, answer A is incorrect. Answer C is incorrect because if the service fails to start, attempting to start it within the DHCP console makes no difference. Answer D is incorrect because it should be a last resort in terms of troubleshooting.

Question 31

Answers A and B are correct. If a service fails to start, you can configure the computer to automatically attempt to restart the service, or you can have the computer automatically reboot. The third option is to have a specific program run. Answers C and D are incorrect because recovery actions do not include the ability to automatically restart the failed service's dependencies nor send an email to the network administrator.

Question 32

Answer C is correct. You can use Network Monitor to capture and analyze network traffic. Answers A and D are incorrect because there are no such utilities included with Windows Server 2003. Answer B is incorrect because you use Network Diagnostics to gather information about the hardware, software, and services running on a local computer.

Question 33

Answer B is correct. You can use the `tracert` utility to view a list of routers a packet must pass through to reach a destination host. Answer A is incorrect because you use `ping` to test TCP/IP connectivity. Answer C is incorrect because ARP is the protocol used to map IP addresses to hardware addresses. Answer D is incorrect because you use `ipconfig` to view the IP configuration of a computer.

Question 34

Answer C is correct. Before installing any new service packs, it is recommended that you test them first to determine any risks and vulnerabilities that they can introduce. Therefore, answers A, B, and D are incorrect.

Question 35

Answer D is correct. The principle of least privilege is based on the idea that a user should log on with a user account that has minimum privileges. Therefore, Mary should create two accounts: one with restrictive permissions that she can use to perform day-to-day tasks and the other with additional privileges for performing administrative tasks. Answers A, B, and C are incorrect because they go against the principle of least privilege by providing administrative access.

Question 36

Answer B is correct. When you see a red X beside a setting after running the Security Configuration and Analysis utility, the value for that computer setting does not match the value in the template. Therefore, answers A, C, and D are incorrect.

Question 37

Answer C is correct. Security settings for a domain controller are automatically refreshed every 5 minutes. Answers A, B, and D are incorrect because they do not represent the correct value.

Question 38

Answer D is correct. The security settings on a workstation or server are automatically refreshed every 90 minutes. Answers A, B, and C are incorrect because they do not represent the correct value.

Question 39

Answer C is correct. When auditing is enabled, events are written to the Security log. Answer A is incorrect because events generated by applications are written to the Application log. Answer B is incorrect because there is no Audit log. Answer D is incorrect because the System log contains events generated by Windows components.

Question 40

Answers B, D, and F are correct. The minimum hardware requirements to install SUS include Pentium III 700MHz, 512MB of RAM, and 6GB of storage space. Answers A, C, and E are incorrect because they do not represent the correct hardware requirements.

Question 41

Answer D is correct. The IP address lease process occurs in the following order: DHCPDiscover, DHCPOffer, DHCPRequest, and DHCPAck. Therefore, answers A, B, and C are incorrect.

Question 42

Answer B is correct. You authorize a DHCP server using the DHCP console by right-clicking the server and choosing the Authorize option. Answers A, C, and D are incorrect because you cannot use these tools to authorize DHCP.

Question 43

Answers A, B, C, and D are correct. For a DHCP server to lease IP addresses to clients, you must install the service, create and activate a scope, and authorize the server. Answer E is incorrect because configuring scope options is not required. Answers F and G are incorrect because Active Directory does not need to be installed on the local server and dynamic updates do not need to be enabled for DHCP to function.

Question 44

Answer D is correct. When creating a multicast scope, you can use IP addresses in the range of 224.0.0.1–239.255.255.255. Answers A, B, and C are incorrect because they represent incorrect address ranges.

Question 45

Answer C is correct. If clients are not configured with the IP address of the default gateway, they cannot access resources outside of their local subnet. Answer A is incorrect because the clients are already successfully leasing IP addresses from the server. Answer B would solve the problem, but it would not be the easiest solution; therefore, it is also incorrect. Answer D is incorrect because configuring the DNS server option allows clients to resolve hostnames but does not give them access outside of the local subnet.

Question 46

Answer B is correct. ISAKMP/OAKLEY is responsible for negotiating security associations before any IP data is transferred. This process includes authentication, hashing, and encryption methods. Answer A is incorrect because it is a management tool used for creating and managing IP Security policies. Answer C is incorrect because the IPSec driver is responsible for securing the data before it is transferred. Answer D is incorrect because the IPSec Policy Agent is responsible for retrieving policy information.

Question 47

Answers A and C are correct. By creating a client reservation for each of the print servers, you ensure that they always lease the same IP address. You must also exclude the IP addresses from the scope to avoid any IP address conflicts. Therefore, answers B and D are incorrect.

Question 48

Answer B is correct. The first elements in a remote access policy to be evaluated are the conditions. The first policy to match the conditions of the connection attempt is evaluated for permissions. If the permissions of that policy deny the user access, the connection attempt is denied. Therefore, answers A, C, and D are incorrect.

Question 49

Answer C is correct. The refresh interval determines how often the secondary servers poll the primary server for updates to the zone database file. Answer A is incorrect because the retry interval determines how often a secondary server continues to contact the primary server if it does not respond. Answer B is incorrect because the serial number is used to determine when the zone data has been updated. Answer D is incorrect because Time to Live (TTL) specifies how long records from that zone should remain in the cache.

Question 50

Answer C is correct. To eliminate any IP address conflicts, the IP addresses assigned to the print devices should be excluded from the scope. Answer B is incorrect because client reservations are configured for DHCP clients that must lease the same IP address each time. Answer A is incorrect because scopes are not defined for individual IP addresses. Answer D is incorrect because there is no option in DHCP called a client exclusion.

Question 51

Answer B is correct. If you place a caching-only server in each branch office, no additional traffic is generated from zone transfers. Answers A and C are incorrect because each of these solutions result in zone transfer traffic on the WAN link or LAN. Answer D is incorrect because a primary DNS server already exists for the zone.

Question 52

Answer B is correct. The authentication protocol must be enabled through the profile settings for the remote access policy. Therefore, answers A, C, and D are incorrect.

Question 53

Answer D is correct. Because there is an existing 044 WINS/NBNS option configured at the scope level with the old IP address of the WINS server, it is overwriting the new one configured at the server level. DHCP options configured at the scope level override those configured at the server level. Therefore, answers A and B are incorrect. Answer C is incorrect because configuring this option defines how the client resolves NetBIOS names.

Question 54

Answer B is correct. If you assign the Server (Request Security) policy, the server attempts secure communications with clients. If the client is not IPSec aware, it is still able to authenticate. Answer A is incorrect because the server responds only to client requests for secure communications. Answer C is incorrect because the server requires secure communications and does not allow sessions for non-IPSec–aware clients. Answer D is incorrect because there is no such default policy.

Question 55

Answer B is correct. To use the Windows Groups condition, you must first create the groups within Active Directory Users and Computers. You should create and configure two policies with the appropriate settings. Use the Windows Groups condition to specify the group of users to which the policy should apply. Therefore, answers A, C, and D are incorrect.

Question 56

Answer C is correct. To clear the contents of the client resolver cache, use the `ipconfig` command with the `flushdns` parameter. Answers A and D are incorrect because there are no such parameters available with the `ipconfig` command. Answer B is incorrect because it displays the current TCP/IP parameters configured on the client.

Question 57

Answers B and C are correct. SRV1 should be using the Server (Require Security) policy. This policy ensures that only secure communications are permitted. SRV2 should be using the Client (Respond Only) policy. This policy ensures that the server does not require secure communications but responds to any requests for it. Therefore, answers A, D, E, and F are incorrect.

Question 58

Answer D is correct. RIPv2 is a routing protocol that you can use with non-persistent connections and that supports password authentication between routers. Answer A is incorrect because implementing static routes means the routing tables must be manually updated. Answer B is incorrect because ICMP is not a routing protocol. Answer C is incorrect because OSPF is not supported by nonpersistent demand-dial connections.

Question 59

Answer A is correct. When you configure a two-way demand-dial connection, the user account names on the answering routers must be identical to the demand-dial interface names on the calling routers. Therefore, answers B, C, and D are incorrect.

Question 60

Answer D is correct. You use the /p parameter to add a persistent route to the routing table. The route will not be removed from the routing table when the router is restarted. Therefore, answers A, B, and C are incorrect.

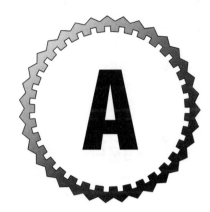

Additional Resources

. . . .

A lot of information is available about the topics covered in Exam 70-291, "Implementing, Managing, and Maintaining a Windows Server 2003 Network Infrastructure," and Microsoft certifications. This appendix distills some of the best resources we've found on those topics.

Web Resources

➤ Microsoft's Training and Certification home: www.microsoft.com/traincert/default.asp

➤ Windows 2003 Server home from Microsoft: www.microsoft.com/windowsserver2003/default.mspx

➤ Windows Server 2003 Deployment Kit online: www.microsoft.com/windowsserver2003/techinfo/reskit/deploykit.mspx

➤ Search TechNet on the Web: www.microsoft.com/technet

➤ Windows 2003 Deployment Guide: www.microsoft.com/windows2000/techinfo/reskit/dpg/default.asp

➤ CramSession's exam information and study guides: www.cramsession.com/

➤ MCMCSE certification resources: www.mcmcse.com/

➤ 2000 Trainer exam resources: www.2000trainers.com/default.aspx?tab=links

➤ TechTarget's Windows 2000 repository: http://searchwin2000.techtarget.com/

➤ Paul Thurrott's SuperSite for Windows: www.winsupersite.com/

➤ Active Network's PC and Windows resource: www.activewin.com

➤ Webopedia's online dictionary and search engine for computer and Internet technologies: www.pcwebopedia.com/

Magazine Resources

➤ *Microsoft Certified Professional Magazine* is directly targeted at those certified by Microsoft: www.mcpmag.com

➤ *Certification Magazine* specializes in information for IT certified individuals: www.certmag.com

➤ *Windows & .NET Magazine* focuses specifically on Microsoft technologies: www.winnetmag.com

➤ *Online Learning* is a resource for professional training and development: http://onlinelearningmag.com

➤ *Computer* magazine is developed by the Institute of Electrical and Electronics Engineers (IEEE): www.computer.org/computer/

➤ *PC Magazine* is a staple for technology enthusiasts: www.pcmag.com

Book Resources

➤ Balladelli, Micky et al. *Mission Critical Active Directory*. Boston, MA: Digital Press, 2001. This book provides the techniques required to design and administer Active Directory.

➤ *Microsoft Windows 2003 Deployment Kit*. Redmond, WA: Microsoft Press, June 2003. This book and CD set includes invaluable additional detailed documentation on Windows Server 2003.

➤ *Microsoft Windows Server 2003 Administrator's Pocket Consultant*. Redmond, WA: Microsoft Press, March 2003. This book covers the core procedures and everyday tasks associated with Windows Server 2003.

➤ Minasi, Mark. *Mastering Windows Server 2003*. San Francisco, CA: Sybex, April 2003. This book contains in-depth information on how to plan, install, and configure Windows Server 2003.

➤ Russel, Charlie et al. *Microsoft Windows Server 2003 Administrator's Companion*. Redmond, WA: Microsoft Press, April 2003. This book details many of the complex features and capabilities of Windows Server 2003. It's a great handbook for any network administrator.

➤ Tittel, Ed et al. *Windows Server 2003 for Dummies*. New York, NY: Dummies Press, February 2003. This guide walks you through the steps to install, configure, secure, and manage Windows Server 2003.

➤ Wells, Linda et al. *Deploying Virtual Private Networks with Microsoft Windows Server 2003 Technical Reference*. Redmond, WA: Microsoft Press, October 2003. This technical reference provides IT administrators with the knowledge required to implement and manage VPNs in a Windows Server 2003 environment.

➤ *Windows Server 2003 Resource Kit*. Redmond, WA: Microsoft Press, October 2003. This reference kit provides in-depth technical information about managing and optimizing Windows Server 2003.

What's on the CD

This appendix is a brief rundown of what you'll find on the CD-ROM that comes with this book. For a more detailed description of the PrepLogic Practice Tests, Preview Edition exam-simulation software, see Appendix C, "Using the PrepLogic Practice Tests, Preview Edition Software." In addition to the PrepLogic Practice Tests, Preview Edition, the CD-ROM includes the electronic version of the book in Portable Document Format (PDF) and several utility and application programs.

PrepLogic Practice Tests, Preview Edition

PrepLogic is a leading provider of certification training tools. Trusted by certification students worldwide, PrepLogic is, we believe, the best practice exam software available. In addition to providing a means of evaluating your knowledge of the Exam Cram 2 material, PrepLogic Practice Tests, Preview Edition features several innovations that help you to improve your mastery of the subject matter.

For example, the practice tests allow you to check your score by exam area or domain to determine which topics you need to study more. Another feature allows you to obtain immediate feedback on your responses in the form of explanations for the correct and incorrect answers.

PrepLogic Practice Tests, Preview Edition exhibits most of the full functionality of the Premium Edition but offers only a fraction of the total questions. To get the complete set of practice questions and exam functionality, visit PrepLogic.com and order the Premium Edition for this and other challenging exam titles.

Again, for a more detailed description of the PrepLogic Practice Tests, Preview Edition features, see Appendix C.

Using the PrepLogic Practice Tests, Preview Edition Software

This Exam Cram 2 includes a special version of PrepLogic Practice Tests— a revolutionary test engine designed to give you the best in certification exam preparation. PrepLogic offers sample and practice exams for many of today's most in-demand and challenging technical certifications. This special Preview Edition is included with this book as a tool to use in assessing your knowledge of the Exam Cram 2 material while also providing you with the experience of taking an electronic exam.

This appendix describes in detail what PrepLogic Practice Tests, Preview Edition is, how it works, and what it can do to help you prepare for the exam. Note that although the Preview Edition includes all the test-simulation functions of the complete retail version, it contains only a single practice test. The Premium Edition, available at PrepLogic.com, contains the complete set of challenging practice exams designed to optimize your learning experience.

Exam Simulation

One of the main functions of PrepLogic Practice Tests, Preview Edition is exam simulation. To prepare you to take the actual vendor certification exam, PrepLogic is designed to offer the most effective exam simulation available.

Question Quality

The questions provided in the PrepLogic Practice Tests, Preview Edition are written to the highest standards of technical accuracy. The questions tap the content of the Exam Cram 2 chapters and help you review and assess your knowledge before you take the actual exam.

Interface Design

The PrepLogic Practice Tests, Preview Edition exam-simulation interface provides you with the experience of taking an electronic exam. This enables you to effectively prepare for taking the actual exam by making the test experience a familiar one. Using this test simulation can help eliminate the sense of surprise or anxiety that you might experience in the testing center because you will already be acquainted with computerized testing.

Effective Learning Environment

The PrepLogic Practice Tests, Preview Edition interface provides a learning environment that not only tests you through the computer, but also teaches the material you need to know to pass the certification exam. Each question comes with a detailed explanation of the correct answer and often provides reasons the other options are incorrect. This information helps to reinforce the knowledge you already have and also provides practical information that you can use on the job.

Software Requirements

PrepLogic Practice Tests requires a computer with the following:

➤ Microsoft Windows 98, Windows Me, Windows NT 4.0, Windows 2000, or Windows XP.

➤ A 166MHz or faster processor is recommended.

➤ A minimum of 32MB of RAM.

➤ As with any Windows application, the more memory you have, the better your performance will be.

➤ 10MB of hard drive space.

Installing PrepLogic Practice Tests, Preview Edition

Install PrepLogic Practice Tests, Preview Edition by running the setup program on the PrepLogic Practice Tests, Preview Edition CD. Follow these instructions to install the software on your computer.

1. Insert the CD into your CD-ROM drive. The Autorun feature of Windows should launch the software. If you have Autorun disabled, click Start and select Run. Go to the root directory of the CD and select setup.exe. Click Open, and then click OK.

2. The Installation Wizard copies the PrepLogic Practice Tests, Preview Edition files to your hard drive; adds PrepLogic Practice Tests, Preview Edition to your desktop and Program menu; and installs test engine components in the appropriate system folders.

Removing PrepLogic Practice Tests, Preview Edition from Your Computer

If you elect to remove the PrepLogic Practice Tests, Preview Edition product from your computer, an uninstall process has been included to ensure that it is removed from your system safely and completely. Follow these instructions to remove PrepLogic Practice Tests, Preview Edition from your computer:

1. Select Start, Settings, Control Panel.

2. Double-click the Add/Remove Programs icon.

3. You are presented with a list of software installed on your computer. Select the appropriate PrepLogic Practice Tests, Preview Edition title you want to remove. Click the Add/Remove button. The software is then removed from your computer.

Using PrepLogic Practice Tests, Preview Edition

PrepLogic is designed to be user-friendly and intuitive. Because the software has a smooth learning curve, your time is maximized because you start practicing almost immediately. PrepLogic Practice Tests, Preview Edition has two major modes of study: Practice Test and Flash Review.

Using Practice Test mode, you can develop your test-taking abilities as well as your knowledge through the use of the Show Answer option. While you are taking the test, you can expose the answers along with a detailed explanation of why the given answers are right or wrong. This gives you the ability to better understand the material presented.

Flash Review is designed to reinforce exam topics rather than quiz you. In this mode, you will be shown a series of questions but no answer choices. Instead, you will be given a button that reveals the correct answer to the question and a full explanation for that answer.

Starting a Practice Test Mode Session

Practice Test mode enables you to control the exam experience in ways that actual certification exams do not allow:

➤ *Enable Show Answer button*—Activates the Show Answer button, allowing you to view the correct answer(s) and full explanation(s) for each question during the exam. When this is not enabled, you must wait until after your exam has been graded to view the correct answer(s) and explanation(s).

➤ *Enable Item Review button*—Activates the Item Review button, allowing you to view your answer choices and marked questions, and to facilitate navigation among questions.

➤ *Randomize choices*—Randomizes answer choices from one exam session to the next. Makes memorizing question choices more difficult, therefore keeping questions fresh and challenging longer.

To begin studying in Practice Test mode, click the Practice Test radio button from the main exam-customization screen. This enables the options detailed in the preceding list.

To your left, you are presented with the option of selecting the preconfigured practice test or creating your own custom test. The preconfigured test has a fixed time limit and number of questions. Custom tests allow you to configure the time limit and the number of questions in your exam.

The Preview Edition included with this book includes a single preconfigured practice test. Get the compete set of challenging PrepLogic practice tests at PrepLogic.com, and make certain you're ready for the big exam.

Click the Begin Exam button to begin your exam.

Starting a Flash Review Mode Session

Flash Review mode provides you with an easy way to reinforce topics covered in the practice questions. To begin studying in Flash Review mode, click the Flash Review radio button from the main exam-customization screen. Select either the preconfigured practice test or create your own custom test.

Click the Begin Exam button to begin your Flash Review of the exam questions.

Standard PrepLogic Practice Tests, Preview Edition Options

The following list describes the function of each of the buttons you see. Depending on the options, some of the buttons will be grayed out and inaccessible or missing completely. Buttons that are appropriate are active. The buttons are as follows:

➤ *Exhibit*—This button is visible if an exhibit is provided to support the question. An exhibit is an image that provides supplemental information necessary to answer the question.

➤ *Item Review*—This button leaves the question window and opens the Item Review screen. From this screen, you will see all questions, your answers, and your marked items. You will also see correct answers listed here when appropriate.

➤ *Show Answer*—This option displays the correct answer with an explanation of why it is correct. If you select this option, the current question is not scored.

➤ *Mark Item*—Check this box to tag a question that you need to review further. You can view and navigate your marked items by clicking the Item Review button (if enabled). When grading your exam, you will be notified if you have marked items remaining.

➤ *Previous Item*—View the previous question.

➤ *Next Item*—View the next question.

➤ *Grade Exam*—When you have completed your exam, click to end your exam and view your detailed score report. If you have unanswered or marked items remaining, you will be asked whether you want to continue taking your exam or view your exam report.

Time Remaining

If the test is timed, the time remaining is displayed in the upper-right corner of the application screen. It counts down minutes and seconds remaining to complete the test. If you run out of time, you will be asked if you want to continue taking the test or end your exam.

Your Examination Score Report

The Examination Score Report screen appears when the Practice Test mode ends—as the result of time expiration, completion of all questions, or your decision to terminate early.

This screen provides you with a graphical display of your test score, with a breakdown of scores by topic domain. The graphical display at the top of the screen compares your overall score with the PrepLogic Exam Competency Score.

The PrepLogic Exam Competency Score reflects the level of subject competency required to pass this vendor's exam. Although this score does not directly translate to a passing score, consistently matching or exceeding this score does suggest that you possess the knowledge to pass the actual vendor exam.

Review Your Exam

From the Your Score Report screen, you can review the exam that you just completed by clicking on the View Items button. Navigate through the items, viewing the questions, your answers, the correct answers, and the explanations for those questions. You can return to your score report by clicking the View Items button.

Get More Exams

Each PrepLogic Practice Tests, Preview Edition that accompanies your book contains a single PrepLogic practice test. Certification students worldwide trust PrepLogic practice tests to help them pass their IT certification exams the first time. Purchase the Premium Edition of PrepLogic Practice Tests and get the entire set of all new challenging practice tests for this exam. PrepLogic practice tests—because you want to pass the first time.

Contacting PrepLogic

If you want to contact PrepLogic for any reason including information about our extensive line of certification practice tests, we invite you to do so. Please contact us online at www.preplogic.com.

Customer Service

If you have a damaged product and need a replacement or refund, please call the following phone number:

1-800-858-7674

Product Suggestions and Comments

We value your input! Please email your suggestions and comments to the following address:

feedback@preplogic.com

License Agreement

YOU MUST AGREE TO THE TERMS AND CONDITIONS OUT-LINED IN THE END USER LICENSE AGREEMENT ("EULA") PRESENTED TO YOU DURING THE INSTALLATION PROCESS. IF YOU DO NOT AGREE TO THESE TERMS, DO NOT INSTALL THE SOFTWARE.

Glossary

. . . .

authentication
The process of confirming the identity of a user, typically by a username and password. Windows Server 2003 supports several authentication methods, including Kerberos v5, NTLM authentication, passport authentication, and digest authentication.

authorization
The process of granting or denying a user, group, or computer access to network resources through permissions and user rights.

automatic updates services
Enables operating system updates to be downloaded and installed automatically. This ensures that systems stay up-to-date with the latest updates.

caching-only server
A form of a DNS server that is not responsible for maintaining or updating any zone information. It simply resolves name requests to IP addresses on behalf of DNS clients and caches the results.

capture filter
Filter configured within Network Monitor to specify the type of traffic that should be captured for analysis.

Challenge Handshake Authentication Protocol (CHAP)
An authentication protocol that uses the Message Digest 5 (MD5) hashing scheme to encrypt responses. With CHAP, the server sends a challenge to the client. The client then generates an MD5 hash result and returns it to the server.

delegation
In Windows Server 2003, this is the ability of an administrator to distribute certain administrative tasks to other individuals or groups. In terms of DNS, a portion of a domain namespace can be delegated to another server that will then be responsible for resolving name-resolution requests.

Device Manager

A tool included with Windows Server 2003 that can be used to manage hardware as well as troubleshoot hardware problems.

DHCP clients

Clients configured to automatically obtain an IP address from a DHCP server. By default, Windows 2000, Windows XP, and Windows Server 2003 clients are configured as DHCP clients.

DHCP database

Database that stores information about client leases.

display filter

Filter configured within Network Monitor after data has been captured to specify the type of traffic to display.

domain

An Active Directory hierarchy component. Domains define the administrative and security boundaries within an Active Directory hierarchy. A domain can be created by installing Active Directory.

domain controller

Computers that are used for storing directory data, user authentication, and directory searches. A computer can be configured as a domain controller by installing Active Directory.

Domain Name System (DNS)

System used to translate host names into IP addresses. DNS is included as a service with Windows Server 2003.

Dynamic Host Configuration Protocol (DHCP)

A protocol used to dynamically assign IP addresses to devices on a network. It can also be used to provide DHCP clients with optional parameters such as the IP address of the default gateway. DHCP in Windows Server 2003 can be integrated with DNS.

dynamic update

Feature that enables a DNS client to automatically register and update its own host record with a DNS server. It can be used in conjunction with DHCP so that clients can update their resource records when IP addresses change.

Event Viewer

The tool used to view the contents of the Windows Server 2003 log files.

forward lookup zone

A forward lookup zone maps hostnames to IP addresses. When a client needs the IP address of a hostname, the information is retrieved from the forward lookup zone.

Group Policy

An administrative tool that can be used to administer various aspects of the client computing environment, from installing software to applying a standardized desktop.

Internet Authentication Server (IAS)

Microsoft's version of a RADIUS server. To ease the administrative overhead of managing multiple RAS servers, you can implement a RADIUS server to centralize the authentication of remote access clients and the storage of accounting information.

IP routing

Routing is the process of sending a packet from the source address to the destination address. Because all IP packets have a source and destination IP address, it is possible to deliver them to the proper location.

IP Security Monitor

Tool that can be used to validate that communications between hosts are indeed secure. It provides information such as which IPSec policy is active and whether a secure communication channel is being established between computers.

IPSec

A set of protocols used to support the secure exchange of data at the IP layer using encryption. In Transport mode, only the data portion or payload is encrypted. In Tunnel mode, both the header and the payload are encrypted.

iterative query

With an iterative query, the DNS server uses zone information and its cache to return the best possible answer to the client. If the DNS server does not have the requested information, it can refer the client to another DNS server.

lease

DHCP clients can be assigned an IP address from a DHCP server. The lease duration determines the amount of time a client can use an IP address assigned from a DHCP server before it must be renewed. The default lease time in Windows Server 2003 is eight days.

Network Diagnostics

A support utility that can be used to identify and isolate connectivity and network problems.

Network Monitor

A tool included with Windows Server 2003 used to monitor and capture network traffic. It is useful for troubleshooting network problems.

Open Shortest Path First (OSPF)

A routing protocol that uses the shortest path first or link-state routing algorithm. OSPF routers calculate the shortest path to each host and share that portion of the routing table.

Point-to-Point Protocol (PPP)

A communication protocol used by dial-up remote access clients. PPP has become an industry-standard communications protocol because of its popularity; it provides support for multiple network protocols, including TCP/IP, IPX/SPX, and NetBEUI.

primary zone

Type of zone that maintains the master writable copy of the zone in a text file. An update to the zone must be performed from the primary zone.

recursive query

With a recursive query, the DNS client requires the DNS server to respond with either the IP address of the request or an error message that the requested name does not exist.

Remote Access Service (RAS)

Service that enables remote clients to dial into a Windows Server 2003 server and access network resources as though they were physically attached to the network.

resource records

The data within a DNS zone file. Windows Server 2003 supports a number of different types of resource records.

reverse lookup zone

This type of zone allows for reverse queries, or the mapping of an IP address back to a hostname. Reverse queries are often used when troubleshooting with the NSLookup command.

Routing Information Protocol (RIP)

A protocol that allows routers to exchange routing information. It is designed for use with small- to medium-size networks. RIP routers periodically exchange entire routing tables.

scope

Determines the pool of IP addresses from which a DHCP server can assign IP addresses. Every DHCP server must be configured with at least one scope.

secondary zones

Zone type that stores a copy of an existing zone in a read-only text file. To create a secondary zone, the primary zone must already exist, and you must specify a master name server. This is the server from which the zone information is copied.

secure baseline

Establishes a set of rules or recommendations that outline the minimum acceptable security configuration for new installations.

Security Configuration and Analysis

Windows Server 2003 includes a tool known as the Security Configuration and Analysis tool. Using this tool, you can analyze the current security state of a server or workstation by comparing the existing settings against an existing template.

security templates

Holds a number of security settings that Microsoft considers to be appropriate for a server, domain controller, or workstation. Windows Server 2003 includes several default templates with preconfigured security settings based on various computer roles. Custom templates can also be defined.

Shutdown Event Tracker

This tool enables an administrator to monitor why users shut down or restart their computers. When Shutdown Event Tracker is enabled, users are prompted to provide a reason as to why they are shutting down or restarting a computer. The information is then recorded in the system log.

Software Update Services (SUS)

One of the options now available for distributing updates. SUS consists of two components: the server and the client. The server (which can be running Windows 2000 or Windows Server 2003) downloads updates from Microsoft and stores them locally for clients to download without having to retrieve updates themselves from Windows Update servers on the Internet.

stub zones

This type of zone is new in Windows Server 2003. A stub zone maintains only a list of authoritative name servers for a particular zone. The purpose of a stub zone is to ensure that DNS servers hosting a parent zone are aware of authoritative DNS servers for its child zones.

System Information

This tool provides configuration information about the local computer or a remote computer.

System Monitor

A tool included with Windows Server 2003 that can be used to monitor the real-time performance of system components as well as services and applications. System Monitor can be used to collect and view real-time performance data, view data saved in a counter log, and present captured data using various views.

Task Manager

This tool can be used to view a variety of information about the local computer. Task Manager displays the applications and processes currently running, provides performance and network statistics, and shows any users currently connected to the computer.

Transmission Control Protocol/Internet Protocol (TCP/IP)

An industry-standard suite of protocols that enables two hosts to establish a connection and exchange data.

zone

A database file that contains the resource records for a single domain or a set of domains. There are three types of zones in DNS: a forward lookup zone for mapping names to IP addresses, a reverse lookup zone for mapping IP addresses to domain names, and a stub zone for determining which DNS servers are authoritative for a zone.

Index

How can we make this index more useful? Email us at indexes@quepublishing.com.

How can we make this index more useful? Email us at indexes@quepublishing.com.

Q

R